SUMMONED AT MIDNIGHT

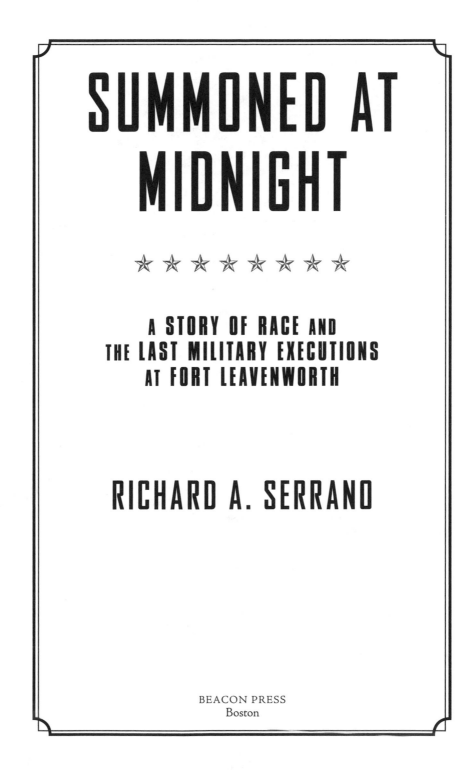

SUMMONED AT MIDNIGHT

★ ★ ★ ★ ★ ★ ★ ★ ★

A STORY OF RACE AND THE LAST MILITARY EXECUTIONS AT FORT LEAVENWORTH

RICHARD A. SERRANO

BEACON PRESS
Boston

BEACON PRESS
Boston, Massachusetts
www.beacon.org

Beacon Press books
are published under the auspices of
the Unitarian Universalist Association of Congregations.

22 21 20 19   8 7 6 5 4 3 2 1

This book is printed on acid-free paper that meets the uncoated paper
ANSI/NISO specifications for permanence as revised in 1992.

Text design and composition by Kim Arney

Library of Congress Cataloging-in-Publication Data
Names: Serrano, Richard A., author.
Title: Summoned at midnight : a story of race and the last military
executions at Fort Leavenworth / Richard Serrano.
Description: Boston : Beacon Press, [2018] | Includes bibliographical references and index.
Identifiers: LCCN 2018025939 (print) | LCCN 2018053896 (ebook) |
ISBN 9780807061039 (ebook) | ISBN 9780807060964 (hardcover : alk. paper)
Subjects: LCSH: Discrimination in capital punishment—United States. |
African American soldiers. | United States—Armed Forces—African
Americans—History. | Discrimination in the military—United States. |
Discrimination in criminal justice administration—United States. |
Executions and executioners—United States—History—20th century.
Classification: LCC HV8699.U5 (ebook) | LCC HV8699.U5 S44 2018 (print) |
DDC 355.1/3325—dc23
LC record available at https://lccn.loc.gov/2018025939

Für Elise

Many of my friends fled into the service,
all to be changed there, and rarely for the better,
many to be ruined, and many to die.

—JAMES BALDWIN, *The Fire Next Time*

The problem of the Twentieth Century
is the problem of the color-line.

—W. E. B. DU BOIS, *The Souls of Black Folk*

CONTENTS

PROLOGUE

In the last half of the 1950s, all eight of the white soldiers on the army's death row at Fort Leavenworth, Kansas, were spared. Their crimes were heinous, unthinkable, and little disputed. Rape, murder, the worst of the worst. Yet the white inmates served only a few years on death row and eventually were paroled and returned home.

During this same period, the army hanged only black soldiers—eight men in all. Their crimes were no less shocking than the white soldiers'. But the stark disparity in the men's outcomes reflected the nation's troubled road toward integration in the US military and the racial dynamics of the country leading into the civil rights era. It also drew sharp political attention.

Then, in the first weeks of the new Kennedy administration, in 1961, the fate of yet another condemned soldier, the last man on death row at the time, came up for reconsideration. He was a black army private from the Old South, younger than all the rest of the doomed men and just as guilty. Suddenly, debate over his fate became a fulcrum on which the past nearly six decades have pivoted. Would he be spared or, like his fellow black soldiers, summoned at midnight to the army gallows?

SUMMONED AT MIDNIGHT

Chapter One

★ ★ ★ ★ ★ ★ ★ ★

ARMY JUSTICE

Snow was coming, and another cold front was settling in. American soldiers at Camp Roeder in the eastern Alps were already shivering in their army outpost in Occupied Austria. The rifles, tanks, and mortars of World War II had gone silent for ten years, but the Allied forces still patrolled the rugged German border. Now, on this first day of winter, December 1954, ice and snowflakes whitened a small stream outside Salzburg. The creek would freeze overnight. Christmas was just a few days away.

Private First Class John Arthur Bennett, a handsome man with deep-set, dark brown eyes, had been posted there only a short while, part of a US Army headquarters battery. He served as an ammunition handler and drove an army truck around the sprawling American compound. The young man had recently won a National Defense Service Medal and a Sharpshooter Badge. He also had taken survival training.

Though he was far from home, the army seemed a good fit for the eighteen-year-old soldier. He worked hard, drew "excellent" performance ratings, and like any smart soldier, kept his head down. His commanding officer liked him—a lot. The army promised him a future. That is why he enlisted. His brothers had joined up, too; one was promoted to sergeant major while serving in Europe and the Far East.

Each morning brought Bennett steady work, a paycheck, and a path out of the poverty and segregation of his hometown in southern Virginia. But Bennett was a black soldier in a still largely white man's army, and before the sun came up after that December 21 snowfall, he stood arrested for sexually assaulting a white Austrian girl and leaving her for dead in a snow-dusted brook. The US Army charged him with rape and attempted murder. Her belongings were recovered near the creek, and Bennett, exhausted and frightened under questioning by military police, signed what army officers and military prosecutors called a "confession."

Local authorities insisted that Bennett be handed over to Austrian authorities; they had no death penalty, and their maximum punishment for rape was twenty years. But the army instead court-martialed Bennett, in what his defense and appellate lawyers derided as a show trial to ease the anger of local Austrians after a decade of Allied occupation. An all-white jury of two army colonels, four lieutenant colonels, two majors, and a captain deliberated for twenty-five minutes and sentenced him to death by hanging. Bennett was placed in chains and leg irons; shipped to a brig in Mannheim, Germany, then a holding cell in Pennsylvania; and finally to the army's notorious death row deep inside the "Castle," formally known as the United States Disciplinary Barracks at Fort Leavenworth, Kansas.

The army's death row was dug into a partial basement below the Castle walls. For six years, Bennett was housed in a solitary cell along a steel-and-iron tier called "Seven Base." Most of the other condemned soldiers were already there when Bennett arrived, and they soon adopted him as the youngest among them sentenced to die.

Unlike all the rest, he was not a murderer. Others had shot fellow soldiers to death, even army officers. Some had slain civilians, and several had murdered children, including the young daughter of an army colonel. In the years between Bennett's military trial and when he finally left death row, he watched as the lives of all eight of the condemned white soldiers, most from middle-class homes in the North, were spared. Not only were their sentences commuted, but all eventually were paroled and set free.

The army hanged only black soldiers in those half-dozen years—eight in all—summoned at midnight to the gallows. The army chose that 12 a.m. hour because it saw no reason to wait for any last-minute reprieves as a doomed man's last day wore on. And at midnight, it hoped, the others on death row would be sleeping and the rest of the prison silent.

Like Bennett, these eight black prisoners were products of a harsh American South, born into poverty and raised under Jim Crow, trying to fit into an army that had been ordered to desegregate. Each died without money or means.

One black army private from Tennessee, Louis M. Suttles, was executed for killing a taxi driver in Missouri. Shortly after his arrest, he was taken into a small room packed with men brandishing firearms and a woman drawing her finger across her throat. An army investigator scanned the crowd and warned Suttles, "How would you like to have about ten of those fellows get hold of you?" Married with two young daughters, he insisted army police had scared him into confessing. But Suttles's case drew few supporters and certainly no Washington insiders or high-priced attorneys.

Six weeks before his hanging, Suttles's mother, Mrs. Gentry Collier of Chattanooga, wrote the Eisenhower White House, her handwriting neat though she was partly illiterate. "I am begger for his life," she pleaded. "I am the only one he got to look to he dont have a father he Die when Louis was small I am cripple." She added, "[H]e was a good boy both white and colored love him he ant never have ben in trouble tell he was in the army."

All on death row, white and black, clearly recognized that in the late 1950s, none were treated alike. There were no written Jim Crow rules on the army's death row. White military guards served them all the same meals, offered them the same books and magazines, and sent them to the same showers and the recreation yard. But everyone realized that a completely different and dual system permeated beyond those basement walls. Attorneys trained in capital litigation represented white soldiers waiting to be hanged. Sympathetic editorial write-ups lobbied to save their lives. Often the public rallied around them, too, launching letter-writing and fund-raising campaigns and other petition drives. In the end, high-ranking army officers, military judges, and Washington power brokers in the Eisenhower administration and on Capitol Hill helped save their lives. The white soldiers had far less to fear.

One, Maurice Schick, an army master sergeant, killed the eight-year-old daughter of a US Army colonel in Japan, slowly strangling her to death, a murder he later admitted. Long after his release in 1979, Schick spoke proudly of his military service. He claimed he enlisted only to escape the drudgery of the coal mines of western Pennsylvania, and yet was grateful that the army, the courts, and President Eisenhower had given him a second chance to rebuild his life on parole. But unlike Bennett and his other black comrades, Schick also could thank Washington politicians, teams of defense lawyers, and community organizers for his release. Even his victim's parents forgave him. "I never regretted joining," reflected Schick, later as a free man in Florida. "I don't hold the army responsible for anything that happened to me. It may sound phony, but I did love the country."

There lay the starkness between white and black soldiers sharing that death row bunker. Eight white soldiers spared, eight black soldiers hanged. Bennett was the last soldier remaining on the army's narrow death row tier. There he sat alone, confined in the sub-basement of the Fort Leavenworth prison. After two stays of execution, his legal appeals rolled into the spring of 1961, outlasting the Eisenhower administration and reconsidered in the first hundred days of the new Kennedy presidency. By then, if the army hangman came for Bennett, too, this soldier born into an old plantation slave family in rural Virginia would go down for a half-century and more as the last one executed in America. Rape at that time was still a capital crime in the US Army, much as it was still stamped into the legal books in the segregated South. Old ideas held fast—the derogatory image of black men as sexual predators, the ideal of the white woman as above reproach. Even in Bennett's hometown in southern Virginia, just glancing at a white woman or not crossing the street when she passed could send a black man to prison, if not into the clutches of a lynch mob.

In the 1950s, America was changing, however slowly and however grudgingly. Many of the old prejudices stubbornly remained, even as cautious civil rights efforts gained strength. The US Army that triumphed in two world wars with the courage and leadership of white soldiers was tested by a new Washington policy of forced integration, put in place by the Truman administration. President Truman's Executive Order 9981 in July 1948 was meant to end discrimination in uniform, and the armed forces in the 1950s became a community laboratory to determine whether the two races could live and work together. According to Truman's edict, each soldier was to be valued on his individual performance, not by the color of his skin. The great hope was that the army would become an institution where men of all races would train and sometimes fight together.

★   ★   ★

During WWII, black soldiers primarily worked as backbenchers in supply units and mess halls, digging trenches or laundering uniforms; many actually preferred it that way, wanting no part of combat. At the time, their commander in chief, President Franklin Roosevelt, signaled little interest in making antidiscrimination a top policy for fear the Democrats would lose the South.

James Rookard, a soldier from Cleveland driving a truck for Uncle Sam, reasoned, "What's the use of going out and fighting when you're second-class citizens? What good is that?"

Secretary of war at the time, Henry Stimson, was asked by a white congressman who commanded black troops in World War I to explain why black soldiers were not serving in combat in the 1940s. He replied that most were poorly educated and "have been unable to master efficiently the techniques of modern weapons." His comments outraged black America. William Dawson, a black congressman from Chicago, called it "a gratuitous slap in the face of many thousand Negro Soldiers in the army." The black press was more to the point, mockingly headlining their newspaper stories, "Too Dumb to Fight."

A black corporal named Rupert Trimmingham took a chance in April 1944 and wrote a letter to *Yank*, a weekly army magazine published during the war. He never expected them to print the letter, but the editors did. He laid out his protests over how he and eight other black soldiers were mistreated during a stopover at Fort Huachuca, Arizona. "We could not purchase a cup of coffee at any of the lunchrooms around there," Trimmingham wrote. "As you know, Old Man Jim Crow rules. The only place where we could be served was at the lunchroom at the railroad station but, of course, we had to go into the kitchen." Worse, about two dozen German prisoners of war were allowed to dine under guard in the station lunchroom, where their meals were served, and Trimmingham said, they enjoyed "quite a swell time." He asked, "Are we not American soldiers? . . . Why are we pushed around like cattle?"

Trimmingham's angst triggered an equally angry response, including from white soldiers, and *Yank* printed several of their letters, too. Other soldiers wrote to Trimmingham directly; he received 287 letters in the first three months. "I am a Southern rebel," one white soldier, Corporal

Henry S. Wootton, wrote the magazine. "But this incident makes me none the more proud of my Southern heritage." Four other soldiers, with Italian, French, Swedish, and Irish heritage, wrote from the war front in Burma, where they were serving alongside black outfits in the jungles. Racial slights in the United States, they worried, "are knocking down everything that we are fighting for."

Many black soldiers rushed to save democracy overseas. On the war's first morning, when the Japanese attacked Pearl Harbor in December 1941, a black, third-class navy messman named Doris "Dorie" Miller swung into action. A farm kid from Waco, Texas, his ship the USS *West Virginia* hit by two torpedoes, he manned a .50-caliber machine gun and fired at enemy planes. He was highly decorated for this act of bravery, including winning the Navy Cross. But, he was abruptly returned to his mess hall duties, only to die two years later when his new ship was torpedoed.

Other black soldiers carried messages under fire, rescued wounded white soldiers, and protected abandoned trucks and other war equipment. Nine enlisted black men and one officer lost their lives in a German tank trap. A pinned-down black soldier operated a radio for forty-eight hours without help. Even General Patton, who believed black soldiers inferior, climbed atop a half-track truck and rallied a group of black GIs.

"Men," he began, "I would never have asked for you if you weren't good. I have nothing but the best in my army. I don't care what color you are, so long as you go up there and kill those Kraut sonsabitches." Patton realized history would be marching with them. "Everyone has their eyes on you and is expecting great things from you. Most of all, your race is looking forward to you. Don't let them down."

Many white soldiers did not care to share the front lines with blacks, and Southern whites especially worried about blacks returning to the States expecting to be treated equally among their white neighbors. Or worse, having learned to fight, they might turn their anger against them. Black troops initially were trained and posted at domestic military bases in the Jim Crow South, something many local communities not only did not like, but came to fear and defy.

Some in Washington urged tolerance. "I think we will have to do a little educating among our Southern white men and officers," First Lady

Eleanor Roosevelt cautioned the secretary of war in 1942. To the assistant secretary a year later, she advised: "The feeling among the colored people is very sad and I think they should be given a chance to prove their mettle. I feel they have something to gain in the war."

FBI Director J. Edgar Hoover accused her of fomenting black activism. "If she wasn't sympathizing with them and encouraging them, they wouldn't be speaking out like this."

Change was slow to come at home, where all soldiers, black and white, hoped to return. In Massachusetts in 1945, four female black officers and privates in the Women's Army Corps drew a year at hard labor. The women were court-martialed for refusing to carry out menial work washing dishes at a local hospital, complaining they were chosen "because of their color."

First Lieutenant Virginia Lawson of Tulsa, Oklahoma, announced, "I have been to work but I don't think I can go on. Put my name down for a court martial." A general later spared the women the prison time, ruling on a technicality that the court was improperly convened. But the insult still stung.

★   ★   ★

In New York, the National Association for the Advancement of Colored People (NAACP) asked Grant Reynolds, a black army chaplain and attorney, to assess the state of black men in uniform in Europe. In a series of dispatches near the war's end, titled "What the Negro Soldier Thinks About this War," he uncovered a deep dread of returning to a still-segregated America. "The Negro soldier needs no one to remind him that this is his country," Reynolds wrote. "He knows this. But he knows also that there is a lot of unfinished business about individual human decency that he would like to see cleared up before he becomes a corpse for *any* country."

Many black soldiers serving stateside found a war of monotony, given little to do. "Here I am again and gripes are foremost as usual," black Private James Pritchett wrote in January 1944 to a new army unit investigating allegations of discrimination in the ranks. He was based at a headquarters regiment in Camp Livingston, Louisiana, to guard German prisoners there. Pritchett pleaded, "This is a hell hole. Believe it or not, but the German P.W.s have more rights and freedom."

Truman's order desegregating the armed forces was still up against entrenched reluctance. The first real test came during the Korean War. Thurgood Marshall, then with the NAACP, traveled there to review the cases of thirty-nine black soldiers court-martialed on the peninsula. General Douglas MacArthur promised he would not find "the slightest evidence of discrimination," yet Marshall discovered an abundance. Of eighty-two army trials, fifty-four were for black soldiers. White officers investigated almost every case, and most of the charges were for "misbehavior in the presence of the enemy." The trials were hurried, in rapid assembly-line fashion. Four that ended in life sentences were completed within forty-five minutes or just under an hour. "Even in Mississippi," Marshall remarked, "a Negro will get a trial longer than forty-two minutes, if he is fortunate enough to be brought to trial."

In visiting MacArthur's headquarters, Marshall counted only three black faces working as civilian clerks, none in uniform. He reviewed an elite honor guard, with not a black among them. "Headquarters had a football team, all white. There wasn't even a Negro in the headquarters band," he quipped.

But it was not just the army. Near the close of the Korean War in July 1953, Representative Adam Clayton Powell Jr., a black congressman from Harlem on the House Labor Committee, wrote in disgust to the assistant secretary of the navy: "Will you be kind enough to advise me why your office continues to assign roughly one half of the Negroes in the United States Navy to work as messmen?" He added bitterly, "No one is interested in today's world in fighting communism with a frying pan or shoe polish."

At the time, a research team called Project Clear was evaluating race and battlefield conditions in Korea. To little surprise, white infantrymen had little good to say about their black comrades. "I don't believe that anyone could ever make a fighting outfit out of them that would be reliable and could be counted upon at any time," a white battalion commander said about black troops. "I was with them in basic training and we had some blacks who were plenty all right. But most of them just chased skirts and drank and talked all the time, even when the rest of us wanted to sleep. A man was afraid to go to a bar alone, 'less he run into about twenty of them with their razors and long knives," said another white GI.

A general officer openly mocked the black infantryman: "We've got two niggers in our squad and they keep us laughing all the time. One day we were laying a minefield and suddenly we were fired upon, and we piled into the jeep. But that colored boy wouldn't get into the jeep. He just ran on ahead of us down the road. Then he sat down and took off his shoes and said, 'I can't go on because my feet are tired.'"

This was the army Private John Bennett was conscripted to when he enlisted a year after the fighting in Korea ended. He followed two of his older brothers into the armed forces. One brother, Ira Bennett, gave twenty-seven years to the army. He served through the early days of forced integration and came out as a sergeant major.

"At the start the army was hard on black people," Ira Bennett remembered. "If you were a lower rank you caught hell going through. Because I did. I went in like everybody else and I worked my way up. And that's how I got to where I was when I retired. I had no opportunity to do anything but what they say. And I thought it rough. You had nothing to say on your behalf. It was always what they say. It wasn't like it is now; it was altogether different. When I first went in, I went to Fort Knox, Kentucky, for basic training. The white guys would get to go out, and they would get breaks but not the black guys, and it was that way all the way through. If you were white you had better opportunities."

Ira Bennett often wondered why his younger brother John joined up, likely to shake the poverty and racism in rural southern Virginia. But he never discouraged his younger brother from enlisting: "When I left home he was just a little boy. But when I saw him in prison he was a man. It made a big difference to see the change, and he was a prisoner. I've never been so sad in all my life."

★   ★   ★

In short, the experiment of integration was largely resisted, despite years of chances and adjustment. By the late 1950s, the army's court-martial process and its military prison, the Eisenhower administration, and federal and military judges never truly accepted a balanced system of criminal justice. Not when it came to capital punishment and not over the worth of a man's life.

Across the country, the death penalty won support and lost it. As crime rates peaked and plunged after the 1950s, so went interest in capital punishment. States outlawed it and sealed off their execution chambers, then reopened their doors. Supreme Court justices struck it down, and Congress and state legislatures enacted new capital statutes. When thin plastic needles replaced knotted ropes, lethal injection seemed a humane antidote to appease a wary public. When those executions went bad, they were halted, too.

For the army, the president as commander in chief stood as final arbiter for death row soldiers. Eisenhower was the last president born in the 1800s. He grew up in Abilene, Kansas, but his real home was the army, a white man's army. A four-pack-a-day smoker, as supreme commander he led the Allied campaign to liberate Western Europe by sending young white men into battle, championing them with battlefield honor. Black soldiers served primarily in back-end support units, much as Bennett later would, driving a supply truck in Austria. As president, he never really embraced the civil rights agenda. He did send federal troops to the school crisis in Little Rock, Arkansas, but only when the Supreme Court forced his hand. He preferred instead a policy of "gradual" change in race relations. Most of the early civil rights victories were won without him.

Today, the United States is in the throes of a new collision over race and criminal justice. The nation's prisons and death rows are bursting with a disproportionately high number of black and Latino inmates, and Washington shows little willingness to confront the disparity. The Black Lives Matter movement erupted in full swing as citizens registered their anger over police killings in the nation's cities. Sixty years after John Bennett's death penalty, many would argue that little has changed. But, the energy behind these protests has encouraged activists and academics to retrace our footsteps and reveal the painful disparities between how the military, the White House, and the courts have historically treated our nation's white and black soldiers.

"The crucial question concerning capital punishment is not whether people deserve to die for the crimes they committed," Bryan Stevenson, executive director of the Equal Justice Initiative, has written, "but rather whether we deserve to kill." Some call this challenge for an equal system of justice the final barrier to overcome in the civil rights movement launched in the time of John Bennett, the army executions, and the late 1950s. In 2017, African Americans made up less than 13 percent of the national population, yet represented 42 percent of those on state and federal death rows, and 36 percent of those executed, according to Department of Justice records. Protect Our Defenders, an organization that studies military justice and sexual assault cases similar to John Bennett's, found black soldiers were still twice as likely as whites to be disciplined and court-martialed. "The military," announced that group's president, Don Christensen, a former air force chief prosecutor, "has known about these numbers for decades." The Pentagon responded that every man or woman who wears the uniform should expect "an environment free from unlawful racial discrimination."

When Bennett was on death row, army executions were carried out on a wooden gallows under the cover of midnight. There was no public outcry on their behalf; no protesters filled city streets; no committees studied army abuse. Few argued then that army justice, if justice at all, was tragically uneven. That kind of discrimination was hidden away in the late 1950s, buried long ago in dusty case files in the National Archives and Eisenhower Presidential Library. The files for the doomed white soldiers who eventually were set free are chock full of legal motions, petition drives, press editorials, and official Washington decisions to grant leniency. The files for black soldiers who were hanged are thin and bare, often a mere smattering of letters, typically from a frightened mother or perhaps a wife, or maybe the hometown pastor of a condemned man. Mostly it was their mothers. Only in opening those bare files and reading those few, often misspelled letters can those black voices at last be heard.

* * *

The old Castle prison at Fort Leavenworth towered above the Missouri River bluffs. By Bennett's arrival in 1955, it had been there for half a century, built by prison labor and on the backs of straining army mules that hauled the brick and river limestone up the cliffs. Its silver dome and eight cell wings jutted out like bayonet spikes. Here were housed the worst who ever wore the army colors.

The army gallows were built in an abandoned power plant on the prison grounds, a short march from death row across the prison courtyard.

Otherwise, the doomed men were held for long stretches in near to-tal lockdown. Seldom was the monotony broken, and like most of the prisoners, Bennett rarely had visits from his family; the trek from his hometown in rural Virginia to Kansas was far too expensive on a share-cropper's wages. His mother, ashamed and worried, could not bear to see John stripped of rank and wearing the drab gray uniform of death row.

When Eisenhower approved his death sentence in 1957, Bennett seemed, among all the black prisoners, the one most likely to live. He was the youngest of the group, and many of the older convicts, white and black, tried cheering him up, boosting his spirits, hollering out to him from the quiet of their own cells. "Ben" and "Bennie" and "Little Ben," they called him, inmates and guards alike. When a small rat slipped through a crack in his cell floor, guards let him keep the rodent. When he asked to work on a prison loom weaving floor rugs, they brought him one.

Bennett often spent his precious fifty-five minutes of recreation time each day alone in the prison yard, his arms pulled out of his long cotton sleeves, which were wrapped tightly around his waist, firing a baseball at the Castle walls. His pitching arm grew strong and his fastball deadly. He dreamed of someday joining the baseball team for the general prison population, which like most things was off-limits to death row soldiers. He imagined riding the bus with other army convicts to Kansas City or Topeka in a bright red uniform and starring on the pitcher's mound.

Each spring, guards and inmates alike watched in awe as Bennett practiced pitching on the prison courtyard, throwing hard against the Castle walls. His fellow death row prisoners rallied around him at night, too, especially when Kansas thunderstorms kicked up outside. Rain and lightning had frightened Bennett since he was a child in the Virginia tobacco fields. When rain splashed the high, narrow, death row windows, as many of the other prisoners recalled, Bennett often buried his teeth into his pillow.

*   *   *

During Bennett's years on death row, three black soldiers did make it out alive, but their cases were exceptional. One was certified mentally insane after killing a fellow soldier in Germany. At times, in his cell, he hallucinated that he was "not really a colored person" or that his father or stepfather was Adolf Hitler. He spoke of "tremendous mental strain" in the army, especially with forced integration.

Another stabbed an army pal in Tokyo in what turned out to be self-defense. The private confessed to a Catholic chaplain, and high-ranking army officials believed the confrontation simply had gotten out of hand; he never meant to kill his friend. "He was trying to save his own life," the soldier's mother insisted to President Eisenhower. "He is a very good and devout Catholic child."

The third was a suicidal air force mechanic. He shot a military policeman in Okinawa and aimed the .45-caliber pistol at his own head. He squeezed, but the chamber was empty. His father, an exasperated Philadelphia minister, had warned army recruiters not to accept his son. But the military took him anyway, soon to realize its mistake. "The army courts . . ." his father lamented. "That's where the trouble began."

Like them, Bennett also struggled with mental illness, and lifelong epilepsy. Despite his impoverished and troubled youth, he was welcomed into the army at just seventeen. In basic training, army supervisors considered sending him home because of nagging headaches and his initial inability to adjust to military life.

*   *   *

Soldiers have long memories, the prisoners and guards of Fort Leavenworth perhaps the longest of all. Even after the old prison was torn down and replaced by a new, modern facility, the clattering prison racket, the slamming of iron bars, and the screech of the green door swinging open at the end of the death row hallway haunted them. Colonel Leonard Becicka was plagued in his nineties by memories of serving as an official execution witness. A Minnesota farm boy, on D-Day he had splashed ashore at

Utah Beach and fought across Europe, then later in Korea and Vietnam. Becicka gave thirty years to the army. But it was watching a military hanging in Kansas that troubled him the most. "I was director of custody and I would visit him every day," he recalled. "To witness his death, it was very traumatic for me."

Bennett's final judge would be John Fitzgerald Kennedy, a Democrat, a liberal, a Catholic who, during the 1960 presidential campaign, helped free Dr. Martin Luther King Jr. from a Southern jail. And Kennedy's new White House was deeply troubled about executing any man for rape. It also thought it "awful" that Eisenhower had ordered only black soldiers hanged. If, after all these years, Bennett's victim and her family in Austria could be found, and if they urged mercy, then surely Kennedy would spare Bennett. Critical new evidence was emerging, too. Bennett's epilepsy left him confused and disoriented, and succumbing to "blind staggers." An army medical board recommended life; so too did a nationally recognized psychiatrist in Topeka, Dr. Karl Menninger. Bennett may well have been under a blinding spell during the attack in that snow-sprinkled field near Salzburg.

His lawyer, young civil rights advocate Jerry Williams, had canvassed for Kennedy for president in his Danville, Virginia, community. Now he hoped his champion would save Bennett's life. With Bennett scheduled to hang on Kennedy's watch, at one minute past midnight on April 13, 1961, Williams filed an urgent plea for a presidential commutation. He presented fresh evidence of Bennett's mental disorders and the disparity between his crime and those of the white murderers whose lives had mattered.

But Bennett's execution date came at one of the most trying times in the untested Kennedy White House. Russia launched the first man into outer space. Kennedy signaled his approval for the Bay of Pigs invasion, a plan with tragic consequences. Anger erupted over racial slights on the one-hundredth anniversary of the start of the Civil War. That war and its armies had failed to put an end to a dual system, North and South, black and white. Now Kennedy was confronted with another matter of race— the army and military justice.

On the prison yard at Fort Leavenworth, Bennett kept hurling his baseball at the brick and limestone Castle walls. His legal appeals had dragged slowly on through the Eisenhower administration. Beyond those walls, the civil rights movement coalesced and gathered strength. When Kennedy replaced Eisenhower in the White House, Bennett's legal team was tentatively hopeful. And out in the crisp sunshine, the death row soldier fired as if every pitch nudged him closer to a presidential reprieve, a reduced sentence, and, he believed, a spot on the prison club's baseball roster. "I'll be there," Bennett would shout to the prison team manager. "I'll be there! I will!"

Chapter Two

* * * * * * * *

AUSTRIA

Anna Aschenbrenner remembered John Bennett well. She worked as a waitress at the Gasthaus Haimbucher, a popular hangout the American soldiers called "Francis' Place." She was new to the job. She recalled that he spent five hours or more drinking at the inn that day in December 1954. He ordered at least eight large bottles of beer, a liter of cognac, and some sloe gin. But she thought him polite enough.

"He left alone," she told US Army authorities. "In my opinion, the soldier was not drunk at the time of his departure." He turned toward the door in his well-pressed Class A wool uniform with an army insignia, holding his cap in his hand.

"He asked me for a girl named Margaret or Margit," she recalled. "I didn't understand clearly." But, she said, "He only asked for her." She remembered he had been there twice before. "He always asked for the girl," she told army police.

Private Harry W. Marks Jr. told officials the two of them drank and spoke quietly, just small talk, army chitchat, how the black soldier "mentioned to me that he was from headquarters battery," little things like that. "He was a Negro, very light, small trim moustache. He was in uniform, wearing his Pfc stripes" to signal his rank, private first class. Camp Roeder was filled with soldiers, a bustling army outpost with a large ammunition depot, and Marks did not expect to see the man again. Soldiers came and went, rotating in and out. "At no time do I remember him telling me his name," Marks said. "He did not mention to me that he was going any place in particular either, but that he was going to walk down the road. Then he left."

Bennett wandered toward the border with Germany, and customs inspector Karl Gruber stepped out of his guard shack. "The colored man came from Austria and intended to cross the foot bridge to Bavaria," Gruber recalled. "I told him that for American soldiers it was prohibited to cross at that point." The soldier presented his ID, but Gruber pointed toward another river span for American GIs. As the soldier turned to leave, the only defining feature the guard could recall was a small mole or birthmark on the man's face; he seemed lost. "But he was not drunk," Gruber insisted.

Fifteen-year-old Gottfried Sima, riding his bicycle, spotted Bennett walking near the river. The teenager worked in the Camp Roeder mess hall and knew him as "Bannert." He recognized him as the truck driver who delivered the morning milk to the camp kitchen. He had been pestering the boy about a woman named "Marianne," a village prostitute.

"Bannert mentioned that he was going to look for her in Siezenheim," the boy told army police. Gottfried could describe the soldier well, as having a "brown-yellow complexion, slim build, mole on the face, small mustache, rank Pfc."

"I cannot say if he was drunk. He appeared to be sober. He was not staggering."

Caecelia Wagner was ironing in her kitchen when someone pounded on her door. The doorknob twisted sharply and a soldier burst inside, demanding in broken German, "Wo Margit?" She was startled. "Nicht hier," she replied, no Margit in her home.

"I told him that I would show him Margit," she recalled. "I went outside and the Negro soldier followed me. I immediately rushed back in and locked the door. The soldier went around and looked through the kitchen window. He came back to the door, where he again kept knocking loudly for several minutes."

He might have been slightly inebriated, "a little drunk," she suspected. She was all the more worried because there were "never any other colored soldiers" in her neighborhood. This one, she remembered, had "black sparkling eyes." He acted in a "strange way," she said, "by his eyes."

Her brother-in-law, Isidor Egger, dismissed him as another pesky GI looking to buy a date with a local woman. "I assumed that he wanted a girl, and showed him the direction of the gravel pit, the residence of girls associating with American soldiers," Egger recounted to army police.

Stefan Baier spied the soldier through his kitchen window. There are no girls, Baier told him. The soldier spotted Baier's wife inside and then "went rapidly into the woods surrounding our house." It frightened Baier, especially when the soldier "threw a wild glance at me and a sharp glance at my wife." Baier could smell the alcohol and reached for a piece of firewood. "If he had done something, I would have knocked him down."

John Bennett circled in and out of the woods, across a field, and along the Muehlbach stream. Hans Hrdlicka and his wife, Maria, heard him clomping up the outer stairs to their second-floor apartment.

"Do you have Americans?" He wanted a woman. "Fraulein!" he shouted. He pointed to his overcoat. "Have you American?" Hrdlicka escorted him back outside, and the soldier followed him to the brook where Hrdlicka scooped his water for the night. "The Negro soldier seemed rather excited," he thought, watching him stumble away.

Into a final house the soldier barged, a two-story stone structure with a red-tile roof. The head of the local customs unit and his wife were home awaiting the return of their eleven-year-old daughter from a shopping spree in nearby Salzburg. The husband guided the American soldier back through the kitchen and out the door, pointing down a paved street, where "women live who entertain intimate relations with U.S. soldiers." But the soldier misunderstood. He started off in another direction, down a dirt road toward a pasture and a small stream.

The moon was rising into a long solstice night. The daughter of the customs unit head was riding the bus home. She had purchased sewing supplies for her mother, a zipper and a belt. She had delivered a package for her mother and picked up a farmer's calendar at a bookshop. She was dressed snugly in her dark gray coat and yellow shawl with green checks, a green sweater, red pullover, and a blue skirt. The bus reached her stop, and she started walking the rest of the way home. Her brown shoes led her across that field, toward that creek.

✶　✶　✶

The girl was raped and left for dead in that near-frozen creek, and army headquarters was quickly alerted. The chief of staff in the tactical command ordered a "blanket search of the entire limits of Camp Roeder."

Military police in steel helmets, sidearms, and regulation green scarves fanned across the region in hot pursuit. Investigators knocked on doors in Siezenheim, jotting down statements from housewives and others about the black soldier and his blazing dark eyes. Private Marks, still drinking in the gasthaus, remembered the soldier was from headquarters battery. Agents learned that Private First Class John Bennett had been off duty on an all-day pass and had just returned.

Around 8:15 p.m., a captain and two master sergeants found Bennett in the camp movie theater. They frisked him and spotted bloodstains on his clothing. Bennett resisted giving them the key to his wall locker. He said he gave the key to Private John A. Gray for his laundry. Gray told police he was playing pool in the company dayroom a little earlier that evening when Bennett purchased a sandwich and a can of beer. Bennett had shaved his mustache. "He did not appear to be drunk or drinking," Gray reported. As for the locker key, he denied Bennett gave it to him. Police ripped the locker open and recovered Bennett's trousers, torn at the hip pocket.

Two more soldiers had seen him in the company latrine, scraping mud from his boots. His bunkmates said Bennett claimed he had visited Munich, but that was nearly three hours away. Bennett blanched. He was placed under arrest while sitting in the company movie theater.

The news flashed through Camp Roeder. Many felt Bennett, an easy-going, get-along kind of soldier, was likely drunk, and police had the wrong man. But Sergeant John F. Kane, chief army investigator, was not so sure. "He did not appear to be drunk," the sergeant would recall. "He had very good control over his faculties."

In the noisy squad room, army interrogators kept Bennett awake. For hours, he sat on a lumpy sofa as police pumped him with coffee. From Siezenheim came sketches and photographs of the farm field. Bennett later would claim to army superiors that police threatened him with an army pistol, hours into the interrogation. Exhausted, he told them yes, he had sex with the girl. But he never forced himself on her. Sergeant Kane walked to the typing pool and pecked away at his notes. He returned and asked Bennett if he would sign the "confession." Sergeant Kane swore him in, and Bennett hunched over the three pages, scanning them one at a time.

"Not exactly aloud," Kane remembered. "He was sitting there, sort of mumbling. I could make out that he was reading it." The sergeant held out an ink pen, and Bennett scribbled his name. Then he collapsed, sound asleep.

They woke him at sunrise and drove thirty minutes to the field the girl's father had seen him walk toward after bursting into their house. Nearby were the brook and an old barn. It was a field full of weeds and underbrush, wet from the previous night's ice and snow.

"Bennett may have been nervous, he may have been afraid," Sergeant Ray Lindamood remembered years later, the images of that morning hard to forget. "He appeared to be cooperating with us though. He took us to the location where the thing occurred." They plodded around the muddy pasture and kicked away fresh snow, inching along the creek and into the barn. Army investigators found one of the girl's brown shoes and the calendar she was carrying home.

"As we were leaving, we saw the father again. We were walking up near this barn," Lindamood would recall. "I had John Bennett handcuffed to me. The scene was tense and the father looked Bennett over. He was in uniform and he had the biggest gun strapped on him I'd ever seen. But he was very level-headed."

The sergeant thought of the many times the army heard complaints from local prostitutes who "screamed rape" if they were not paid enough. But this felt vastly different. Here sat this young soldier, still fresh-faced and in terrible trouble, and a young girl in a hospital.

Bennett was locked inside the Camp Roeder stockade. "This building was old, like an old horse barn," remembered Corporal Louis Johnson. "Or a converted cow barn." Eight officers guarded fifteen inmates under a black slate roof and iron bars. The outside perimeter was walled in by ten-foot-high barbed wire, four-foot rock fences, and stone barricades. The cell windows were blacked out, not to shut out the light but to hold back the cold. Three naked light bulbs dangled from the ceiling. Bennett's cell brought up the rear of the tier, and a guard glanced inside every quarter hour. His bunk was anchored by chains to the cement floor. He was given a towel, a toothbrush, and a bar of soap.

There only a few weeks, Bennett opened up to Johnson. They chatted about the army and shared stories from the old South; Bennett poor and black from plantation Virginia, the corporal a white soldier from Tennessee. They talked about life in Siezenheim—the small homes on one-acre tracts. The half-dozen brothels that serviced Camp Roeder were vestiges of the old way, a reminder that Austria ten years after the war still fell under the boot of the Allied occupation.

"They got a lot of the GI trade," Johnson remembered of the brothels. "Five dollars would get you the works." The parlors were strictly off-limits, and a soldier could draw a fourteen-day suspension for patronizing them. "But they wouldn't bust anyone for it," he recalled. Bennett told him about his last night out there. Other prisoners were locked up for far less, drinking or disobeying orders, common soldier scrapes. Bennett was, by far, their biggest prize. Johnson listened carefully. "At that time he didn't seem too scared," Johnson remembered. "He didn't realize either what he had done. Not until he was court-martialed."

The army filed criminal charges against Bennett for rape and assault with intent to commit murder. Two days before Christmas, Lieutenant General William H. (Old Bill) Arnold, who oversaw Camp Roeder—with great flair, down to a coterie of aides, chauffeurs, and each evening a glass of single malt—announced a court-martial for January. At the Judge Advocate General's office, army prosecutors signaled they would seek the death penalty.

General Arnold resisted demands that Bennett be given over to the Austrian justice system. Arnold had been there a year and a half, and when he arrived, he welcomed local guests to a camp reception and promised to increase the military's cooperation with the surrounding community. The general said the army would start returning local property and processing damage claims.

"The necessity for understanding the people with whom we live is essential," he instructed his troops. Someday, the occupation would end; Austria would regain its sovereignty. "When we leave this country," he predicted, "we will be long remembered as friends." To ease tensions, the camp held Christmas parties for Austrian children and the elderly. The general's wife donated a hundred dollars' worth of wool for children's blankets.

Wounds of war still scarred the community. As late as 1953, workmen discovered a five-hundred-pound bomb in a ruined building less than one hundred feet from Camp Roeder headquarters. During Hitler's rise to power in the 1930s and throughout World War II, the Austrian people had largely embraced the Nazi regime. Austria, after all, was the fuhrer's birthplace, and on the first page of his *Mein Kampf*, he urged its return to "the Great German Motherland." From his Chancellery, he summoned their young men. For four weeks after his troops "annexed" Austria, vast crowds celebrated their native son. And by war's end, his Aryan Reich lay crumbled, his vaunted empire destroyed. Allied bombers even descended on Hitler's Obersalzberg mountain retreat in Austria, and his own SS troops set it afire in retreat. But they spared the beauty of Salzburg; the city's majestic river spires survived the shelling. And with Austria in defeat, many hid their Nazi past.

"It's really turning out to be a long war," an American soldier wrote home to his parents in November 1945. "It seems as if officers will be here forever." He was based in Gallspach, in upper Austria, and from the first days of the occupation, the soldier disliked the Austrian people. "If anything that I hate it's some of these people to tell me how innocent they are of the war. I think much more of the one who admits he was a Nazi and let it go at that."

Victor and vanquished learned to live together, and the United States did try to partner with the Austrians. The parents of Pennsylvania soldier Bill Billet collected funds to purchase socks, hats, gloves, toys, nuts, candy, and fruit for fifty Austrian orphans "adopted" by American servicemen. A freedom "way station" was mobilized to accommodate escapees fleeing the Iron Curtain in Germany. General Arnold offered parole to the last of five Austrian war criminals still held in the American zone. His army flew rescue missions for Austrian children sick with scarlet fever and whooping cough. Just a week after Bennett's arrest, Captain John Hayes and Private William L. Pruett perished in one of the training flights as their L-17 aircraft plunged toward Linz. The plane burned upon impact, lighting up the snow-covered hillside.

"We were an occupying army in a defeated country," wrote Major Robert Harlan Moser, an army medic at Salzburg. He was there at the time of Bennett's arrest in 1954 and through the army drawdown, and he sensed how American soldiers straddled a delicate line between overseeing Austria and trying to build up the defeated countryside.

"The Austrians I met all seemed pleasant and gracious," he recalled. "It was difficult to realize that they had been among the most rabid Nazis in the Third Reich." In three years, Moser met only "a handful of honest people who admitted they had been party members. But the vast majority would not acknowledge they even heard of 'National Socialists.'"

Salzburg still had its moments—the music festivals and the white-capped Alps that brightened in spring with mountain flowers. And winter, when Salzburg and the Siezenheim countryside sparkled and Christmas brought midnight Mass and a visit to Oberndorf where "Stille Nacht" had been composed.

"It was a magical night," Moser reminisced. "Gentle flakes drifted down embracing the landscape with a coat of white down, an angelic children's choir with voices soft and soaring." And, yet, "I could never get over the Jekyll-Hyde paradox of Austrians and Germans, capable of such sensitivity and beauty and such cruelty and horror."

Despite his previous commitments to partnership with the Austrians, General Arnold refused to bow to the growing clamor for a local trial by the Austrian courts. Many local citizens were angered that the attack had occurred on their soil and insisted Bennett be turned over to them for trial. Despite the gravity of the crime, many also were upset about the looming death sentence. In their country, Austria had no death penalty. Rape brought a maximum of only twenty years. Yet to prove that the US military could deal with its own errant soldiers and not operate like Hitler's Gestapo, just the previous May, a Camp Roeder army jury had given Private Carlos P. Johnson seventeen years hard labor for crossing the Iron Curtain into the Soviet sector. The army's court-martial system could handle Bennett just as well, the general insisted. This was a military matter.

Yet everything about the Bennett case continued to outrage Austrian locals. Many were furious that an American predator had been set loose inside their homes. On the witness stand a few weeks later, Stefan Baier, speaking on behalf of his entire community, described the chill that still hovered over Siezenheim.

"We don't even dare to leave our houses at night," he testified in Bennett's court-martial. Many families deeply distrusted the GIs. The occupation had gone on far too long; ten years was too much. "They all feel sorry and feel the same pity I do," Baier testified.

Asked to identify the soldier, Baier balked on the witness stand. He could not bring himself to glance at the defendant sitting in uniform at the defense table.

"He threatened the child," Baier said. "He is not worthy of being pointed at."

The judge, Captain Bueford G. Herbert, a no-nonsense officer from Kentucky, ordered Baier to comply. "Point to the man," he demanded.

Baier shook his head. "I cannot do that," he replied.

The judge ordered him to raise his arm, and when Baier did, the judge again insisted, "Then you can point to the man you are talking about! Do you understand what I told you to do, Mr. Baier?"

"Yes, I understood it."

"Why do you not point to the man?"

"Because I am unable to do it."

The judge pressed him harder. "You mean you are physically unable or that you do not know the man and cannot recognize him? Do you understand that question?"

Baier's head swayed back, and he fainted.

The war had ended a decade earlier; many like Baier felt it was time the Americans left. But Austrians were also aware of the camp's power in their community. American troops' patronage of their businesses and restaurants brought in $30 million a year—a quarter of all the salaries and wages paid in Salzburg. The occupying army was the city's largest employer. Nearly twenty thousand Salzburg residents relied on the camp for income. Five million dollars in building contracts would be defaulted upon.

Nevertheless, the attack occurred outside the army camp, and Bennett was off duty on a daylong pass in their town, at their doorways, and inside their kitchens. Why wasn't he turned over to local authorities for trial? Why shouldn't they sit in judgment? But the army would not budge. General Arnold simply felt a Camp Roeder court-martial could handle this matter best, internally.

Some local leaders continued to press for an Austrian trial and for Bennett to be brought to justice on Austria's terms. If the army would not give him over to local authorities, they demanded the United States punish him no more than the maximum sentence that Austrian law allowed for cases of rape—twenty years in prison.

Bennett himself spotted an Austrian ambassador in a camp hallway inquiring about his case. Protesters marched outside the camp gates; others crowded around the courthouse doors.

"I am an Austrian and an old lady and I should like to plead for mercy for the young American soldier," wrote a woman who identified herself as A. Lenz. She had seen his picture in the local papers, light complexioned, dark-set eyes, a troubled look. "He seems to be such a mere boy that I can't help feeling pity for him." Perhaps, she wondered, "he did not fully realize the weight of his crime." She pleaded against death. "Do him mercy," she begged the general. "Do not take his life. Give him a chance. He is so young."

The local protests were remarkable, if for no other reason than Austrian citizens were demanding a lenient punishment for Bennett, hoping to keep him alive. But General Arnold and army prosecutors saw stark differences. To them, a black soldier had sexually assaulted a white girl. In army terms, even as late as the mid-1950s, such a crime was repugnant to army decorum and army conduct, only to be dealt with by Bennett's swift execution. Those beliefs had been drilled into the army, where for decades, many of its enlisted men and corps commanders had come into uniform after a childhood raised in the American South. Even President Eisenhower, the former army high commander who later was confronted with Bennett's appeals, believed it "was necessary" for Bennett to die in order to send a harsh lesson to US troops and bolster overall army discipline.

Elise Demus Moran's husband had been an Austrian general in the First World War; he later was imprisoned by the Gestapo. She too was held briefly behind bars. Now seventy-one years old, she canvassed the community for signatures opposing the death penalty. "White Men Beg for the Life of their Colored Brother," she titled her petition. Moran met with army lawyers and, wary of her place as a citizen of Occupied Austria, she told the camp commander, "Please, dear General, don't be cross for me an old woman using your precious time but my heart drove me to take this step."

★   ★   ★

Until Bennett's arrest and the resulting Austrian outrage, Camp Roeder had had a reputation of being a slow, quiet outpost. Renwick C. Kennedy, an army chaplain from Alabama, described life for an occupation soldier as anything but glamorous.

"There he stands in his bulging clothes," Kennedy told his diary, "fat, overfed, lonely, a bit wistful, seeing little, understanding less—the Conqueror, with a chocolate bar in one pocket and a package of cigarettes in the other."

Life was structured around small social events. In one week in early March 1953, two visiting generals attended graduation ceremonies at the camp's mountain training center. An Austro-American group planned a folk dance. Two Salzburg men were arrested for stealing gasoline from army vehicles. Ping-Pong tournaments were staged on Sunday afternoons, Tuesdays were bingo nights, and a "Black Cat" scavenger hunt was planned for Friday the thirteenth. An accidental grenade explosion slightly injured two army privates, and the camp's dental clinic was busy "drilling, filling and pulling" teeth, as the camp newspaper, the *USFA Sentinel*, so brightly reported. Seventeen down in the paper's crossword puzzle called for a two-letter word for a Teutonic deity in German mythology. Despite the tensions between conquerors and conquered, a tenuous, peaceful co-existence had been wrought.

The Bennett case with its racial undertones changed everything. Many recalled two other US soldiers recently court-martialed for rape in Austria. They were imprisoned for twenty years, matching the Austrian punishment for sexual assault. They were white soldiers though, and the death penalty was never considered.

For Bennett, the stakes were grievously higher. The color of his skin alone seemed to demand that. Washington's attempt to desegregate the army quickly upset the caste system of white officers overseeing black grunts.

"The black men, they all congregated in their own little area," one white veteran recalled many years later, after serving in Salzburg and Vienna. "We tried to get along. It just didn't always work out that way."

Bennett's court-martial proceeded as planned, the prospect of death weighing heavily. In the final days of December, Major James F. Donovan, chief of psychiatric services, wrote the army's first assessment of Private John Bennett.

"The soldier was born in a rural zone of Virginia," noted the psychiatry chief. "Father is forty-four years of age in poor health and a retired laborer. His mother is forty-two years of age and housewife, who suffers from high blood pressure. Family relationships apparently were fair. The soldier got along fairly well in school, finished the seventh grade when he quit to go to work at age fourteen. Held minor common labor jobs until August 1953 when he volunteered for the draft." Bennett, the major added, "apparently had been in no previous difficulty."

Of his difficult childhood, all Donovan wrote was: "He began his sexual activities around ages of 4–5 and began actual intercourse when he was around 12–13 years of age. He has been extremely active in this area since that time and has at least one living illegitimate child. In addition he has a history of drinking excessively since about age of 15, and on occasions he has used marihuana."

Prosecutors would seize upon the Donovan summary to argue for a death sentence. His mental status, Major Donovan wrote, "reveals a dull, apathetic, frightened, young Negro soldier whose fright is in reference to the situation in which he finds himself. He displays no concern for the little girl in this act but is anxious only in the area of what might happen to him." In the end, Donovan did not delve deeper into Bennett's troubled background, nor did he report upon his family history of mental illness. The majority of the report was gleaned from a short interview with Bennett and a brief review of his military records. Nevertheless, for army prosecutors, this became Exhibit A for the court-martial jury.

"There is no evidence of psychosis or neurosis," Major Donovan concluded. Rather, Bennett's "judgment is extremely poor. He has little or no insight." He continued bolstering the prosecution's case. "This man possesses an extremely unstable personality structure. . . . He finds it difficult to resist sexual impulses because of his lack of moral code, his low intellectual level and because of overindulgence in alcohol. This inability to resist impulsive acting out is *not* due to a mental illness per se, but to an extremely poor organized personality structure."

In a second medical consult, Bennett described to army doctors his seizures, what his mother told him was epilepsy. His head throbbed over his right ear. He would faint or go "running around trying to hurt someone." As a teenager, the seizures gave way to "blind stuppers." He lost any sense of himself, everything blended into a single color. For a while, he boxed with friends "but couldn't stand the blows to the head." Three times, he complained to army doctors, he said, "but no follow-up has been done." He admitted the rape but denied the attempted murder. The examiners concluded nevertheless: "No neurological disease." The exam, however, turned up a low IQ score of 67, which, years later, would suggest he may have had a developmental disability.

The army next sent him to Landstuhl, Germany, for more medical and psychological evaluations that also uncovered no psychiatric or neurological diseases. Lieutenant William J. Reid, a psychiatric social worker, interviewed Bennett at length.

"He claims that his adjustment to work and superiors has been good, and there is no record of disciplinary difficulties," Lieutenant Reid found. Bennett admitted this was the first time he had "messed up." His only complaint was the "dizzy spells." They came on frequently, he said, almost every other day. He felt weak and his stomach cramped. "I have to lie down for a while." To ease the pain, he drank heavily. He rattled off the names of his good buddies who joined him at the local bars. Beer, hard liquor, cognac, all of it made him happy. He told of visiting the gasthauses to pick up prostitutes. There was a girlfriend back in the States though, and he wrote her regularly. He also had worries over his parents' poor health. All in all, he mostly spent his off-duty hours writing letters, sleeping, or drinking with army pals.

Upon further inspection, Bennett's family history showed he was the fourth of seven children. His father, Percy Bennett, was a "passive, easygoing man." Lieutenant Reid concluded that he "was permissive, at times lax, regarding [his children's] behavior." His mother, Ollie Bennett, might scold John for some childish infraction, and then he and his father would share a "laugh over it." His mother though, Bennett told the lieutenant, was a "more aggressive, hot-tempered person afflicted with chronic high blood pressure." She "would at times lose control of herself and scream at them." Two older brothers, Bennett complained, were often "mean and loafing around." His sister, five years older, seemed always "after him," urging him to help around their house and small farm. He did not like the farmwork. He labored only "to keep going." Mostly he spent time with friends. They shared aspirin and drank wine or corn liquor. Sometimes he smoked "refers" and liked to "hot-rod."

Bennett also told Lieutenant Reid about the "blind stuppers" and dizzy spells. "I act crazy," he said. He would fight and run about the house; once he even drove off in his brother's car, though he had no memory of it. At fifteen, he was injured in a car wreck and had cuts across his leg, arm, and face, but was never diagnosed with a concussion. He enlisted at seventeen and was kidded a lot by his fellow soldiers. Not bullied, just teased harshly. Bennett was young and looked it. He started growing a mustache when a sergeant mocked him as a "little girl."

Major Donovan C. Senter, chief clinical psychologist at the army hospital in Frankfurt, Germany, also assessed Bennett. He put the soldier through a battery of "Draw-A-Person" tests, having him sketch people in different poses. Major Senter found "some evidence of internal confusion," his report stated, part of Bennett's court-martial file. Bennett drew extensively, a sign of "considerable anxiety." Evidence of "psychopathy and aggressiveness" emerged in how Bennett's figures were depicted, with their hands stuffed in their pockets. He showed "evidence of virility striving" by adding elaborate buttons, pockets and a belt, collars and hats. He gave his male characters hats to hide their baldness. He seemed "fearful and withdrawn" because he drew small people in large crowds, bunched together. And his figures were tilted, what the major termed "evidence of disorientation." Major Senter claimed it was a phenomenon often associated with schizophrenia. He reported that Bennett suffered from "external pressure and danger," evident in how the prisoner described his fear of storms. This soldier, Senter concluded, lacked any "strong, stabilizing purpose" in life.

Lieutenant Colonel T. A. Kiersch, chief of neuropsychiatry at Frankfurt, reviewed the test reports and clinical summaries and, in another gift to army prosecutors, discounted any mental disorders. Bennett, Lieutenant Colonel Kiersch determined, was not mentally ill. Even if the spells suggested a hint of epilepsy, he said, "It is not felt that his conduct as reported on the date of the offense could even remotely be considered an epileptic seizure."

A separate three-member medical board at the US Army Hospital in Salzburg also found "no medical disease" and "no psychiatric illness." One board member was Major Moser. However, his memoirs years later confused key details about the Bennett case. He wrote that two soldiers confessed to the rape, that the girl was just seven years old and was murdered. The major also blamed the attack on black prejudice against white Austrians.

"They considered Austrians as *untermenschen* [racially or socially inferior], not real people; one could take liberties," he asserted rather grandly. "This dispassionate racial blast, from black soldiers who undoubtedly had suffered their own outrages of discrimination, caused me several sleepless nights."

At Camp Roeder, the army assigned Bennett a new defense lawyer. They met only once to prepare for trial, even as the prosecution's case was building against him. Most damaging was Bennett's signed confession. He was eighteen years old, and admitted to having sexual intercourse with the girl but denied that he tried to kill her, or that he threw her in the icy creek. He said he left the post on an authorized pass and visited "several sites, a girl friend and several bars." He met up with some friends, and they rode in an army truck to Siezenheim.

"We went to Francis' Gasthaus where we got to drinking Christmas beer, cognac and sloe gin," he told Sergeant Kane. He claimed he did not know the names of the men he was drinking with, but he confirmed leaving the bar alone. He described the customs man on the river bridge and later meeting a fellow soldier—a "boy," Bennett called him—and they shared a half bottle of cognac.

Bennett's recollection of a second soldier was never corroborated. Neither the army nor his defense lawyer found this individual, and there is no evidence the army even tried. No one else was charged in the case or brought to testify as a witness to the attack. Clearly, that night of his arrest, exhausted and scared, Bennett was trying to shift his story to deflect blame from himself.

Other prosecution witnesses filled in other gaps though. Captain Floyd M. Wilson recounted how his wife called to him, "Come downstairs quick!" He ran to the kitchen and saw her helping a small girl into the bathroom.

The captain's wife, Helga Wilson, told police she had been cooking supper when the girl appeared at their door.

"Will you help me?" the girl pleaded. "Will you please help me?"

Wilson thought at first the girl was a beggar, "until she told me that a Negro had strangled her" and tossed her into the stream behind their apartment. She wrapped her in a comforter on the couch. "She was cold. She was shaking." She handed her a hot-water bottle and poured some hot milk with butter and sugar, but the girl could not steady the glass. Her mind racing, Helga Wilson lit a cigarette and tried to think— "What do I do next?" She suddenly realized she did not even know the girl's name."

"Gertrude," the girl said. "But my mother calls me Gertie."

The girl was interviewed by US army police in the hospital. Her statement was short, only a page and a half. Anastasia Lindamood, married to the US Army sergeant who helped investigate the case, served as translator. Anastasia was driven to the hospital, and army officials also picked up the girl's father, the customs chief.

Inside, the girl rested alone in a hospital bed, a yellow room with yellow walls. Her two long dark braids hung over her feather pillow. Next to her was "an old-fashioned German type doll." The girl turned her gaze from the window as the police, the interpreter, and her father entered. Her father was short and slender, clean shaven, and "extremely calm," Lindamood recalled. They all looked at the girl; a clean white sheet covered her to her chin. "Her eyes were brown and large and very, very hollow," Lindamood remembered.

The girl answered their questions. "This Negro soldier said to me in German, 'Come along.' . . . The Negro soldier choked me with both hands . . ." She tried to scare him, shouting an English word she knew from her father, "MP," for military police.

"No," answered the soldier. "Nix MP."

★　★　★

At 8:30 in the morning, January 31, 1955, just six weeks after the crime, John Bennett's court-martial opened at US headquarters in Salzburg, all eyes searching Bennett sitting stoically at the defense table in his crisp army uniform. Sergeant Eugene W. Cadwell stood among the guard detail in the rear. Even with Bennett's back to him, he could sense that Bennett appeared uninterested, as if he never expected to be found guilty, much less a death sentence. "He looked as if he didn't care if anything happened or not," Cadwell recalled years later.

Another courtroom guard, Staff Sergeant Marvin Jacobsen, believed Bennett was resigned to his fate. "He didn't seem to want to eat much. He was pale looking. He wouldn't talk hardly any," the sergeant remembered. "I think he knew he'd get the max." Each morning, Jacobsen drove the hand-cuffed Bennett in an army jeep from the jail to the courthouse. Bennett was dressed in a gray Class A uniform with black boots and garrison cap. "Austrians would line the streets," Jacobsen recalled. "They wanted to see him."

Nine jurors were chosen. They all were white officers—two colonels, four lieutenant colonels, two majors, and a captain. Two were supervisors in Bennett's same headquarters section, part of his direct chain of command. In less than fifteen minutes of questioning, the panel was asked only a few questions. Could they set aside local newspaper stories about the assault and Bennett's arrest? Yes. None of the jurors acknowledged any "conscientious scruples" with regard to the death penalty. The judge asked only one of the white officers on the jury panel if he could be impartial, noting "the accused is a member of the Negro race." Yes, he replied.

Bennett was arraigned and pleaded not guilty. The judge addressed the jurors: "Probably few cases have come up for trial in U.S. Forces Austria with so much advance notice and advance publicity as has attended this one." All that had to be set aside. This decorated army jury in this military courtroom, these nine Americans in Austria, would sit in judgment. A white army would decide the fate of the black soldier.

Chief prosecutor Captain Howard Vincent stood before the jury. In his opening statement, he described Bennett drinking the Christmas beer, searching for a woman, and carrying the girl toward the creek. He also, later that night, "took some precautions to cover his part in the affair, ate dinner and went to a movie." Vincent called thirty-five witnesses to describe Bennett's odd behavior, pounding on doors, bursting into strangers' homes, their descriptions of his wild, blank eyes. Most, like Sergeant Gilbert Romero, suspected he was suffering from some kind of spell.

"If he had something to drink, I don't believe it was more than one or two," the sergeant testified. "But he looked kind of peculiar because this man didn't motion with his hands. Just stood with his hands down." The look in his eyes, that was the thing.

The border-crossing officer testified; the housewives, too. Stefan Baier was so afraid to point to Bennett that he fainted on the stand. Caecelia Wagner was asked whether it was difficult to tell black people apart.

"Do you find that Negroes are easy to identify?"

"Not so easy," she said.

"They all tend to look alike?"

The girl's mother recounted how the soldier burst into their house, and an hour later, she and her husband rushed to the army captain's home to find their badly injured daughter.

"She was very pale, gray, and very disheveled," the mother remembered. "She had dark circles under her eyes . . ." The prosecution focused next on the alleged cover-up. Private George Burkett described Bennett later that night as carrying his combat boots. His pants were ripped. "I noticed a tear, and I asked him how he tore his trousers. He told me had been skiing at Berchtesgaden [in the Bavarian Alps] and that is how he tore them, and he went from Berchtesgaden to Munich. Burkett paused. "I asked him how he could have made it to Munich and back that day, and he just said that he had been to Munich. I told him that was pretty hard to do."

Lead investigator Sergeant Kane described Bennett's confession, and defended bringing his pistol to the interrogation—not to display it threateningly, he maintained, but strapped under his zipped-up windbreaker so Bennett realized he was armed. Bennett's defense lawyer, Captain James H. Boyle, suggested his client had been coerced into confessing. He asked Sergeant Kane about the need for a firearm.

"You would hardly expect trouble with another man when there were a lot of other men wandering around in the office, would you?"

"Oh," said Kane, "we have had it."

"But you thought things would go easier this evening if you had a gun?"

"No, sir. It is common practice, sir."

The defense lawyer did not give an opening statement and offered just seven defense witnesses. They spoke well of Bennett and his army service, but none provided an alibi. Sergeant Homer Persinger tried to compliment Bennett and other black soldiers under his command, only to end up insulting them.

"He stayed busy all the time," the sergeant testified. "I never had to look around for him. When there was no work to do, he was always standing around waiting. In the morning he would get his truck. One boy worked one day and then another."

Captain Vincent again addressed the jury.

"Gentlemen," the chief prosecutor stressed, "his confession is full of admissions of force although he didn't know it at that time probably. He probably thought if he said he didn't use any force on her that would excuse it."

In an army courtroom filled with Salzburg and Siezenheim citizens, in a country long under heel during the Allied occupation, the chief prosecutor also praised the US Army's judicial system. "This accused has gotten one of the fairest trials that any accused probably in the history of the United States ever got," he proclaimed. "The facts of this case show that there was no excuse for it, whatever. The proof is extremely strong—circumstantial and real. . . . There is nothing else to do but find the man guilty."

Captain Boyle rose next. The defense attorney was fully aware of the public outcry, in this room, on this army camp, and throughout Austria. "This case has been tried and developed and commented on in the newspapers, in the press, by word of mouth, by rumor and by conversation," he said. "A vast amount of what we call 'public opinion' has been built up." That, he said, is really what "the defense must combat."

The best argument he had was a defense of mistaken identity. Were Bennett's stares blank or some sign of a mental blackout and not drunkenness at all? The prosecution centered its case on the sexual assault, he argued, "and spent very little time" on the second charge of attempted murder. "This case is not airtight," Captain Boyle cautioned. He suggested that attempted murder was added to the charges to make sure Bennett was executed: "The inclusion of that charge, if this were not a serious case, I would say is laughable. There is no evidence, really serious evidence" of attempted murder. "There is nothing to show it."

During a trial break, the girl's father approached the prosecution table and asked if his daughter could testify in person. He wanted her to clear her name, he said, especially after Bennett's confession asserted "she appeared as though she wanted to go with me." Without that, the father insisted, a not-guilty verdict would be "damaging" to her reputation, especially in a country still under US control. The family was willing to risk the trauma of her testifying in court rather "than take the chance of her being hurt" in the community if Bennett was acquitted.

The judge, Captain Herbert, cited an army psychiatry report that her physical and mental health remained delicate; she should not be questioned anymore and certainly not brought in to testify. But the prosecution insisted; it relished the emotional impact of that moment, the Austrian schoolgirl confronting the eighteen-year-old American soldier. It could easily sway any juror holdouts. The defense objected but was overruled. The judge agreed to invite her. But he adjourned the trial for a week to give her more time to recuperate, and the defense to prepare for the inevitable.

The court reconvened the morning of February 8. For a lineup, Bennett was seated in a chair in the back, next to three other randomly selected "colored soldiers." Would the girl with her emotional trauma and the darkness of that night remember the right man? It clearly was an odd arrangement, something police normally would have done long before the trial with a lineup or photographs. But the army again was skirting the rules. With John Bennett in this racially charged trial, prosecutors were aiming for maximum impact—and all before the jury.

She took her seat, and the prosecutor, through a German translator, asked if she knew not to lie.

"It's a sin," said Gertie.

"What happens to people that tell lies?"

"They are not believed by other people if they always tell lies," she answered.

"Anything else happen to them?

"And God punishes them."

She was brave that day, calm and direct, not hesitant. Her dark hair was still knotted in braids, her fingers twisting in her lap. She was small, but she was forceful.

"I got out of the bus and there is a hill, and the Negro walked down that hill," she explained. "I saw him but I continued on walking. He was walking behind me. Then I tried to let him pass because there is a dark narrow road and I was afraid."

She told all of them, the American soldiers in their bright, brisk uniforms crowded in the front of the courtroom, the big police guards along the back and sides, the military judge high up on his courtroom bench, and her Austrian countrymen, too.

"No!" she said. She begged the man as he dragged and carried her off and how she later pretended she had drowned in the creek. "I closed my mouth tightly and then he left."

There was one issue left, one matter yet to clear up; then she could go home, they promised her.

"Gertie," the prosecutor began, "I want you to look around the room here and take all the time you want to, and then tell me if you see that man in the room, or if you don't see him, or if you don't know."

"There, I believe," she answered. "The one who is lighter in color."

Captain Vincent walked to the rear of the courtroom. He stood behind the first black soldier. "Is this the man?" he asked.

"No," she said.

He stood behind Bennett. "Is it this man?"

"Yes," she said, and she pointed.

She was done; she had spoken. She left and the lawyers addressed the jury again. The prosecutor emphasized her positive identification. "You saw the expression on her face when she pointed her finger at the accused sitting at the back of the room with the other colored soldiers," he told the jury.

But Captain Boyle for the defense believed her identification hazy. "She didn't know whether his lips were thick or thin. She thought maybe he had a moustache. She didn't remember whether he had a hat or not. She didn't know whether he had stripes or not because she couldn't see it. It was half dusk."

The jury began deliberating at 1:35 p.m. They returned just one hour later. They found him guilty on both charges. For the start of the punishment phase of the trial, the judge asked the now-convicted soldier if he wished to testify. Bennett stood. "Sir, I wish to remain silent," he announced.

Only three defense witnesses were called to the stand, and they were largely inconsequential. They spoke about Bennett's good conduct and hard work. His supervisor, Captain William M. Fuller, offered high praise. "To my knowledge there had been no trouble as far as the military is concerned," he said. "He had not appeared on my battery punishment book. He had never been in any trouble or had never been brought to my attention for any wrongdoing . . . I had no occasion to even call him on the carpet."

Not a troublemaker?

"Not by any stretch of the imagination."

An asset?

"Yes," Bennett's captain testified. "The man was an asset to the unit and a morale factor. He was always joking, not in a wise attitude, but he had a jovial manner. He had a happy-go-lucky attitude throughout. I could not attest to his intelligence level or anything of that sort. He has his Pfc stripe." Even after Bennett's arrest, when Captain Fuller rated the young soldier "excellent" in character and efficiency, the captain still felt compelled to add: "This man has a very likable personality . . . And most things are treated with a winning smile as he looks for humor in everything."

The testimony, the evidence, the arguing were done, the trial nearly complete. Bennett still declined to speak. Captain Boyle rose and praised Bennett's work ethic and soldier camaraderie. "He is only a private first class. He is not high in rank, and yet he did his job in such a manner that it inspired other men."

The defense lawyer stressed that the assault occurred on Austrian soil; maybe they should have turned this over to Austrian authorities. "This crime happened while the man was stationed in a foreign country—in Austria, and the person injured was a citizen of Austria," he pleaded.

Captain Vincent disagreed. "The accused is not an Austrian. He is an American," the prosecutor argued. "And the good that men do, I agree with the defense counsel, lives after them. The evil lives after them too."

The jurors deliberated again, this time a mere twenty-five minutes. They returned to the courtroom, their vote unanimous. The judge read it aloud.

"The court," he told Private John Bennett, "sentences you to be put to death."

Bennett did not flinch and the court adjourned. Guards descended around the now-condemned soldier.

"We put extra guards on him," Sergeant Jacobsen remembered. "Double as many, six or more. There was a hurry; a rush to get him out of there." Their concern was a possible attack by angry Austrians lurking outside the courthouse, near the camp gates, or pacing around the army jail. "Some of the civilians would have lynched him," the sergeant worried.

In two weeks, the Judge Advocate General's office (JAG) quickly reviewed the court record, the evidence and testimony, and a trial transcript. The crime was "heinous," the JAG declared; Bennett did not merit clemency. "Therefore," the JAG office concluded, "the sentence as adjudged should not be disturbed." The ruling made little mention of Bennett's background, just that he was poor and from Chatham, Virginia, that his parents were in ill health, and his grandfather died "in an Insane Asylum." That same day, General Arnold approved the death sentence and ordered Bennett moved for six weeks to the US Army Europe Military Prison in Mannheim, on Germany's Rhine River. In the spring, the prisoner would be shipped to the US Disciplinary Barracks at Fort Leavenworth, the army's death row in Kansas.

Everything was moving fast, and still Bennett showed little emotion. More likely he was confused and frightened again. He had had little schooling in rural Virginia. He had spent little time in the white man's world outside his family farm near Chatham. Now here he stood an ocean away, a mentally disturbed, young black man in handcuffs and leg irons and in the worst trouble of his young adult life. He had put his faith in the

United States Army when he raised his hand and swore his allegiance to the flag. Now under a sentence of death and bound for death row, all he had left was to still trust in the army to save him.

The Mannheim jail was an army collection point for prisoners bound for the United States, and for a newly convicted soldier like Bennett, a devilish place. One prisoner had slashed his throat in the shower. Another was hauled off to a "dungeon" cell. A third attacked a guard with a baseball bat. But of all the prisoners, John Bennett instantly became the main attraction, the only one sentenced to die.

"The first thing I'd see in the morning was a report on Bennett and it almost always said he had been up at night walking his cell," recalled a Mannheim jail guard. "A model prisoner."

Bennett was housed in the maximum-security B Building. He was held just down the hall from the command office on the second floor; that way the staff could keep a close watch on the new man. His cell consisted of a bed, a seatless commode, and a porcelain washbasin. His water came from a spigot in the wall; he pressed a button to drink. He slept on a bed with a mattress, two sheets, and a cover. Wake-up call sounded at 7 a.m., "and the cells had to be spotless," the guard said, "as fine and clean as any hospital bed." Bennett swept and mopped his own floor, and was not allowed back on the bed until 5 p.m. That meant spending most of his day on his cell floor, his back pressed against the wall. If he so much as creased his linen, a guard platoon would rip the bed out and issue him a replacement made of two-by-fours and a metal frame, six inches off the ground. Act up some more, and he would be punished with a bare prison diet—eighteen ounces of bread a day. Bennett understood the rules in Mannheim. To prevent suicides, no belts or belt loops were allowed. In that cold German winter, he huddled in a green fatigue jacket.

The guard who watched over Bennett liked him. He came to know him well. "No trouble at all," the guard remembered. His name was Maddox, and he too was being transferred to Kansas. He would become the army's hangman.

Chapter Three

* * * * * * * *

THE CASTLE

The man who gave his name to the old fort died chasing a small buffalo. An attorney from the East Coast, Henry Leavenworth had expected to devote his life to the law. But unlike other men of privilege, he cast his future with the US Army and the opening of the American West. Sent "out there" to scout the best location for a new army encampment, the young officer chose not the eastern banks fertile with low-lying farm ground but the towering river bluffs on the other side. He settled on a spot high above the Missouri River just before it makes its mighty swerve east. There he plotted a new fort facing west, for the army to shepherd wagon trains, Mormons, and gold prospectors coming to tame the continent. Leavenworth brought discipline to the frontier.

Tall and thin, with a long nose and steely eye, Leavenworth served as an "Indian agent" in the Northwest Territory and a lieutenant colonel exploring the upper Mississippi. In 1823, he struck a treaty with marauding Arikarees and four years later was ordered westward in search of that new cantonment. From St. Louis, his regiment pushed off in keel boats after the April snow melt. Three weeks later, they happened upon the perfect site.

From its earliest days, good and evil spirits descended upon Fort Leavenworth. The site began as a great military adventure, but frontier pestilence held sway. Some of it was stirred up by rotting vegetables in the river bottoms. Mosquitoes carrying malaria buzzed up the bluffs, too. When the six-year-old son of an army lieutenant died at the Kansas fort, parents transferred their children to school across the river in Missouri.

"A great deal has been done, much more in truth than could have been expected of a garrison so reduced by sickness," reported two army

inspectors general in 1829, the second year of the Leavenworth cantonment. "Still the work is not half accomplished, either as to labor or dis-
bursements of money. A good hospital had been erected, and four houses,
originally intended to quarter one company each, have been put up and
very nearly completed."

That same year, Lieutenant Otis Wheeler wrote to his sister in New
Hampshire, pitying the pleasant but also dismal life in Kansas. "We have
a garden just in front of our quarters," he told her. "At least 12 acres just
coming up, grape vines, four hundred plum trees and everything that is
good under way."

For two years, Lieutenant Wheeler led a company at Fort Leavenworth
and boasted his was the healthiest of the eight companies there. And yet,
he wrote, "I have lost ten or twelve men since I came here, by death, but
I could not help that." Others, though, wrote movingly of the new army
post, the unfolding frontier, and the gold-green patchwork prairie.

"A speck of civilization in the heart of a wilderness," John Treat Irving
Jr., the author of *Indian Sketches* and a nephew to Washington Irving, declared after a visit in 1833. "There is nothing here to tell of war; and but
for the sentinels upon their posts, the lounging forms of the soldiers or the
occasional drum as the signal for the performance of some military duty,
we would not have known that we were in the heart of a military station."

The frontier spread vast and open, lovely and treacherous. On the
river bluffs, soldiers mounted a brace of bronze cannons, cast in Paris for
French kings. The army hammered out peace negotiations with native
tribes, swapped furs and weapons, and launched immigrant trails to Santa
Fe and the Oregon territory.

Despite the struggles of settlement, for his achievement, Leavenworth was promoted to brigadier general. He set out once again in
1834 with four hundred army troops to subdue native warriors in the
Southwest. Many of his men fell sick with fevers, and most believed
their leader had succumbed to malaria along the marshy river banks. As
he died in a hospital wagon near Cross Timbers, the general confided
he had badly injured himself trying to lasso a young buffalo; his horse
tripped in a gopher hole. "I have killed myself in running down that
devilish calf," he despaired.

In death his reputation grew, and so too the fort that bore his name. In the beginning, it was nothing more than a shantytown of makeshift tents and huts on slab quarters carved from bark and timber. In a year's time, the fort housed enlisted men in frame-and-brick buildings with basement kitchens and a post infirmary. Officers and their families toured the countryside on horseback and carriage. The frontier painter George Catlin recalled the region fondly. High above the Missouri River cliffs, the land sprawled lush in corn-gold sunflowers and tall grass, home to roaming buffalo herds and sometimes marauding native warriors, the skies threatening with summer heat, winter whiteouts, and spring tornadoes. Beyond that swerve in the river, looking west past the bluffs, the prairie opened like a frontier quilt. There lay America's future.

Fort Leavenworth stood guard during the Bleeding Kansas attacks and the Plains Indian wars. For a while, the army imprisoned the Brule chief Spotted Tail within its walls. Upon his release, he became a lifelong advocate for peace, even as other warrior elders derided him as "fat, soft and supine." And so, in time, Fort Leavenworth's reputation would be staked less on winning the West and more on filling another pressing army need: a national military prison.

Following the Civil War, army prisons often appeared small and unruly, more like county jails than penitentiaries. Up to thirty stockades and prisons blemished the American landscape, many decrepit. Each commandant ruled his own stockade. Some prisoners were branded or forced to wear stripes, many were chained or beaten. Some were shot. Guardhouses often were sloppily built, with long-term offenders crowded in among petty thieves. The scattering of jailhouses was difficult to maintain, and costly.

In the 1870s, Washington dispatched a board of visitors to Canada to study military prisons there. The panel came away impressed. What was needed for the United States was a uniform system, a central facility to "maintain discipline in the army, to reform offenders and repress repetition of military offenses." The most prevalent of crimes was the sin of desertion, something no army could tolerate. Even in the time of General Leavenworth, the army was losing up to half of its enlisted men as runaways. The adjutant general called it a "progressive evil."

In May 1874, the army settled on Fort Leavenworth as an ideal location for its centralized military prison. It redesigned the arsenal buildings, expanded the quartermaster section, and soon took in 225 soldiers behind a new stretch of walls built from local brick and limestone. Inmates were fed milk and ten ounces of oatmeal for breakfast. The lunch call included more milk, plus cornmeal, pork or beef, and two pounds of potatoes. Dinner was no feast either: a half pint of milk and fourteen ounces of sourdough. Prisoners fashioned army corn brooms and barracks chairs, and soon were stitching together thirty thousand pairs of shoes a year.

By century's end, the army's new central prison, guardhouses, and cell blocks already were vastly overcrowded with men stacked into jail dorm rooms, and conditions were unsafe. In response, Congress funded an even larger prison for Fort Leavenworth, one to confine up to twelve hundred convicts. New construction was launched in February 1906, and the plans were elaborate: a grand archway entrance and new cell houses, with cell wings to join the ends of the old prison structures. Prisoners were assigned to "work gangs," and convicts chipped away at rock quarries, pressed bricks, and cut stones. They planed boards at a new prison sawmill. If anyone slipped out of line, two or three guards might beat them with clubs or a rifle butt. The convicts were required to ask permission for almost everything. If anyone even looked as though he might escape, a guard was cleared to shoot. Constant troublemakers were locked in underground cells.

For five years, the construction slogged on. Not until shortly before America entered World War I was the United States Military Prison rechristened the United States Disciplinary Barracks. The first large wave of inmates, culled from that first World War, was confined in its eight jutting prison wings. Capacity soon reached twenty-five hundred prisoners. The massive silver dome, a huge cap over the prison rotunda, could be spotted for miles. It stood sentry over the river heights, steady and solemn, the army's maximum-security prison high on the embankment. At its front gate were tacked the letters "U.S.D.B." and below that a prison motto: "Our Mission—Your Future." Everyone called it the "Castle." That imagery instantly stuck, with the prison's high unscalable limestone walls, its center courtyard, and a rotunda topped by that large silver dome. The main gate could be a welcoming place for short-timers, but the cell wings were impossible to leave for anyone doing hard time, especially men on death row. For soldiers who had been trained to march in open fields and camp outdoors, the Castle stood sturdy and menacing, like a medieval fortress from a far-off era in Europe, or even Austria.

The "Mutiny of 1919" erupted at the close of World War I. As the war ended, many prisoners wanted their sentences commuted. When no clemency was offered, 150 prisoners dropped their tools in an organized strike. At nightfall, they torched a storehouse. In the morning, inmates were lined up and ordered to return to work. The 2,300 prisoners refused to cooperate. Tempers steadied only when Colonel Sedgwick Rice, the prison commandant, promised to forward their grievances to Washington. Several months passed without commutations, and anger flared again. A gang of inmates looted a warehouse. Prisoners held as conscientious objectors were placed in lockdown.

"They watched the disturbances from the windows," Colonel Rice recounted. "They shouted and encouraged the prisoners in the yard to resist the authorities." But the colonel seemed little concerned. "There was no riot or general disturbance," he said, dismissing the affair. Only six guards were injured, and one prisoner suffered a bullet wound to the leg.

By 1944 and the peak of World War II, the Castle was brimming with violence. More than three thousand prisoners were locked inside; others were jammed into extra "rehabilitation wings." Another 17,500 soldiers convicted of minor crimes passed under the Castle archway. In the summer of 1945, violence peaked during three days when fourteen German soldiers were hanged in a warehouse elevator shaft, executed for killing fellow German prisoners they suspected of cooperating with American guards. They were buried in American soil in the prison's hillside cemetery just outside the Castle walls.

By the 1950s, attitudes around imprisonment had changed. The judge who would preside over an appeal hearing for Private John Bennett praised the Castle for its "success" in rehabilitating inmates. Army leaders offered psychological testing and vocational training. Prisoners took classes in carpentry, plumbing, accounting, or college algebra. For those who never finished the fourth grade, basic schooling was mandatory. Anyone except the men on death row could try out for a coveted spot on the prison baseball squad. Otherwise, the average day for the prison population was preparing chow in the kitchen or spooning grub in the cafeteria. Inmates stacked books in two prison libraries, washed shirts in the prison laundry, and pressed them in the dry-cleaning plant. Others slopped hogs on the prison farm, any kind of work to kick-start a man's life. "What a prisoner accomplishes while inside the walls," said Colonel Weldon W. Cox, prison commandant during Bennett's last year there, "is partly his responsibility."

The army was not unique to prison reform. State penitentiaries also were redesigning their facilities, stressing rehabilitation over incarceration. At Fort Leavenworth, the days of hard prison labor were dying out; the rock pile was knocked down, and the ball-and-chain was wrapped up. Inmate haircuts no longer had to be regulation army-style, and silence was not required at mealtime. Rank-and-file prisoners were treated to weekend movies. A hobby shop kept convicts busy, and a gym was opened. There were even trampoline exercises and a string-and-dance band. Sometimes the songs aired over the institution's in-house radio system. The station also carried *A Talk with Your Chaplain* program in the evening, and *Dateline: USDB* posted updates on prison rules. In December, the staff handed out Christmas cards for inmates to mail home.

Prison security still came first. By the time Bennett arrived in 1955, 561 officers patrolled the Castle. Twelve sentry towers loomed over the Castle perimeter. Army sergeants and privates who patrolled the tiers and prison yard often felt more like teachers or mentors. "They are not merely guards," Colonel Cox stressed. The entire staff, the commandant announced, "has a tremendous influence on the prisoner's attitude and his progress toward rehabilitation." He also stressed, "They are constantly on the alert."

The walls stood high and firm, up to forty-one feet at spots, some reinforced with concrete blocks. But to Donald Powell Wilson, a psychologist for three years at the prison, the Castle seemed like a miniature army regiment. The men had been stripped of rank and yet each morning rose from their cells and fell into line. "They pass the flag in the courtyard," Wilson marveled. "They look up at her. 'Hi, Old Girl,' they say softly." Army convicts as a class, Wilson believed, were "hotly patriotic. There's no country like America, no flag like hers . . . They are Americans to the death."

Most who worked the tiers and all confined inside would never forget those years. "It was a pretty mild place," thought Lieutenant Louis H. Diamond, the legal officer. "There were cells and bars but there were officers too. It was a place to work except there were people in jail. And it was high up over the river and pretty imposing."

First Sergeant Kenneth Kramer loved working the Fort Leavenworth cell blocks. He even remembered the commandant proudly showing off thank-you letters from former inmates. "Some of those guys had made it, and they were never coming back," the sergeant boasted. "It was an outstanding fantastic tour."

Others were not so fond of the gloomy Castle, the stifling Kansas weather, or the dreary prison surroundings. Joan Bateman's husband, John, served as a prison psychiatrist. The couple was raising two small children, the youngest born in the post hospital. They shared an apartment on the fort, and sometimes she spied prisoners in work details around the grounds close to her home. "I was terrified," she recalled, especially on those nights when her husband worked late. "I would be there alone with my daughter and I'd sit there in the dark with the windows open to get some air and you'd wonder who's going to be wandering around."

Some trustees, those prisoners with good behavior records, were permitted outside for chores. In September 1956, three of them slipped over the river bridge and stole a car in Missouri. They made it nearly to St. Joseph, forty miles north, until a night watchman spotted one of them traipsing along a railroad track. A fifty-man posse on foot cornered the other two in a cornfield.

Three more trustees, who were housed in barracks just outside the Castle walls, made a break for it in February 1959. They hoofed it north for Atchison, Kansas, a twenty-five-mile march, hijacked a car, and headed east. Police picked them up in St. Louis. A month later, two more trustees working a trash detail slugged a guard and stole his uniform. They tied his hands with shoestrings, snatched his keys, and lit out in his car. Police caught them in a heavy patch of woods nine miles north of the prison.

There was no magical exit, not by that route. If a prisoner hunkered down, obeyed the rules, and won parole, he would be led back out under the Castle arch to the gravel driveway and freedom. He was handed several meal tickets, twenty-five dollars, and a bus ticket or railroad fare home. Others, after a 1959 federal court decision, were returned to active duty. Most departed the army Castle for good, typical at that time for recidivism rates. Most soldiers never came back.

★   ★   ★

For nearly ninety years, the Castle prison anchored the far end of Fort Leavenworth, twenty-six buildings crammed within brick and limestone walls, including the round turrets and the huge receiving-room rotunda, the spokes, and cell wings. By 2000, the prison showed its age. Walls creaked, the foundation had settled, and cells floors were cracked and cramped. In 2004, a new prison was opened as demolition crews tore down the old Castle walls. It took five months to rip everything apart, a wrecking ball smashing through the last cell wing in January 2005. Six thousand truckloads of debris hauled away nearly a century of progress and hard times. The bulldozers drove off and the graders moved in. The army had itself a new parking lot on what was once the Castle grounds. But the billowing ash and the water hoses never washed away all the difficult years there.

Black soldiers around the nation were treated to a different system of army justice. That simply was how army life had always been, how all the black recruits imagined it would be. The long arm of the law swung heavily against them; the scales of justice tipped the other way. And sometimes that reality could have devastating consequences.

Prison life in Fort Leavenworth was marked by the same social tensions felt outside its walls. Racial strife and prison riots were long remembered through the decades.

In 1901, an army veteran was arrested in the city of Leavenworth, Kansas, for the rape and murder of nineteen-year-old Pearl Forbes. She was white; Fred Alexander was black. He enlisted at twenty-one and served as a private at Fort Huachuca in Arizona Territory. He had returned home to Leavenworth.

After his arrest, a white crowd collected outside his jail cell. One held up a rope. Alexander insisted he was innocent; for safety, police moved him to the nearby state penitentiary in Lansing, Kansas. A white mob of five hundred followed. Some with shovels and pickaxes tried to wrench up railroad ties and break into the state prison, so police returned Alexander to the Leavenworth county jail. "Tell my people and friends goodbye," he cried to the jail warden. "I am not the guilty man."

A thousand angry white men broke through a side entry, smashed his cell lock with a sledgehammer, and hauled Alexander onto the courthouse lawn. They slashed him and demanded a confession, but Alexander persisted.

"I didn't do it!" They cut him some more. Then the woman's father, William Forbes, raised a hand in silence. "Don't hang the brute," he said. "Let's take him out where he murdered my daughter and burn him."

They tied him up in a wagon and clattered down Lawrence and Spruce streets, mothers holding infants chasing after the mob; boys and girls racing behind them, too. Five thousand people converged on a ravine, doubtless many of them white soldiers from Fort Leavenworth. This was the community where they lived. They chained Alexander to a railroad tie and emptied Standard Oil kerosene over his head, twenty-two gallons in all. "Throw it on the nigger!" some shouted. Pearl's father struck a match and lit the former soldier on fire.

In 1906, when the army started building the Castle, three black soldiers working at the fort were involved in what the papers called an "alleged riot" on a downtown bus in the city of Leavenworth. They were sitting in the rear on Christmas Eve when the white conductor asked for their fare. One soldier swore he had already paid, and the conductor barked back, "You niggers are getting too fresh around here." More threats were hurled. The conductor reached for a baton. Someone on the station platform tossed a rock through a bus window. Police arrested the black soldiers and returned them to Fort Leavenworth as prisoners.

In 1910, Fort Leavenworth came within days of legally executing an infantryman. Private Charles O'Neil murdered his young lover, Minnie, a French immigrant. She had attended a dance at Fort Leavenworth, and that sent an enraged O'Neil rushing to her doorstep. Army officers encouraged the couple to sort things out, but O'Neil drew a revolver and shot her.

"I was jealous," O'Neil confessed. He was tried in federal court in Kansas City, Kansas, and sentenced to die. There were no army gallows then, and engineers hastily built a makeshift platform behind the prison walls. O'Neil was less than a week from the noose when state officials, led by the Kansas governor, lobbied President Taft to halt the execution. He intervened and commuted the sentence to life in prison. Private O'Neil was white.

When the United States entered World War I, scores of black conscripts had been arriving to assist the army's effort, only to be insulted by the local press, particularly so in Iowa. "Pie-Eating 'Cullud' Lad at Soldier City Sho-Nuff in Love," guffawed the Des Moines *Capital*. The Des Moines *Evening Tribune* quoted a Southern black soldier joking, "Say man, I nevah was in de United States befoh I came to Ioway."

In the summer of 1918 at Camp Dodge, Iowa, three black soldiers from Alabama were hanged on the parade ground. The army convicted them of "assaulting and outraging" a seventeen-year-old white girl. The entire force was ordered to assemble under a broiling sun and stand at attention as Privates Robert Johnson, Stanley Tramble, and Fred Allen met their end. Johnson and Tramble had confessed; Allen insisted he never "touched the girl." On July 5, all three were marched onto the parade ground and up the scaffold steps. All the white troops were wearing their sidearms; black soldiers were directed onto the parade ground too, but without arms. The prisoners approached the gallows singing. "At times the voices of the doomed men sank almost to a whimper," reported the *Capital*. "Then rose to a shriek." The men prayed too. "God save my soul!" cried one. "Have mercy!" called another. As the thud from the trapdoor echoed across the parade ground, several black soldiers fainted; a fourth bolted toward the scaffold until white guards stopped him.

A race riot broke out in May 1947, this one inside the Fort Leavenworth prison. The fight began amid rumors of President Truman's plan to desegregate the armed forces. To test it, soldiers from segregated cell blocks were ordered to assemble in the dining hall. They were to share meals in the same cafeteria, even though they were assigned separate tables. For many of the white inmates, that was too much.

"They would not go to breakfast," complained Colonel Graeme G. Parks. A veteran of both world wars, wounded in the second, the colonel quickly lost patience. "They would go now or go without food. They still refused to go and then locked the inner door of the wing and began tearing the place to pieces." Eight prisoners were court-martialed.

"The emotion that moved them is primitive and simple," the *New York Times* editorialized. "A man in a disciplinary barracks has for the moment little to be proud of. He feels inferior. And if he happens to have been born with a white skin he may build up his self-esteem by looking down on others who happen to have been born with black or brown skins. Like any of the rest us in a similar position, the Negro resents this attitude. Trouble follows."

A white prisoner, Dewey D. Osborne, a thirty-year-old Tennessean, was stabbed to death; six other inmates and five guards were injured. Guards fired hundreds of tear gas canisters as more fighting erupted in one of the prison wings. Colonel Parks, the commander of the barracks who had just arrived at his new post, warned black prisoners that the gas and smoke would intensify if they did not stop. Guards cut off water and food deliveries to the cell wings. The 213 black inmates and 514 white prisoners surrendered.

★　★　★

Not until July 1943 did the army carry out its first execution at the Fort Leavenworth Castle in a case that foreshadowed John Bennett's. Both men were black, and their victims white. Both were young army privates who had been drinking heavily when they sexually assaulted females in secluded areas at night. Each was subjected to police lineups and each confessed. Both also tried to change their stories.

Levi Brandon, a twenty-three-year-old soldier from Kansas City, Kansas, was arrested in January 1943 shortly after two young females reported they were sexually assaulted. One, a sixteen-year-old waitress, ran three blocks to a city of Leavenworth police station. She told officers that "some negroes" approached and frightened her, and one forced her into an alley and raped her. He also threatened to cut her throat. "You wouldn't want to die, would you?" he warned. She described him as short and stocky, "of the colored race, not real dark and not real light, dressed in an army suit with no overcoat." He also wore his army garrison cap. The second victim, who was twenty years old, reported to police that she was accosted in

Kansas City, Kansas. Forcing her into a wooded field, the soldier smacked her across the top of her head with some kind of blunt weapon and began to sexually assault her. "Scream and I will kill you," he threatened. She screamed anyway, and broke free when he ran off. She remembered the man as "short, stocky, a light-skinned negro, wearing an army uniform with an overcoat and cap."

Police scoured the Kansas City and Leavenworth neighborhoods. They rode city buses hunting for men in uniform matching the assailant's description. They learned that Brandon had been away from Fort Leavenworth on an off-duty pass, just like Bennett, although Brandon's pass was good for three days. They arrested the soldier at the home of a relative, handcuffed him, and locked him inside the Fort Leavenworth guardhouse. The waitress was brought to the fort and, peering through a cell window, positively identified Brandon. She also was asked to view what army reports describe as a lineup of "three negro boys"—they were soldiers, actually—but she ruled them out.

As with Bennett, the army wasted little time in bringing Brandon to trial. However, at his court-martial in February, he chose to testify in his own defense, unlike Bennett. He admitted he had been drinking heavily during those three days—straight shots mostly. "I went crazy," he agreed. "The whiskey was working." But then he tried to repudiate a written statement he earlier had given army investigators. He said he confessed to harming the females only to protect a married woman he actually had been seeing. He did not want the husband to suspect Brandon was interested only in the man's wife. Army prosecutors dismissed that story as ridiculous. He was convicted, and though he had hoped for a fixed prison term, he too was given death.

His commanding general in Omaha approved the ultimate sentence, as did the War Department in Washington. Three military judges on an army board of review affirmed the conviction and sentence as well. "Even considering the possibility that accused may ultimately be released for good behavior," the board wrote, "because of old age there would be no question of a re-occurrence of this happening." And the board was not persuaded by three letters in March and April from Brandon's mother, Edith Griffin. She begged for clemency, but the board of review turned her down. "He will be hanged from the neck until dead," the board ordered.

Levi Brandon was hanged from the Fort Leavenworth gallows on July 26, just six months after his arrest. Justice was swift, and secret. Only military authorities were allowed to witness the hanging, with a single army chaplain. Brandon's nearest relative was notified of the execution in advance but did not attend. The local newspapers gave the hanging a mere four paragraphs.

A year later, the army was expecting more executions. The command staff produced thick manuals laying out official *Procedure for Military Executions*. The protocols were repeatedly updated—1944, 1947, 1953, and 1959—as the army continued refining.

The last update came four years into John Bennett's stay on death row. The electric chair was no longer an option by then, but soldiers could still face a firing squad. Eventually death by musketry, typically only used during war, was discarded, too. That left only the rope. Staff director Neal Harrison, a World War II veteran wounded by a German gun nest in the Battle of the Bulge, wrote the final protocols. They did execute one white soldier, an army warrant officer held over from the Truman era. Bernard J. O'Brien from Texas committed the unpardonable sin for an officer and a gentleman. Desperate to get out of a failing marriage, he clubbed his wife to death with an entrenching shovel, then propped her body in his car and crashed it into a tree, making it appear to be a traffic accident on a German highway. "Just wanted to make her suffer," he told his army jury at his 1952 trial.

O'Brien was arrested long before John Bennett joined the army, and was dead before the army became serious about carrying out executions at Fort Leavenworth. Not until March 1, 1955, three weeks after Bennett's conviction in Austria, did the steady string of hangings begin—all of them black soldiers, and all hanged at midnight, in accordance with the most recently updated protocols.

The command staff designated escort details and let convicts select a chaplain "of the prisoner's choice." The new policy set in 1953 and 1959 assigned army medical officers armed with stethoscopes, poised and ready at the foot of the platform: "It will be his duty to determine the extinction of life in the prisoner." Guards would change the soldier from prison garb into a "regulation uniform," though stripped of "decorations, insignia, or other evidence of membership" in the US Armed Forces. "Likewise, no such evidences will appear on any clothing used in burial." And "when reasonable," the soldier would be treated to a last meal and permitted a "Bible, Rosary, or similar religious articles during the execution." In his last hours, the man would be given "sufficient writing paper and envelopes," though not all letters were forwarded. The army never explained why.

Like everything else, though, the command left nothing to doubt: "The hood will be black, the outer surface of rough materials split at the open end so that it will come well down on the prisoner's chest and back." A collapse board was kept handy in case the prisoner fainted or his feet gave way, or he refused to cooperate.

> The rope will be of Manila hemp, up to 1¼ inches in diameter and approximately 30 feet in length. The rope will be boiled and then stretched while drying to eliminate any spring, stiffness, or tendency to coil. The hangman's knot will be used in the preparation of the noose. That portion of the noose which slides through the knot will be treated with wax, soap, or grease to insure a smooth sliding motion . . . The noose will be placed snugly around the prisoner's neck in such a manner that the hangman's knot is directly behind his left ear.

The knot sometimes ended up behind the wrong ear. Things often went wrong in the dead of night. "The officer charged with the execution will face the prisoner and read aloud to him the charge, finding, sentence and orders," stipulated the 1959 manual.

> He will then notify the chaplain and the prisoner that a brief time will be allowed the prisoner for any last statement. After a reasonable time, he will have the sergeant from the main guard place the hood over the prisoner's head and bind his ankles. The sergeant of the execution party will then adjust the noose around the prisoner's neck. The sergeant of the execution party will then place himself in position at the trigger and upon a signal from the officer charged with the execution, will spring the trap.

Master Sergeant William H. Maddox Jr. eventually took charge of execution details inside the Castle. Like John Bennett, Maddox had been transferred from Mannheim to Kansas and was posted at Fort Riley, Kansas, a two-and-half-hour drive down freshly paved Interstate 70, the "Eisenhower Highway." He helped hang Japanese army general and prime minister Hideki Tojo and other war criminals in the Far East and later served as a military policeman and jail guard in Germany during the Allied occupation. He seemed the perfect pick, a natural choice.

But it was as a farm boy of seven that Maddox learned how to kill a man. One night, a neighbor attempted to rape his mother while his father was away. She resisted and he stormed off, vowing to return. At sunrise, the neighbor stomped back up the yard, this time wielding a shotgun. But Maddox's father had returned and was waiting, standing out front with a shotgun of his own, double-barreled with buckshot. His father fired first and slammed the man in the shoulder.

"He didn't go down so my dad fired again, grazing him in the head," Maddox remembered. The man fell but still would not quit, crawling around the yard, inching closer to his gun. "My dad reloaded for the third time and stood over him and shot him once more, killing him in the dirt." His father served sixteen months of a two-year sentence. To the young, wide-eyed boy, "it was worth every day of it."

Maddox joined the army in 1935. He was born in Kentucky, raised in central Texas, and first put on a uniform when he was twenty-one years old, tall, skinny, very pale, and eager to succeed. The army saved him. He was working twelve hours a day on a Texas spread for a dollar and dinner, or about twenty-six dollars a month with Sundays off. He had no insurance, no hospitalization, just a blazing Texas sun in the heat of the Depression.

"If a horse kicks me and breaks my leg, I'm through," he realized. "The closest hospital is seventy-five miles away in Palestine, Texas. You didn't see a doctor or go to a hospital in those days, unless you were bleeding to death. But in the service you got twenty-one dollars a month, room, clothing, board and a thirty-day leave. I didn't have to worry anymore about where my next meal came from."

He carried his Texas temper into the army and the fighting in World War II. "I got busted for cussing out a line sergeant," he remembered. His unit was pinned down for nine days by enemy fire, one of his four men was killed, and Sergeant Maddox grabbed a radio phone and yelled for another officer to come out and fight himself. "I unloaded on him," he conceded. A week later, his superior gave him a choice: a general court-martial or demotion from master sergeant back to private. "I remember standing there in front of him, ripping off the stripes myself, telling this commander to keep those stripes but be sure to tell the boys where they came from."

At war's end, he mustered out. He traveled the world, to Naples and the Suez Canal, seeing Singapore and the Persian Gulf. When his army savings ran thin, he wandered back to Texas and drifted around the state. He worked six weeks for a detective agency at a Gulf Coast refinery. "I made up my mind. I had ten years in the service and I needed ten more for retirement. I told my boss I was going to re-enlist. He looked at me crazy-like and said I must have rocks in my head. I said maybe. But I left. I went down to the induction station in Houston, threw up my hand and said 'I do.'" The army sent him to Japan for more than three years and detailed him to the Sugamo Prison, a fifty-five-year-old fortress near Tokyo that the United States converted for war criminals. He started as a security platoon officer but eventually wore those sergeant stripes again.

Hangings became Maddox's specialty, Sugamo his classroom, 1948 his year. Sometimes, he recalled, they "dropped" four Japanese criminals at a time, every thirty minutes. "I was the lever man. I put on the anklets and I set the ropes. And I pulled the lever that sprung the traps. The first thing I learned was to do it fast. Quick. Once he starts up those steps, make it a short time from then on." He knew to strap a man's ankles so he could not block his fall. He knew to spring the trap forward "to keep the man from pitching and breaking his jaw on the edge of the platform." He used two kinds of black hoods—one was cotton, the other included a zipper near the forehead for a priest to sprinkle Holy Water. The rope must be hemp and had to be boiled first. He would hang 210-pound weights on it to stretch it out. "Make sure it doesn't bounce like a rubber band," he cautioned. He learned to loop the rope over a man's head and secure the knot behind his left ear. "That," he said, "was the keeper."

The firing squad was ordered for Japanese Colonel Satoshi Oie. He died for civilian atrocities. Driven at night from Sugamo Prison to the firing range, he was so calm he not only slept, he snored. They tied him to a post, fearing he might fall asleep again. But Oie thanked everyone, including the six men aiming rifles at his chest.

In all, Maddox said, he managed or participated in sixty-seven executions—sixty-five with the rope, one by musketry, and one by the electric chair. The electric chair execution was in the summer of 1959 in Nebraska where he helped put to death Charlie Starkweather. Charlie was a lost teenager on a two-month, two-state killing jag across Nebraska and Wyoming with his even younger, fourteen-year-old girlfriend. The girl served seventeen-and-a-half years and was paroled; Charlie got the chair. "He had this great big red hair, and how composed he was to the end," Maddox marveled. "We strapped him in and he joked how light the straps were. He even tried to tighten them. Then we zapped him with three bolts."

Sergeant Maddox was proud of his calling and forever grateful he could serve his country. "It's a job. It's a nasty job," he swore. With a chuckle, he added, "But none of us, none of us, are going to get out of this world alive."

Despite the pride he took in his job, Maddox did have a small quirk. He was a man of disguises. He worried constantly someone related to a person he had executed—a brother, a son, a father, a wife even—would hunt him down. He grew beards and mustaches and shaved them off. He wore baseball caps and cowboy hats or went bald-headed. "We've got too many idiots here in this world," he once complained. "I don't want a bunch of midnight callers."

The army taught him many things. Most importantly, he would say, he learned that crime not only does not pay, but "it comes with punishment." Maddox had his own problems, though. He could admit that, as an old retired man. He and his wife, Virginia, a former elections supervisor, shared a small home on Topeka's east side, their five children grown and gone. He was addicted to gambling, he confessed, and most of his life never cared much for religion. But he was a proud man, a loyal soldier, a self-described

"Texas hangman." He gave his best years to the army, through World War II, the occupation, and finally in Kansas. After retiring in 1962, he worked another seventeen years as a training officer for the Kansas Department of Corrections and a guard at the state diagnostic center. He died in the autumn of 1999, at the age of eighty-five. They buried him in Topeka with full military honors in a cemetery called Mount Hope.

*   *   *

When Sergeant Maddox transferred to Germany after World War II, the Mannheim prison was partly the ruins of an old German palace, most of it blasted apart by bombers. Rummaging around the debris, Maddox stumbled upon a guillotine.

The prisoners were a sorry lot. Most had no family dependents in Europe, and nearly half were young black soldiers in for bar brawls or burglaries. John Bennett's crimes far exceeded the others.

In 1955, Maddox helped herd several hundred prisoners, including Bennett, onto a North Sea ship near Hamburg bound for the States. In New Jersey, they boarded an old prison train, seventy-six convicts to a railcar, the windows barred, and an armed soldier monitoring them from a guard cage. They were dispersed to small army jails around the United States, or, for the lucky ones, given a trip home on parole. Sergeant Maddox ended up at Fort Riley, and Bennett, the Fort Leavenworth prison.

Soon a call came to Fort Riley from the prison commandant. Maddox learned he would be assigned occasional special duty whenever an execution drew near. The army would now lean on his experience. Every year or so, he gathered his execution tools and left his ranch home in Topeka. He headed down the new Eisenhower Highway, his collapse board, ropes, restraining belt, handcuffs, and ankle straps clanking around in the trunk of his car; in the backseat he stuffed his tape, a hood, and a knife.

In a box in a closet at home, Sergeant Maddox kept newspaper clippings and meticulous records. He pasted them into a five-hole spiral binder. He saved copies of his written orders and the names of the doomed, down to their weight, height, and age, "overall drop" rates, and "pully-to-trap" ratios. He recorded their religion, if they had one, the date of their death, and the hour it arrived, always at midnight. He even ordered the caskets. "Bill Maddox was a typical master sergeant," remembered Harrison, the prison staff director. "He was all business and nothing else."

Before he did anything else though, Sergeant Maddox stopped in at death row, called "Seven Base." It was just beneath Seven Wing and in the dim half-light, he took a long look at the next man in line, always a black face. He jotted down some final measurements and checked to see if the prisoner had recently suffered any head or shoulder injuries, cuts or bruises. "Otherwise, and you might not know it, but there's a good chance you could jerk his head off," he later explained. Then he let out his big Texas grin. "You sure as hell don't want to do that."

Chapter Four

★ ★ ★ ★ ★ ★ ★ ★

SEVEN BASE

Three times a day, food was delivered to death row. A guard or trustee left the kitchen for the Castle rotunda, turned onto Seven Wing, circled down to Seven Base partially underground, swung through a sally port, passed several checkpoints, and entered the long, cold, concrete corridor. By the time the meal trays arrived on death row, the warm food often was cold.

Everything about Seven Base was bleak. The walls, the floor, and the ceiling were painted drab gray; a green iron door opened and closed at the end of the narrow hallway. Thin windows high on the ceiling were ground level outside and offered a fleeting glimpse of spring grass; in summer, several peacocks strutted about the Castle yard, gifts from an army colonel in California.

Each inmate's name was posted above his cell door and the doors were double locked. Guards opened them by turning an all-brass Folger Adam key. Steel plates near the bars had been newly replaced with an expandable black metal grille, and the doors stood six feet high, sliding to the left. Each was eleven feet by eight feet. A bare light bulb wobbled from above, and an air vent hummed high up on the wall. The floor was concrete. Each man was issued a bed, a locker, a sink, and a commode. The bed frame was solid steel, covered by an army mattress and blankets. Shoes were tucked neatly under the bed, a single pillow on top. Toiletries were stored in the steel metal locker. No calendars or posters were permitted on the walls. Pictures from home belonged inside the locker, and the locker was kept shut. Earphones for the prison radio system dangled from the wall.

The inmates would wake to a thread of sunshine through the windows and strain to hear the thinning notes of an army bugle outside or the gravel crunch of car tires. On an especially good morning, they might catch a woman's soft voice. Once a deer slipped onto the courtyard, and prisoners heard army guards laughing as they struggled to corral the enemy invader. In a high wind, the flag snapped sharply and the inmates might catch the flash of colors. Out on the prison yard for some brief exercise, they watched the sunlight as it slanted in between Castle towers four, five, and six, over the walls, and through the fence to warm their skin.

"You eventually throw your mind out of gear," recalled Maurice Schick, ordered to die for killing an army colonel's daughter in Japan. "You lose time. One day became another day and then another day. You'd see things on TV but you couldn't understand any of it. You never saw a rock 'n' roll show so you didn't understand rock 'n' roll." Inevitably, some of the prison racket from above seeped down to death row, an echo of what the rest of prison life was like.

"There was a high, low rumble," Schick remembered. "Sort of a distant noise. And there was no tuning it out. It was there. You knew it was there. You lived with it. It was human noise, doors slamming, whistles blowing. Pretty soon it was there so much it didn't register. And you didn't miss it when you left." He added, "You can't have a couple thousand of guys living stacked on top of each other without noise." All the inmates largely learned to tolerate one another, make friends, discuss their cases, and weigh their legal appeals. Few secrets could last long in a cadre of men sentenced to death. "We knew exactly what each other did," said Schick, "down to the weapons and the victims and the anger that caused it all, the booze and the drunks and the army rules." But the prisoners were careful not to delve too deeply into another man's misfortune. "That was one area of privacy we granted each other. Because other than that we had no privacy. You never had your light turned out. There was a guard looking at you twenty-four hours a day."

On death row, they wrestled with daily fears. Floor rats scurried under their beds. Night thunder and bolts of lightning banged against the windows. Food was cold and the Kansas summers scorching. News from home was fleeting. The next execution hovered constantly at the edge of their thoughts. Whenever a hanging date arrived, army boots came stomping down the death row hallway.

Once a career soldier, a veteran of the Battle of the Bulge, Schick re-peatedly railed against authority on death row. He detested the guards who wore the army colors, resentful because he once had been a master sergeant with ribbons pinned to his chest too. "They have to get some kind of satisfaction, a kind of power thing, because there's nobody more helpless than an inmate locked in a cell." He struck a guard; he swore at an officer who refused to pry open a window. Twice he was thrown into "The Hole," an underground pit the prisoners derided as "Dungeon Base." The door was hinged with a narrow food slot.

"You could hear nothing," Schick groused. "Time was meaningless. You'd think and think and think, thinking about everything you ever did in your life. You'd talk to yourself, sing until your voice gave out."

Death reared up as their common enemy, not for its finality but for how long it might take before those heavy army boots came clomping down the tier again. Who was next?

"All of us had the idea that if was a valid thing then take us out after the trial and shoot us," Schick said. "Get it over with. Keeping us there on death row year after year after year, you only got all the more resolved to live, until you died."

Everything took forever—the clock, the food, the head counts. The endless stretch of time could break a man. Schick read thirty, sometimes forty, paperbacks a month, a good number for someone who never cared much for books. Something as trivial as the daily guard change could seem momentous.

"You knew it was daylight because the day hacks came on," Schick remembered. "You knew it was night because the night hacks were on. Sometimes you'd just as soon be dead." Or not, he admitted. "When one of your buddies got hung you'd lay there thinking about it. They'd call him out and he was gone."

Another inmate, Richard Hagelberger, always believed he would make it out. "I never thought I'd be executed," he said. "I'd think about how to make up for time lost too, how things would be different then."

Hagelberger kept his nose down and his feet in line. A school dropout from upstate New York who enlisted to escape the reformatory, he hoped his good behavior would win out. When others wasted their recreation time playing table tennis or goofing off, Hagelberger turned his fists on a punching bag.

"There wasn't much to do otherwise," he recalled. "I'd just walk around, punch on the speed bag a little bit. They later put in handlooms. We could go over there and weave rugs, sometimes two at a time. You were never out long enough to finish a rug. But it was something different to do rather than sitting there. You get tired of sitting in the cell."

He buried his head inside paperback books, completed mail-order courses, anything to shift his mind off prison rules, prison guards, and army death. He tried to forget helping to kill two men in Germany. "I'd quit high school when I went in the service and I was frustrated at times. Especially when somebody else came in while you were already down there and then they got their sentence commuted before you did."

Unlike Schick, Hagelberger could be extra friendly with the guards. "Big brother!" he called out. Hagelberger remembered, "After a while you get used to it and you don't pay attention to them. You lay there, you sit there, you continue doing what you're doing. It takes a while to learn how to put something so distasteful out of your mind. But you just want to forget it there."

Twice, his mother, stepfather, and sister visited Fort Leavenworth; otherwise he was the loner on the tier, far different from the boisterous Schick. "It's just that you were in individual cells and you weren't with the others that much," Hagelberger explained. "You really didn't strike up strong friendships. Maybe you were scared to. I didn't talk too much about my case; I really didn't want to know about theirs. It didn't make any difference. We were all there in the same boat."

Many nights Hagelberger lay awake imagining smiling guards parading him out of his cell, past the cheers and applause from the other men in their cells, and through the big green door at the end of the hall and away to freedom. The door fascinated Hagelberger and all of the death row soldiers. If a man was to die, he would be shackled and marched through the green passageway to a small holding cell called Eight Base where he waited out his final hours. If he was to live, he would gather his few belongings and was escorted through the same big green door and upstairs to join the rest of the general prison population. From there, he might someday win parole. That door fascinated them all the more because of a 1956 hit record, a honky-tonk number called, of course, "The Green Door." It played over and over on their radio headsets asking "What's that secret you're keeping?"

The door seldom swung open, for good or bad. Time moved slowly, measured by the shadows inching across the windows. They knew it was Christmas because the commandant's office sent down a holiday bag of candy. A four-pound box of cookies from home signaled someone's birthday. Heat warmed the men in winter; large air fans cooled them in summer. And a man could swelter in the Kansas summers next to the big river, the marshes, and the open prairie. Soldiers condemned to die lay on their beds in their underwear. Guards, many from World War II and Korea, some later to rotate to Vietnam, reported to work in army shorts.

Command Sergeant Major Shirley Strange ruled the death vault with a single core principle: a soldier sentenced to die had already hit rock bottom. "He has everything to gain because he's already at the end of his rope," Strange maintained. "It's to his benefit to be on exemplary behavior. Because he's hoping like hell to get his sentence commuted and moved upstairs."

Strange was a large man with wavy red hair and a Roman nose; his refuge an eighty-acre spread near Easton, Kansas. He was raised a Missouri farm boy, farmed wheat and milo and hay, fed a few head of cattle, and nurtured his calves. Above all, he struggled to stop worrying about the doomed to die at Fort Leavenworth. He tried hard to treat death row men as he would any other inmate, "with respect." If they had questions, and they had a slew of them, he sought answers. If they were angry, and that was often, he tried to cool their tempers. If they needed help, he obliged.

As head of the death row command, Strange chose the officers who worked the Seven Base detail, and he was selective. "You wanted a good, stable and mature guard, someone completely rational, able to talk to a person, to respond and treat everyone as a human being. Someone to be fair. Someone to be firm and impartial. And you wouldn't want them to become attached to those people." He would instruct his recruits: "You don't carry anything in and you don't carry anything out." In prison hierarchy, death row work was far from glamorous. "It wasn't a desired position. It wasn't a crack detail," he explained. "It was just a necessary part of the institution."

Master Sergeant Orvill K. Lawson, who, with Sergeant Maddox, helped hang Japanese war criminals, had seen enough death by the time he was posted to Seven Base. The son of a railroad boss in Missouri, his family moved across the river to Kansas City, Kansas, and Orvill took up carpentry and worked as a night cop. He enlisted in 1942 and, because of his background, was rushed to the Castle prison because with so many men in uniform for World War II, the penitentiary was filling up. He patrolled the main tiers for two weeks before the army even sent him to basic training. Soon he was in Japan and eventually Sugamo. With the war over and Tojo dangling from an army rope, Lawson tried to muster out, but his commanding officers encouraged him to stay around. An overload of army prisoners from jails overseas were headed for Fort Leavenworth. Sergeant Lawson stayed long enough to become supervisor of eighty-six correctional officers throughout the prison. He sat at a desk in the center of the Castle rotunda and managed the daily prison operations. In his last three years there, he also supervised the woodworking shop and helped run death row.

Master Sergeant Holsey K. Mills perched atop a small stool or metal folding chair on the tier and thought, "I'm here just to check them. I watch them constantly." The only real threat he confronted was boredom. "I baby-sit them." He showed the typical American GI countenance—the weary eyes, the thin grin, and by war's end, the receding hairline. He won two Bronze Stars in World War II and Korea and started at the Castle as a tower guard. He later descended to death row officer, what he preferred to call "a professional watcher."

Sergeant Mills was raised out in the flatlands of western Kansas, so being partially below ground was no bother. What nagged at him were the endless hours. He also called it "eyeball work." He mostly handled the graveyard hours when prisoners likely were sleeping, though few slept well. He kept notes in a death row log, jotting down a few scratches. "If they rolled over in bed, you wrote it down. If they reached for a book to read, you wrote it down." It amounted to constant surveillance, something for army doctors or lawyers to analyze. "You'd keep your eye on a man to make sure he doesn't hang himself," he shrugged. "To see that he don't get sick. If he turns down two meals, you get a hold of the doctor." Some death row men might ask if he had read a recent *TV Guide* or heard some new radio program. He rarely answered back, careful not to become too friendly. "I didn't get personal with a man. I didn't feel sorry for him. It's like combat. If a man gets shot and he's dead, you reconcile it. The man has had his last peace, and you get your mind off that."

Every half hour, Master Sergeant Thompson Biggar rose from his stool, stretched his long arms, and lumbered down the tier, glancing into the cells. "To make sure they were still breathing," he noted. "But it was pretty easy to tell. The lights were on pretty much all of the time." He came from Tennessee and served with a rifle company in Europe during World War II. "Every day you're firing and seeing action," he remembered. "For ten months running." The change from bullets and men screaming to the hovering silence over Seven Base jarred Sergeant Biggar. "The silence rattled me."

Rarely did a doomed man let out his frustrations, though some occasionally banged on bars or slapped the walls. One who killed an army sergeant in Germany kicked apart the black-and-white television. Michael Kunak, who shot an army lieutenant in Texas, tried to climb up in a windowsill. When no word on legal appeals came down, Maurice Schick would cry out, "No noose is good noose!" Others had other ways to shatter the boredom. Abraham Thomas, who murdered four in Germany, might scream for help. Guards rushed to his cell and found a dummy fashioned from bed sheets hanging from his earphone wires. In the corner of his cell crouched Thomas, giggling.

The few outbursts startled Staff Sergeant Richard C. Curtsinger. One-eighth Cherokee and nicknamed "Running Bear," he was part of a combat mop-up team in the Philippines in World War II. "Jungle rot" had scarred his face. He lay in an army infirmary on the Pacific atoll when the bomb exploded over Hiroshima. His war was done and he returned home, still strong and tall, 240 pounds, with hazel-gray eyes and an endearing smile.

Sergeant Curtsinger gave another decade to the Castle in Kansas. On death row, he sometimes "dressed out" black soldiers for their final march to the gallows.

"If I met one today on the street, I wouldn't be ashamed to stop and shake his hand and say hello," he said. "I wasn't trying to make them do hard time. They all knew they were guilty as hell. We didn't need to punish them anymore." Some did, however, protest their innocence or claim they had killed in self-defense. Few believed them. If they persisted, no one listened.

Sergeant Elgie Maiden was barraged by Seven Base prisoners filling out request slips. They wanted fresh sheets, more pencils, and new library books. The sergeant initialed the slips and sent them upstairs for approval. That stoked more questions. What took so long? And more questions. Who won the ballgame? Where's the chaplain? Sergeant Maiden was an early riser. Stuffing a Prince Albert can in his chest pocket, he rolled his own. He initially came to the disciplinary barracks as part of the prison carpentry staff. But with his war record in Europe and on the Korean peninsula, awarded three Purple Hearts and two Bronze Stars, Sergeant Maiden's grit and patience seemed meant for death row work. He watched his charges eat lunch, swat flies, and kick at their walls. Some just paced about in their tiny cells, three steps and turn. One prisoner practiced blowing on a harmonica. "You had to watch them very closely though," Sergeant Maiden advised. "A harmonica would have brass reeds in it that could be made into a key or a shiv." Another, he recalled, "spent a year jimmying with a bar of soap to try to grease his cell lock. A man will do that just to see if he can. But once he's out of his cell, three guards are going to see him immediately anyway. It was all so terribly fruitless."

Sergeant R. W. Pinson had served in a graves registration unit in Korea, hoisting up the army dead into coffins. He helped process some four thousand bodies of American servicemen, checking for personal effects and identifying corpses. "The hard part is to get used to death," Sergeant Pinson cautioned. "At first tears are rolling down your eyes. But after seven days you could whistle while you worked. Until you found somebody you knew."

Seven Base and the midnight executions for this army officer seemed just another dying ground. "I had no sympathy for those men," he said of death row soldiers. "I didn't take any BS from them either." Some of the prisoners even mocked death, asking for the electric chair, repeating a nauseating TV commercial slogan, "You can be sure if it's Westinghouse!" Pinson shook his head. These men did not know death.

Few guards would ever forget death row. Staff Sergeant Ted Ray tried. He moved to a farm in North Carolina. He drifted through two wives. In his new isolation, he refused to own a telephone. Asked about combat duty in Korea, he replied, "Let's not talk about that." The men of death row figured just as heavily into his memories of the army. He still could see condemned soldiers laughing at nothing, talking gibberish, kicking their legs in bed, clutching their pillows for hours.

"But those prisoners with death hanging over them, they seemed to be more relaxed and calm than others," Sergeant Ray realized. More chaplains visited, and Sunday services were popular just off the row. Sergeant Ray thought, "It might have been religion."

Captain Thomas E. Carter had just hit thirty when he was assigned as a Baptist chaplain at the prison. He was thoughtful, measured in his opinions, and deeply religious. He came out of Atlanta; at sixteen, a friend grabbed his elbow and dragged him to a local church group. His involvement in the church saved him from falling completely into juvenile delinquency, on the road to adult ruin. He skipped school, ran away from home, and racked up a series of minor scrapes.

"I could run fast so I always felt a special kinship with people in trouble," Captain Carter liked to say. He interned with a Georgia prison chaplain, joined the army, and in 1958, settled in at the Castle prison and its Seven Base death unit. He dove into his work. He scheduled prisoner appointments, counseled new arrivals, and answered Red Cross messages. He made hospital calls at the infirmary, held daily devotionals and Bible studies, and gave pre-release lectures. In summertime, he wore khakis, sometimes shorts, high socks, and a pith helmet. He and his family, including twin boys and a daughter, lived six houses down from the Castle in a brick and clapboard home. "If anybody came to me with problems," the chaplain said of the death row men, "they didn't have to worry about them anymore. I worried for them. I internalized everything for them. I would tell them 'I didn't kill anybody. I didn't rape anybody. But I'm going to be your best friend and help you deal with this.'"

Some opened up. "They were in a small little world in there, trying to make life comfortable for however long it would last," the chaplain recalled. He set a goal to visit them often, and always on birthdays, Thanksgiving, and Christmas. "Lots of times just to be friendly, just to shoot the bull," he said. He talked to them as they wove rugs, lifted weights in the rec room, or crunched sit-ups in their cramped cells. "I always felt completely safe. If there ever was any problem in the prison, I always felt the inmates would protect me." Often he walked home late. He would sit on his porch and watch the moon dangling over the Missouri River. He drank coffee and prayed for his prison flock. "Deep down, way deep down," he convinced himself, "they're just ordinary people."

Father Anthony A. Dudek, a Catholic priest from Chicago, endured seventeen tours of army duty; saw action in World War II, Korea, and Vietnam; and left the army a colonel. At Fort Leavenworth, he relished the Sunday Masses near Seven Base and the prayers they lifted to heaven. He shook hands with smiling white soldiers whose lives were spared and accompanied grim black soldiers to their hangings. On the battlefield, Father Dudek had ministered young soldiers convinced they would live forever; on Seven Base, he knelt with soldiers about to die. "I just tried to help a man die well."

He enlisted in the chaplain corps in 1942, his mission, he said, "to save the world, to follow these men into battle and glory and to minister to them, to give them the courage to persevere. We marched with them into Germany and we saw death." On Seven Base, he felt the same pull, the same calling. "These men so wanted to live," he remembered. "I didn't crack up. I didn't lose my cool. I just followed my spirit. Nobody got too emotionally involved because nobody knew who was going to die next, or when." It was his afternoons and evenings standing at the door of a cell on Seven Base that he felt he truly performed God's work.

Visit the prisons, the Lord had commanded. "These guys wanted to be prepared for a better world," the priest recalled in his old age, a semiretired assistant pastor in Chicago. "We never talked about dying. We never got occupied with death. We kept death in the back room."

He shared with them the day's news and guessed at "what tomorrow might bring." He realized they were deeply frustrated, some beyond anger, but that they also understood that "I couldn't help them get released. I couldn't get them a commutation." So, he said, "we just shrugged our shoulders together," and every time another man was hanged, "We prayed and had Masses said for them. I will continue to pray for all these men until I die."

"He really felt for us," recalled the prisoner Hagelberger. "I wasn't really into anything but I became a Catholic for him. I went to Mass for Father Dudek." Frank Harris, another condemned man, remembered the priest as short and round, Polish, with an army crew cut, who set up an altar-on-wheels just off the tier. Afterward, the priest would stall the guards "to give us an extra few minutes together before going back to our cells," Harris laughed. "Just because of that alone, we all became Catholics." And because of this, "He wasn't no pious guy. He fought with us. We used to call him St. Dudek." The priest earned his sainthood, Harris said, those many Sundays mornings. "He would look at us and he'd go through the Mass with tears coming down his cheeks."

For twenty-six years, the social worker Joseph A. Thompson worked the Castle and the death row block. He was a supervisor in the psychiatric clinic, and one of the few black professionals in the prison. He drove each morning from his house in Topeka. But unlike the hangman Maddox, Thompson chose the scenic rural roads, the "roller-coaster route," to prepare him for what lay ahead behind those high walls. He showed up at the front gates with his daily newspaper tucked under his arm and set to work.

Thompson was born in Atlantic City, New Jersey, but at six weeks moved with his parents to a family farm outside Topeka. He signed up for Boy Scouts, and when the local white troop refused him membership, he christened himself a "lone" scout and earned an Eagle badge. He served eight years as his community's first black probation officer and, fearing he would miss World War II, enlisted in the army at thirty-five. Part of a military police unit in North Africa and Italy, he gathered enemy captives and herded them to an Allied prison in southern France. He returned to Kansas and interned at the Menninger Clinic. He started graduate school in Chicago studying psychology, but only until his GI Bill ran out. "I left with an ABT," he joked. "All But Thesis." Thompson returned once more to Kansas and was ordained an Episcopal deacon.

At Fort Leavenworth in the late 1950s, he counseled those who needed it most—especially those on death row. He gave his time particularly to the black soldiers. Thompson himself was a grandson of slaves from a plantation in Georgia. His grandmother Massie was nine years old when Yankee general William Tecumseh Sherman swept through the state. His grandfather worked for a doctor in the Confederate army until he snuck off to the Union side. Their grandson Joseph Thompson, a social worker, was tall, lean, and hardworking. He typically slept just four hours a night; he ate little.

He held staff meetings, assigned caseloads, and prepared for medical boards and mental evaluations. Mostly he enjoyed afternoon rounds and regular visits to Seven Base. Down there, prisoners hurled complaints at him, and Thompson listened with a sympathetic ear.

"It was a soldier's right to bitch about his food," he noted. "Food was part of his salary and he got regular GI rations. One guy would complain he got one flapjack while another guy got six. Or a meal was held up. Or the chaplain hadn't come down to see him or a doctor hadn't visited. The complaints could be real or imagined and a lot of the time the complaints were filed just to get somebody to come down to talk. And that was me."

Thompson urged the condemned men to take up hobbies to keep their minds right. They assembled jigsaw puzzles, played checkers with the man in the next cell, and filled in paint-by-number sets.

"You have to reconcile yourself about military justice," Thompson would teach them. "Sometimes you wonder about it but as long as the court-martial was correct and there were no errors, the sentence would stand unless you get clemency." And, as Thompson knew, "they all wanted clemency."

But black soldiers, he soon realized, were the ones called away at the midnight hour, sent to die. "I remember how composed they would be in the end. We liked to think it was because we worked with them, consoled them, talked to them, helped them to get over their feelings. We'd do all we could for them until they went in peace."

The morning after a hanging, as on all mornings, Thompson drove those country roads back to the fort, winding over the river hills and pulling up to the gate just as "those peacocks were screaming and scaring the rest of the men on Seven Base." It seemed to Thompson the birds knew what the night had brought. He walked into his office with his newspaper rolled up under his arm thinking, "I hope no more come to that."

Only three of the black soldiers were redeemed off death row, their death sentences commuted to fixed prison terms. That was a feat in itself, something Thompson long remembered and always took heart in. As one of the very few black members of the prison administration, he realized more than all the rest, from the white commandant down to the white guards, how difficult and impossible it must have felt to be a black soldier sentenced to die at a time and in a place where only black soldiers were hanged.

★   ★   ★

Sherman Gravitt lingered for four years on Seven Base. He was hauled to death row for killing a military police lieutenant in Okinawa. An airman, he tried to shoot himself, too, but the .45-caliber weapon jammed or was empty and he was arrested. Death by his own hand, he came to appreciate, would have been easier than all those years in a compact Seven Base death cell.

"What we hated most was no freedom of moving around," he said. "You're stuck in one place. It was years in one place." He played a little chess or pinochle, other prisoners calling out their next move. He memorized a book offering a hundred different ways to win at solitaire. He sang out loud, shouting the blues a cappella. He picked up snatches of Spanish, "so the guards wouldn't know what I was saying." When the guards caught on, he switched to German.

"We knew, we thought, that if we didn't turn bitter and we survived, we had to be better people when we got out of there," he recalled. "If we got out, we had to come out better than when we came in." Many broke down, crying for hours, threatening guards, throwing things. "It didn't make you a sissy. It made you human," Gravitt decided.

At dawn and the rustling of the peacocks, everyone strained at the windows to see a splash of feathers. "They were a beautiful sight," Gravitt remembered. "Oh God! Someone would whistle down the hallway and we'd get real quiet. Here they come!" It offered, he said, the "only glimpse of life we had there." Other mornings they woke to tires crunching or the echo of a car horn. Was that a goose high over the river? Was that the last clink of a Sunday church bell? "Our imaginations would run wild with something like that."

Executions were seldom, roughly once a year, and that made it all the more excruciating—all those long months of waiting, the nights of uncertainty, the wretchedness when hope was lost. Death row men closely followed their legal appeals, of course, and any court decisions or army orders. They tracked whenever an execution date was set or postponed and then rescheduled. But when their time drew close and death hovered, everyone down there knew it. Most horrid was that approaching, dreaded midnight hour when the other men shivering in their bunks listened quietly, straining hard for a faraway echo of the army's trapdoor.

Inmate Frank Harris swore that if the night air was right and everyone lay perfectly still, they could hear the creak and the thrust that followed. They recognized its unmistakable finality, rattling off the Castle walls. "Everyone stayed awake on those nights," Harris recounted. "You *had* to hear it to know it was real. It was like the sound of a breaking board, not one pop, but like the sound of wood tearing. It would be in the dark of the night, and everyone was afraid to stir, afraid to move, afraid of the death that came in the dark."

Harris had killed a friend in a mess hall knife fight in Tokyo. One of the few fortunate black soldiers, his death sentence was commuted, but he still did not make parole until 2016 at the age of eighty.

Confinement on Seven Base, though, was "the worst hell." He prayed the Rosary, tried to watch the TV, and waited for lights out at ten. After a long silence, one of the prisoners would whisper "blankets down," and the army's death row soldiers tossed their covers on the concrete floor and lay face down with their chins in their fists. They whispered in tones low to the ground so the guards might not hear them as they praised their mothers and cursed old girlfriends, missed home and cherished life before the army. They sought a little personal dignity apart from the ever-present army that meant to kill them. "Being on death row," Harris learned, "you see a guy like you'll never see again. All the pretense is cut away. We know who is really guilty and guilty by intent too."

★   ★   ★

In April 1955, John Bennett arrived at Fort Leavenworth. They marched him through the Castle rotunda and down the stairs, past the sally port, and along the death row hallway. Guards pointed to a cell at the end of row on the far right, his home for the next six years. Before he could turn around, the door clanged shut.

The new man was younger than all of them, more naïve and frightened. He told the other inmates about his Virginia background and his posting in Austria. To great surprise, they discovered that unlike them, Bennett had killed no one.

"We were convinced he was going to get off death row," predicted Harris. "I mean, we were all in for murder, for rape and killing."

Bennett's army service in Europe was far different than theirs, too. "He'd tell us about the tensions and pressures of Austria, of going on alert and worrying about getting involved in a fight, about being put on call and worrying about the Russians," Harris remembered. "That scared him." In time, Bennett opened up a little about his crime. From his troubled youth in rural Virginia, the son of a sharecropper with little formal education wrestled with mental issues. Bennett in uniform often fell into a backwoods sense of not knowing how to behave beyond his own limited world. In the army and far from home, he did not learn to control his drinking, appreciate the opposite sex, or seem to understand how to mature in an organization built rigidly around structure and obedience. "In his own mind, he never raped that girl," Harris felt. "To him it was just that she went in shock and screamed. He said he panicked and threw her in the water because she struggled, and she was white and he was black."

Bennett took months to adjust to the routine of life on death row. Six years later, he would be the last prisoner still there, white or black. And in all that time, prisoners and guards alike long remembered Bennett's first night in his cell near the green door that offered death or salvation. The other prisoners stayed up late, listening quietly. They could hear him sobbing for hours. By morning, when the sun peeked in the windows and the peacocks shrieked, Bennett had chewed his pillow in half.

Chapter Five

★ ★ ★ ★ ★ ★ ★

WHITE DEATH ROW

The army was good to them. Despite all that they had done, the horrific homicides, the dereliction of duty, the shame they brought upon the US Armed Forces, that much was certain. Even after these white soldiers were slotted away in narrow cramped cells on death row, they still enjoyed friends in high places. In army-speak, they still could pull rank. Army review boards and appellate judges would find ways to knock a death sentence down to life. A federal court might consider something in a white soldier's file that suggested some mental illness. Hometown boosters lobbied for their release; newspapers rallied around them as well. Their mothers' pleas frequently graced the front pages. Photographers snapped their pictures, delicately framing the women with tears in their eyes. Washington congressmen from back home would pressure the White House. President Eisenhower's staff would weaken in time. Eventually a new recommendation was carried into the Oval Office. As short as one page or as long as two dozen, it would suggest mercy. The former World War II general signed his name, a slanting cursive crawl tilting to the right. Dwight D. Eisenhower.

The system worked for them. They lived.

★ ★ ★

Michael Kunak slipped into a phone booth at the Leavenworth bus station and called Master Sergeant Orvill Lawson. Just paroled from prison, he held in his hand the grandest prize of all—a one-way ticket home to Baltimore. But before leaving, he wanted to thank his mentor for all his help at the army prison. And Sergeant Lawson was overjoyed. He slammed down the phone and hurried to the bus station. "He treated me like an old-time friend," the sergeant recalled. "He was one of the smartest men I ever knew, a devil of a nice man. If I ever did anything else, that was the one man I helped."

Kunak had deep-set eyes and jug ears. When he entered the army, he brought a raggedly nervous smile. Too young for World War II, too green for Korea, he never came close to combat yet hated everything about the US Army. He enlisted in Baltimore after he dropped out of high school, two months before graduation, but soon wanted out of the uniform in the worst way. He worked as a cook's helper with an Eighty-Second Airborne Signal Company in Texas and regretted that too. He lay awake at night plotting an early discharge. Sometimes evil "thoughts" crept into his head. To ward them off, he would fiddle with army radios, trying to chase the thoughts away. His command officers dismissed his threats as hollow nonsense. Kunak, they said, was "sane and sound." They ordered him back to work.

No one took him seriously until Kunak, nineteen years old, shot Second Lieutenant Harold Bern Williamson near Fort Hood, Texas. They were holding "Exercise Long Horn" maneuvers that spring of 1952, and the stunned lieutenant, hit point blank in the chest, crumpled over dead. As other men rushed for cover, Kunak slowly lowered his carbine. "I don't have any more ammunition," he muttered.

In custody, he warned he would do it again, anything for an army furlough. "I'll kill a man to get out or I'll kill a man who would keep me from getting out," he threatened. "I know I was wrong. It was cold deliberate murder. I expect to be hanged."

Kunak told army police he had not been upset with Lieutenant Williamson. He barely knew the officer and had only spoken to him once or twice. Kunak just wanted out of the service. He had considered punching General Joseph P. Cleland in the nose, sure that insulting a widely respected officer would get him out. He had stolen a pair of boots and left his khaki hat behind with his name attached, hoping to be court-martialed and riffed. He had snuck off on a "fishing trip" and jumped from a seventy-five-foot river bridge, expecting injuries from the fall would send him home. He had tried to stand on his head while riding a motorcycle. But his superiors never wrote him up on charges. They merely dismissed Private Kunak as a harmless army washout.

Finally, he came up with something far more ambitious. As a low-level kitchen aide, he was not permitted to handle live ammunition. So Kunak fashioned a bullet from a brass pellet, added some pieces of yellow metal, and loaded it into a blank cartridge. "I am going to get me an officer," he boasted around camp. Again, no one believed him. But once he was in custody, the army wished it had. "They put me on K.P. [kitchen duties]. That was the last straw," he grumbled to investigators. "There's nothing straight in my mind. I know I was wrong."

By the time of his trial, the lanky soldier had gained weight. The army court-martialed him in June 1952 at Fort Bragg, North Carolina. He testified he was under a "strange impulse" that drove him to kill; he felt "powerless to resist." He confessed, "I knew what I was going to do was wrong and I prayed for it." When the fatal shot roared across the Texas campground, he said, "I felt stunned. Even today I have difficulty bringing myself to realize it ever happened." He spoke with an army medical officer and was counseled by an army chaplain. "I'm mixed up inside," he told them. He had a brother and sister who were in a mental institution; another brother was under treatment. But Kunak blamed himself for the murder in Texas. "I just raised the carbine and fired." The army sentenced him to death.

His case automatically went up on appeal, and three psychiatrists insisted the soldier not only was sane but knew full well what he was doing was wrong. His planning proved it was premeditated murder. Although everyone in his unit disregarded him before he fired that shot—"Killer," they mocked him—Kunak took Lieutenant Williamson's life anyway. The military board of review upheld the conviction; the death penalty was both "legal and appropriate."

Upon review of additional tests from private mental health experts from his hometown, something a white family would be able to afford back then, the Court of Military of Appeals tossed out the death sentence and reduced his punishment to life in prison. Dr. Manfred S. Guttmacher in Baltimore concluded Kunak not only was a "borderline psychotic," but was "a flagrant one." Loyal B. Calkins, a criminal psychologist in Maryland, performed tests that discovered traces of "paranoid schizophrenia."

After less than two years on death row, Kunak was moved upstairs to the Castle's general prison population. It amazed many of the death row guards.

"He would sit with his hands on his forehead," recalled Sergeant Elgie Maiden, suspecting Kunak faked any mental disorders. "You'd speak to him in the morning and he'd grunt." When the library cart rolled down the hallway, Kunak asked for books on chess. "He got pretty good at it," the sergeant remembered. "He even played himself, somehow. The guy was always thinking."

But Sergeant Lawson, the death row overseer and carpentry shop manager, took a liking to the young soldier. He assigned him to his wood-working school and, in time, promoted Kunak to assistant instructor of the carpentry shop.

"He could grasp anything I taught him," Sergeant Lawson enthused. He helped him land a job in the prison pharmacy, too, and routinely lob-bied parole boards on Kunak's behalf. "Every year I helped talk the board into knocking a few years off his life sentence."

Now Sergeant Lawson burst into the bus depot and spotted Kunak across the lobby, chatting with other new parolees. Kunak was free, and beaming that nervous smile of his. Pointing to Lawson, he told the others, "If had had a sergeant like this man in the first place I never would have gotten into the trouble I did."

★   ★   ★

Army misfits Richard A. Hagelberger and John Vigneault joined Kunak on death row in 1952. They were marched in shackles through the Fort Leavenworth gates and down into the bowels of Seven Base. The pair had murdered two Germans in a fumbled robbery. Both confessed, but their confirmed guilt never dampened the widespread attention and support for their release.

When they were both nineteen, the soldiers were stationed at the old Landgraves castle in Germany. They killed Paul Eckart and Lothar

Schlosser during a clumsy robbery attempt on a ride back to army quarters. A manhunt with trained German shepherd dogs tracked them down.

Vigneault stood trial first, his court-martial in the same Nuremberg courtroom where top Nazi war criminals had been tried. Each morning, US caravans drove more than forty German officials and families of the dead to the courthouse as the army sought to prove it could deal harshly with American soldiers preying upon German citizens.

Detractors in the States dismissed it as a "show trial." The American press editorialized that a dual hanging was inappropriate, even with the occupation still underway in Europe. But Vigneault offered little in his defense, even when confronted with his signed statement admitting they were AWOL when he shot the Germans. "Hagelberger egged me on," Vigneault said; it was Hagelberger's idea from the start. They were sitting in the backseat when Hagelberger "signaled" to him. Vigneault aimed the carbine just behind the passenger's left ear and fired. The driver slammed on the brakes and struggled for the door handle. "I raised up and kept blasting at him until the gun jammed," Vigneault confessed.

His lawyer described his client's "feeblemindedness" and troubled upbringing; a "victim of a poverty-stricken childhood," he called him. A mix of "liquor and low mentality" lurked behind the slayings, he said. "He may be guilty of something but not of murder," protested the defense attorney.

Captain Richard F. M. Gowan, an army psychologist, testified that Vigneault "was not fully developed mentally. He has the mental capacity and ability to learn of a child of ten." When the jury voted death, Vigneault sat sharp-faced in his seat. Led away, he broke into tears.

His mother fell apart too. "I don't understand why my boy must die," pleaded Claudia Vigneault of Goffs Falls, New Hampshire. "I can't believe he would do such a thing if he were all right. He was a good boy when he went in the service." John was one of nine children; their father, Rudolph, a carpenter.

"It must be a frame-up," Vigneault's mother feared. "He didn't walk until he was two years old," she wrote First Lady Mamie Eisenhower. When he first tried to join the service, she wrote, "He couldn't read good enough."

She hired an attorney experienced at defending soldiers. Samuel Green of Manchester, New Hampshire, had earlier cleared the records of two

World War I veterans long ago disgraced with dishonorable discharges. Now Green argued that Vigneault had been unfairly prosecuted; a German civilian charged with killing an American would get five years or less, he maintained. And the army, Green alleged, should never have accepted him in the first place: "His mentality is definitely retarded."

The newspapers jumped on the bandwagon. The Newport *Daily News* in Rhode Island claimed the army wanted a dual execution to prove it could punish US atrocities abroad, rather than in pursuit of any fair justice. "Is Vigneault actually a moron, unable to distinguish between right and wrong?" the paper asked. "Has justice actually triumphed in this case?"

Hagelberger was court-martialed in the same Nuremberg courtroom before similarly angry German crowds. He too had confessed, admitting he had urged Vigneault to shoot the men; he even nudged his elbow. Their plan, he contended, was to "kill them both and take the car." He was rather calm about it, too. "I realize that when you point a loaded carbine at a man's head and pull the trigger, he will die," Hagelberger said. When the guilty verdict was read, Hagelberger snapped to attention and saluted. He stood again when they sentenced him to die.

Massive letter-writing campaigns were mounted, and pictures of the handsome young soldiers graced the nation's newspapers. Wardens and cell-block guards advocated for their release. White House aides, congressional power brokers, and other officials eventually fell in line. By 1956, many on Eisenhower's reelection team worried that executing the two privates could cost votes.

Army review boards and appellate courts approved both death sentences. But the new examiners did uncover some disturbing details about Vigneault. Fellow soldiers would hide or throw away items from Vigneault's locker, reducing him to tears. When he was on night patrol, they crept up and heard him sobbing. When a mess sergeant issued an order, Vigneault would just "stand there and stare." A single beer and Vigneault often was drunk; four beers and he passed out. He assumed any woman who talked to him wanted to be his "girlfriend." He would flash a "silly smile" and then cry as she walked away. At the enlisted men's club, he hugged a wall and begged a soldier for a thousand dollars so he could impress a girl and drive her home. He was spotted in a latrine cradling a bayonet. "Everybody is against me," he wept.

Hagelberger and Vigneault left Germany for Fort Leavenworth and separate death row cells. Hagelberger seemed to adjust well. He read voraciously and enrolled in correspondence courses. He wrote to everyone he could think of—the White House and Capitol Hill lawmakers, governors, newspapermen, community leaders, veterans clubs, and ladies auxiliaries. Vigneault sat quietly in his cell.

But Hagelberger later acknowledged, "There was really no difference between us. We were both AWOL. We were both drinking heavily and this happened."

Many death row guards found Vigneault unpleasant. "He'd sit in his bed like an old lady and pretend to rock. He had lots of ways like an old lady. He was real tidy. He'd hum to himself. Hagelberger was different. He always seemed smarter, a pretty nice-looking kid," Sergeant Richard Curtsinger recalled. Sergeant Maiden recalled the guards largely "felt sorry for" Hagelberger. "He was just mad at the system. He didn't physically do anything. He didn't shoot them."

In January 1955, Eisenhower approved both death sentences. Vigneault's execution was scheduled first, and a national campaign kicked in to save his life.

"This boy was very upset as a child, really handicapped," revealed Dr. Anna L. Philbrook, director of the New Hampshire Mental Hygiene and Child Guidance Clinics. At eight, he was still "sucking all four fingers of his left hand constantly and he would fall down in the school room without any apparent reason." He lay on the pavement at recess and in the classroom "scribbled all over his desk, chewed lead pencils and bit colored crayons into small pieces."

His mother reminded the White House that the navy rejected him, but in the army "he was so happy to be a soldier, to fight for his country." Claudia Vigneault realized, though, "that a big mistake had been made. He was scared to death of being over there. He started to drink and missed going to Mass and the Sacraments. The only answer I got was that he was lonely and wished he'd stayed home."

Hagelberger enjoyed a bounty of supporters too. His father, a disabled World War I veteran, died when Richard was seven. His mother abandoned him when he was eight at a children's aid facility in East Aurora, New York. He often ran away. For a while, he lived with a grandmother, in a county boarding home, on a farm for foster children, and with a Lutheran congregation. He sang in the choir, and the church members thought him a "good boy," but he fled them too.

Local probation officer Raymond E. Sullivan tried to mentor the young Hagelberger after he stole a car. "He never exhibited any tendencies of viciousness," Sullivan advised Eisenhower, "but appeared to be a confused and bewildered youth." He hitchhiked across the country "in a vain effort to locate his mother." He returned without her.

His probation broken, Hagelberger enlisted in the army in 1950.

Five years later, his mother, now Mrs. Anna Stacy of Chula Vista, California, visited him at Fort Leavenworth. She returned home and wrote Eisenhower begging for forgiveness on her son's behalf. "I don't believe they had a fair trial over in Germany," she wrote. "We are receiving letters from all over from people who have had sons in World War II, who are hoping and praying that you will commute the sentence."

The White House began to soften on Vigneault. Veterans groups, mental health experts, and lawyers trained in capital litigation lobbied the Eisenhower administration. The New Hampshire state legislature voted unanimously to intercede on Vigneault's behalf. Lawyer Samuel Green advised Eisenhower about Vigneault's poor education: "How he was able to pass the mental test required by the service is unbelievable . . . It is a sad commentary when boys are sent overseas to places where men are needed." In February 1955, both houses of Congress unanimously passed a resolution to spare Vigneault the gallows.

John Lindsay, a navy gunner in World War II and now executive assistant to the attorney general, studied Vigneault's case. Lindsay had run a Youth for Eisenhower Club in 1951; he later would serve in Congress and lead the nation's largest city as mayor of New York. In March 1955, he asked for assurances that if the sentence was commuted to life, Vigneault would never be paroled. This intrigued the president, and two days before

Christmas, he reduced Vigneault's punishment to a fixed, fifty-five-year sentence. He also added a no-parole provision.

"In granting clemency," the president stressed, "I desired to spare his life, but I did so in the belief and hope that my successors will not release the prisoner to society by a further exercise of executive clemency."

In New Hampshire, family and neighbors crowded into the Vigneault home. "It's wonderful!" shouted a brother, Rudolph Vigneault. "We couldn't be happier!" On death row, though, Vigneault took the news quietly.

"That's good," was all he said. He did thank the president. "This Christmas is the greatest my Folks have ever had," he wrote Eisenhower. "But I am still very unhappy. The reason is that Richard didn't not [sic] share the gift with me." But, he added, "If Richard was put to death it would be as if I had killed him with my own hands. . . . He didn't pull the trigger. I DID."

Hagelberger's mother immediately wired the White House asking for the same consideration. An East Aurora lawyer, Anne Mack, wrote too, describing her community's troubled reaction. Why was the triggerman commuted but not his sidekick?

"When the news came over the radio at Christmas," Mack wrote, "indignation was felt at every hand." Republican congressman John R. Pillion of New York requested a fresh review. Death row guards considered it terribly unfair, too.

"A bunch of hooey," spat Sergeant Elmer Peterson. "Hagelberger did a lot of meditating over this," recalled Sergeant Maiden. "But there wasn't a hell of a lot you could say to a guy in that situation. Except it wasn't right. And that ain't telling him a whole lot."

Hagelberger remembered how "I thought any day they'd come and tell me mine was commuted too. Everybody thought naturally the same thing would happen with mine. Then I got word that Eisenhower had upheld my sentence, that I would be executed."

In January 1956, he wrote the president himself. "We wanted the car but without a fight," Hagelberger told Eisenhower. He tried to warn Vigneault not to shoot but "just as I poked his arm the gun fired." He suggested that Eisenhower had commuted the wrong man.

More letters piled up at the White House gates. Congressman Pillion continued to lobby Eisenhower, but Gerald D. Morgan, special counsel to the president, offered little hope. He reminded Pillion that Hagelberger was the "dominant personality and the moving spirit in the killings."

Morgan admonished, "The question of a low mental capacity is not present in the Hagelberger case," unlike Vigneault. But the newspapers pressed harder.

"Don't Hang Hagelberger!" called an editorial in the Chula Vista *Star*. The Chicago *Daily Tribune* warned that "if army justice has any meaning, they should receive the same punishment. It would be a travesty if somebody's pull saved the actual killer and his accomplice was put to death."

The Farmers Bank in Gardner, Kansas, opened a legal defense fund. In East Aurora, Hagelberger's former homeroom teacher released letters he wrote her in his first months on death row:

November 22, 1952—Do you have any guys in your homeroom that are as foolish as I was? If so, give them a warning and use me as an example. Maybe they will change.

January 14, 1953—I had a pretty good Christmas for being locked up. We had a good meal. "Turkey dinner!" In the afternoon we saw a movie. The only thing to mar the holiday was the bad news of my Grandmother's death. I was really in low spirits.

More congressmen applied more pressure, but the counsel's office announced in February 1956 that "[n]o further action will be taken in Hagelberger's case"; the army would proceed. Still more protests followed, more petitions collected to save Hagelberger, more newspaper editorials. But the army, the Justice Department, and the White House would not budge. In early June, Hagelberger rose in his cell as an officer read a Washington telegram announcing he would die on July 6.

"I had hoped any day they'd come down and tell me mine was commuted," Hagelberger remembered. "Instead I got word Eisenhower had upheld my sentence, that I would be executed. And then I knew it. My mind, part of me, already accepted the fact that this was it."

A young Leavenworth lawyer, Edward Stephens, rushed into federal court in Kansas City, Kansas. A year out of law school and working without pay, he had visited Hagelberger several times on death row. Now he filed a petition alleging Hagelberger's right to due process had been violated. The clerk waived the customary $5 filing fee because Hagelberger "was a pauper," and Judge Arthur J. Mellott postponed the hanging. The death row prisoner stared up in amazement. "That sure is good news," he blurted out, stunned again.

Eisenhower had suffered a heart attack a year earlier, and now in late June, severe stomach pain led to intestinal surgery. He was recuperating on his Gettysburg farm in Pennsylvania when aides sent over fresh material on Hagelberger. Like Vigneault, the Pentagon had come to believe the army was never a good fit for Hagelberger either, a consideration reached after the press, Congress, and local groups still hammered away that it was only fair to spare both men. On July 3, the president commuted his sentence as well. Also like Vigneault, he would have to serve fifty-five years without parole. In his tiny cell, Hagelberger snapped his head back when the commandant brought the news. "He did?" the prisoner asked. In Washington, the presidential press secretary explained that Eisenhower felt both men should be treated equally.

And so they were. For twenty years, they served in separate prisons, transferred from Fort Leavenworth to federal penitentiaries in Georgia, New Hampshire, and Texas. They continued to lobby Washington, writing to presidents Kennedy, Johnson, Nixon, and Ford, sometimes the presidents' wives and widows, too, and enlisting new lawyers to figure a way around that no-parole provision. And that worked, too.

In January 1977, in the fading days of his administration, Ford made them both eligible for parole. To hold them so long without hope, he believed, was cruel and unfair. Eventually they walked out free men.

But for Richard Hagelberger, July 3, 1956, mattered most—the day he learned he would not die. "Oh, it was just a new life!" he still rejoiced, years later, living in his mother's California ranch home. Forever he cherished how the guards opened his cell and escorted him down the long hallway, past a line of outstretched hands, white and black, reaching through the iron bars. "All the other guys were hollering 'Good news! Way to go! Great to hear!' They all shook my hand as I walked by their cells. You know their circumstances, but still you're really just so elated you're leaving. They're locked up and you're putting all that behind you."

★ ★ ★

Even the worst of crimes did not send a white soldier to the gallows. Even killing the only daughter of an army colonel did not, in the end, merit death. At Fort Leavenworth, the prisoner could be boisterous and cocky, a loudmouth difficult to manage, someone to send to the Hole for extra punishment. Down there, the death row guards despised him most of all. But he found a way out.

For two days, army police held Camp Zama in Japan on semi-lockdown. Investigators combed through the barracks, summoned soldiers to the squad room, and huddled over bits of evidence sifted from a drainage ditch. An eight-year-old, red-haired girl named Susan, bicycling home from a friend's house, had been drowned in that shallow water, her body discovered by her father, Colonel Jacquard Rothschild. Army detectives were questioning everyone, and every soldier questioned everyone else that fall of 1953. With each passing hour, pressure intensified to find the killer.

"Whoever did this," warned Master Sergeant Maurice Schick, a career soldier speaking for all of the officers and soldiers stationed at Camp Zama, the noncombatants, too, "they ought to string him up."

Two Japanese teenagers had spotted a soldier talking to the girl, and an artist's sketch led authorities on Thanksgiving Day to the door of a yellow frame house on base. After a lie detector test and a dose of truth serum, Schick admitted he was the one who clamped his foot over Susan Rothschild's head in the trickling runoff.

A winner of the Purple Heart in World War II, veteran of the Africa, Europe, and Mediterranean campaigns, he had helped take out German machine gun nests during the Battle of the Bulge. With his green eyes, wavy hair, and wide, bright smile, the army hospital officer was admired by many on the base twenty-five miles from Tokyo. Now Schick was charged with capital murder.

"Just that she was there," he confessed to army police. "I grabbed her and choked her . . . Oh God! I just had an uncontrollable urge to kill her."

Despite his unequivocal confession, few wanted to believe he could be guilty. Colonel Karl D. MacMillan, commander of the base hospital, warned army investigators they had the wrong man. "I felt sure they were wasting their time," he told reporters. Then it fell to MacMillan to visit the Schick home and tell his wife. "I've never had a worse task than that night," the colonel conceded.

Sergeant Curtsinger was working at Camp Zama then, too; he later guarded Schick on death row. "When the girl was missing, Schick even helped organize the hunt," the sergeant remembered. "He said he had a wife and that he was concerned because they had two adopted Japanese kids. And when they found out he did it, nobody could understand it. He was supposed to love kids."

At his court-martial, Schick chewed gum and shuffled papers at the defense table. Some days, he sobbed in front of the jury. Two Japanese doctors called by the defense determined he could not distinguish right from wrong. But four army psychiatrists for the prosecution testified he was sane. Schick declined to testify. But prosecutors read his signed statement and presented evidence that he would have recognized Susan from visits to the hospital.

"She is a colonel's daughter," Schick complained to army police after his arrest. "She has everything in God's world anybody would want. My children's father is a master sergeant. He is knocking down $700 a month. I am knocking down $250 a month. It isn't fair. It isn't fair at all." Schick said he purposely sought out Susan Rothschild.

"That's why I hated her, and when she turned her back I choked her. I wanted to make it look like a sex crime . . . I stood up and put my feet on her throat . . . I threw her into a moat. That's when she died." Schick conceded that he had only one regret. "I'm sorry it was not a boy. If it had been a boy he would really have been the apple of the old man's eye."

From the witness stand, the girl's father described his heartbreak. "He did discover her body," their only other child, Ron Rothschild, remembered years later. "She was late coming home and they knew she occasionally took a shortcut. There was an irrigation drainage ditch system and she would ride her bike through there if she was running late."

When the jury sentenced him to die, Schick stood, saluted sharply, executed a military about-face, and returned to his seat with an oddly frozen grin. On death row, he considered himself far superior to the other doomed men in separate cells. "I was a master sergeant," he bragged years later. "I had four rows of decorations I could wear. I had my Purple Heart and Bronze Star, wounded in France and a German sniper to handle. I was not as young as the rest of them on the row. I was already twenty-nine when I was busted." He had enlisted, he said, "to get out of the coal mines in western Pennsylvania. Bethlehem Steel owned the town. My father was a miner. In 1941 the only way out was to join the service."

On Seven Base, Schick would send away for seed catalogues, boasting he planned to buy a farm. He bragged that he had once built apartment complexes in Florida. He claimed he had up to seven thousand dollars stashed in a bank. Asked by guards to enter or exit his cell, he typically had to be told it was an order.

"He was the kind of guy who would play any angle he could think of to maybe get a favor," recounted Sergeant Maiden. Most guards dismissed him as a coward; they often could hear him crying on his bunk. Yet Schick would demand better food than what came down on the prison trays. When he visited the prison dentist, Sergeant R. W. Pinson remembered, he cried "like a baby."

What mostly frightened Schick though, and all of them, was when orders came in for another hanging. "He was always shook up that it would be his turn to die," recalled Sergeant Pinson. "He'd go all to pieces." He may not have liked the prison food, but he gained weight, and everyone saw through him.

"Schick would say that no sentence could punish him more than that of having to live with knowing what he had done," prisoner Frank Harris remembered. "And he had killed a colonel's daughter."

The military board of review affirmed the death sentence, finding him "beyond a reasonable doubt mentally responsible for his acts." The Court of Military Appeals noted that his "psychotic"-like behavior emerged only when he was drinking, and Schick had been drinking for five hours before he came across the girl. It too approved the sentence.

But like other white soldiers on death row, Schick was blessed with an army of supporters—in Japan, Washington, and Kansas. Even Susan's family forgave him; her mother met with Schick's wife, Jeanne, and offered their prayers. "Mrs. Schick is a wonderful person, and her two girls have obviously been brought up in a warm and loving atmosphere," announced Phyllis Rothschild. "My husband and I feel that Sergeant Schick is a sick man and we have no personal feeling of bitterness or revenge." The Rothschilds asked that "all help and aid" be given to the Schick's two adopted Japanese daughters. "They always expressed a position that tragedies happen, and the best way is to forgive and move on," their son later explained.

Jeanne Schick defended her husband, at first. The night of the murder, he returned home and "happily" played with one of their daughters. He volunteered as a Boy Scoutmaster and taught Sunday school. Their daughters were well cared for, she said, "and for the first time in their orphaned life they have known what it is like to be loved and a part of a family group."

She had met her husband in 1945 while he was recuperating from war wounds in West Virginia. He lost one of his crutches while struggling down the street; she helped him up and he treated her to a cup of coffee. They were married four months later.

She soon discovered his darker side. In England at war's end, he stripped naked at a USO club. In 1952, at Camp Fuji in Yokahama, he pounded his head against a wall. "They're all dead!" he screamed. Two months before he killed Susan, he tried to strangle a fellow soldier. Military doctors, his wife complained, never treated him well; the army should never have taken him back in a second enlistment after the war. "He is a sick man," Jeanne Schick warned. "He is not normal."

Others also rallied around him. In 1956, Dr. Winfred Overholser, once president of the American Psychiatric Association, advised Eisenhower that Schick was misdiagnosed in Japan. "Even by the rigid army standards, Schick was properly entitled to a verdict of acquittal by reason of insanity," the doctor wrote. "Since serious doubt as to his sanity exists I

urge as strongly as I may that the sentence of death be commuted." In Topeka, Dr. Karl Menninger and his staff found Schick suffering from peri-
odic schizophrenic episodes. He developed "extensive inner fantasies" and
"impulsive aggressive behavior." Menninger termed Schick "at this time,
permanently and incurably ill."

Schick remembered his visit with the famed psychiatrist. "It was very
clinical, very cold, pure," he later recalled. "When I went in he forced the
guards to take the chains off me. I had a dog collar and belly chain and I
was handcuffed to a guard. I had a three-link ankle chain too. Dr. Menninger ordered them off; he said he couldn't talk to me with those chains
on. And he told the guards to sit outside. That shook them up to no end.
They were uncomfortable until they got me back in chains."

In July 1957, US Army Secretary Wilber M. Brucker urged Eisenhower to sign the death warrant. "The sanity issue has been thoroughly
and legally resolved against the accused," he counseled the president. "I
recommend that the sentence be approved and carried into execution."

Attorney General William P. Rogers concurred. "There is no other basis in the record to support a recommendation for executive clemency." It
had been four years since Susan's murder and Schick's trial.

Others disagreed. Former army sergeant George W. Dull of Pennsylvania, a Korean War medic and rifle company veteran, served under
Schick at the Camp Zama hospital. He knew the Rothschilds and "their
lovely daughter Susan," he told Eisenhower. "Susan's mother first brought
her to the dispensary to be treated for a sty [sic] on her eye. I saw her later
when she cut her foot in or near the hotel's outdoor pool."

The morning after the girl's body was recovered, "there were a number
of us at the hospital who immediately suspected Sgt. Schick," Dull continued. "I believed him to be mentally ill—and that belief remains." He added
that Schick "had been involved in an unfortunate escapade shortly before
this matter," referring to his choking a fellow soldier. "Mr. President, I wish
to ask you to consider commuting his sentence to life imprisonment."

By Christmas 1958, Phillip Areeda in the White House Counsel's office had reviewed the crime reports, trial testimony, and the psychiatric
exams. A recent Harvard Law School graduate and newly appointed assistant special counsel in the White House, Areeda found buried in the

records other wartime-era atrocities carried out by Schick, including his admission that he killed two children in France. Some of the material had been unearthed by Leavenworth attorney Homer Davis, who often represented men on the army's death row, white and black.

"If these premises are accepted," Areeda wrote to his boss, White House counsel David W. Kendall, "one must doubt the propriety of imposing the death penalty upon Schick." He felt that Schick had long suffered from psychosis, some of it war related. He thought Schick mentally ill rather than a serial killer. He added, "I recommend commutation."

Not until February 1960 did Attorney General Rogers change his mind. According to newly discovered army records, Schick was treated by hospitals on seventeen different occasions, including thirteen months of psychiatric care, and six outpatient consultations or examinations. He was separated from the army in March 1946, and the army accepted him back just two years later. There lay the dilemma for the White House. Eisenhower's army had re-recruited a man it knew was dangerous, and now Schick, in uniform, had killed a colonel's daughter. Dr. Karl Menninger summed it up, "The Army knew when they accepted his re-enlistment that this man was mentally abnormal."

In March 1960, Eisenhower decided to resentence Schick to life in prison, without parole. For all his faults, Schick on death row was magnanimous in victory. Years later, he credited Menninger and Homer Davis for "saving me from hanging. They fought for me." Davis also noted that when possible schizophrenia first was mentioned, Schick suddenly started acting like "he thought the girl was an animal, a wolf or a mad dog." Many thought him faking again, and the lawyer just grinned. "It worked."

Schick left Seven Base and rotated through a series of federal penitentiaries, ending in Lewisburg near the Pennsylvania mining country of his youth. The federal Bureau of Prisons put him through a battery of tests, and by the late 1960s, prison exams in Springfield, Missouri, showed his mental failings had "improved." His parents sought help from their local congressman, and Representative Thomas E. Morgan advised the pardon attorney that Schick "is making a good adjustment."

His mother, Effie Schick, wrote to President Johnson in 1968. "He would like to have his rights restored and also his Army status," she pleaded. Schick, in a clemency petition, credited his time on Seven Base with turning his life around. "The years spent on death row acted as a therapy in that my mental process underwent a drastic change toward a better citizen," he wrote. But being confined with no parole, he said, "dooms me."

He offered to undergo castration if it would win back his freedom. A team of lawyers volunteered to challenge his no-parole restriction before the US Supreme Court; they argued it was cruel to hold an inmate with no hope of leaving prison. The court in December 1974 turned them down. Schick's supporters aimed next at President Ford. In April 1975, the head of the Pennsylvania Jaycees urged Schick's release. J. J. Parker, warden at the prison in Lewisburg, also recommended parole. Schick had recovered from a massive heart attack and dreamed of working again in the medical field. But he was done with the army; he had no interest in a third enlistment.

"He had nightmares" after World War II, a prison progress report found. "Schick said he had had enough of killing."

As he had done with Hagelberger and Vigneault, President Ford lifted the no-parole status in January 1977. Two years later, the once decorated army master sergeant at last was freed at the age of fifty-six. He left Pennsylvania for South Florida and worked not in health care but as a nighttime convenience store clerk in West Palm Beach. The once handsome army officer lived until he was seventy-nine; he gained even more weight and his hair thinned out. "I let myself go," he griped. "I got fat on death row."

★   ★   ★

On a glorious summer evening in 1954, Private Roy Travis Dunnahoe found himself lost in the Bavarian forest. He had spent that July afternoon drinking at several country inns. As he tried to make his way back to town at dusk, he came upon a thirteen-year-old Munich boy. Startled or scared, perhaps delusional, Dunnahoe opened his army pocket knife and started slashing at young Wilhelm Seiber. That night, he returned to his barracks with blood stains splotching his army uniform. His army cap and knife blade were missing. Dunnahoe leisurely showered and fell comfortably asleep. The boy's body turned up in the woods after dawn.

Dunnahoe made a poor infantryman. He was lazy and uninterested and frequently punished for disappearing from his post, stealing away without permission. His army superiors found him difficult to handle.

Twenty-three years old and a native of Arkadelphia, Arkansas, he downed several beers and set off on foot through the Schleissheim Forest, thinking, he later said, he might find a woman on the other side. When he instead spotted the boy, Dunnahoe chased him with his knife.

He offered little to the jury about that evening deep in the trees. The lean-faced private did say that since he was ten years old, he had struggled with fits of amnesia. At first, he could not say for sure what he confronted in the woods. At his court-martial, his defense lawyer presented evidence that the soldier in the darkening woods feared the boy actually was a wild bear. But the private at last broke down on the witness stand and admitted he had indeed killed the schoolboy because Wilhelm upset him.

"The kid laughed at me when I stuttered," Dunnahoe whined to his jurors. "He started grinning like he was making fun of me or something." He stabbed him up to eighteen times in the head, neck, chest, and back. "I just see red when people laugh at me," the soldier testified. He kept on slashing because, by then, "I would get just as much punishment as if I only hit him once." Dunnahoe got death.

The army transferred him from the Bavarian Alps to the Castle fortress in Kansas. On death row, he changed his story yet again, insisting he had fought a large bear in the German woods after all.

"The bear, the bear, the bear," inmate Schick complained. "That's all we heard about, the damn bear." Prison social worker Joseph Thompson recalled that "it wasn't for years later that it got to him: the bear was actually a boy."

Doctors at the Brooke army hospital in San Antonio, Texas, reviewed the case file, studied the court testimony, and analyzed Dunnahoe's background. They concluded he understood what he had done, but simply showed "poor judgment."

In contrast, doctors in Topeka determined Dunnahoe was "suffering from a mental defect, disease, derangement or a character or behavior disorder." The psychiatrists believed he attacked the boy with a few blows and then "saw red," chasing him through the forest. Yet the army board of review ruled that Dunnahoe "had the power and mental ability to reason." The board noted that Dunnahoe calmly "returned to his bunk to sleep" after the "heinous" attack. The panel affirmed the sentence of death.

The Court of Military Appeals, however, expressed doubts. Maybe Dunnahoe knew what he was doing at first, but the alcohol and the "seeing red" blinded him; maybe he could not control himself.

The appellate court found that before the attack, a witness noticed Dunnahoe staggering, "unable to hold his head up and was drunk but he was not very strong drunk," much like John Bennett in Austria. After the attack, the witness spotted him again, now his eyes "glassy and bloodshot," again like Bennett. However, an army police guard did not smell alcohol on Dunnahoe when he returned to camp; rather he thought the soldier "walked and talked normally."

The high court sent the case back to the review board, asking it to consider a finding of "unpremeditated" murder. In April 1957, the board did exactly that, reducing Dunnahoe's sentence from death to life in prison, with a possibility of parole.

Late the next afternoon, the Fort Leavenworth prison commandant ordered the guards to open Dunnahoe's cell. The staff escorted him up to the general prison population, and some years later, he too was set free. Roy Dunnahoe returned to Arkansas and worked awhile for the Razorback trailer company. On Sundays, he and his wife, Wanda, shared a pew at the Pentecostal Church in McGehee, Arkansas.

★   ★   ★

Sergeant Isaac Jackson Hurt died not at the end of an army rope in Kansas but in a comfortable VA hospital in Ohio. On death row, most everyone thought him aloof and cold-hearted. He was tall, thin, and quiet. Later, as a free man, he worked as a night watchman. His new bride cherished him as a "law-abiding, good and moral citizen." One president commuted his death sentence, and another president set him free.

He was arrested in September 1955, accused of the rape and murder of five-year-old Yumiko Nagayama in Okinawa. Her assailant had sliced open her abdomen with a knife and abandoned her body in a beach quarry garbage dump near the China Sea. Her slaying drew uproars over what is still known today as the "Yumiko-chan Incident." Crowds marched down city streets in protest. Several other females had been raped by American GIs, and after Yumiko died, another soldier attacked another child. "Every Okinawan is burning with indignation!" cried the Okinawa *Shimbun* newspaper.

Until then, Okinawans had been counseled not to resist their occupiers. "Do not be anti-American," they were warned. "Do not be angry or criticize, do not talk too much, never lie, always be truthful. . . . Never put your hands above your ears, do not shout, speak calmly." But Yumiko's murder lifted their voices in anger.

A student activist named Irei believed fears of repression would never end until the Americans left their homeland. "In tears," he said, "my university friends and I discussed that these incidents were evidence of racial insult. I was convinced that these crimes would never disappear unless we recover our human rights."

Many demanded that the United States "punish offenders of this kind of case with the death penalty," singling out Hurt. It marked the first meaningful anti-American protests in a decade. Ten years earlier, the island had been ravaged by Japanese and American troops fighting over the string of beaches and coral reefs. The battle for Okinawa cost more than two hundred thousand lives, soldiers and civilians alike, including a third of the island population. Up to ten thousand Okinawan women had been raped.

Two weeks after the girl's murder, Major General James E. Moore spoke in a packed community hall and offered his "deep sympathy" to a community relations advisory council. He promised change, suggesting restricting or ending altogether his soldiers' leave time. But Okinawans knew their economy would suffer if GIs were banned from shops and restaurants. The general also admonished the more strident activists. To suggest that Americans condoned violence, he cautioned, "is an insult to the American people." And he strongly defended the army's judicial system. "There never has been an attempt at whitewashing or covering up any case," General Moore declared.

Mitsuko Takeno, president of the Okinawa Women's Association, argued that the army should immediately turn Hurt over to Okinawan justice. "If this act was committed by an Okinawan, the people would probably surround his house and stone it and indignation will reach its peak and they will probably lynch this person," she warned. "But because of the fact that it was committed by an American, nothing has taken place so far."

Homer Davis, the Leavenworth lawyer who later represented Hurt on appeal, said Hurt should have been either tried in the Okinawa courts or moved to a military courtroom in the States. "The natives raised so much hell because it was one of many rapes our soldiers perpetrated over there," Davis recalled. "People were holding rallies, 5,000 at a time."

Before the court-martial began, Hurt's army lawyer, Captain Julian B. Carrick, asked that the soldier from Kentucky be returned stateside for trial. He cited "the hostile attitude of the Okinawans" and insisted their anger "prevented a fair trial" there.

Before his arrest, Hurt had swilled some twenty beers and partied with prostitutes. When army police caught him, he asked for a cigarette (his brand was Lucky Strikes), and he teased the investigators. "I read the newspaper about the girl's killing," he quipped. "I feel I might have been the one. It could have been me."

At his court-martial, the prosecution's best witness was a scared nine-year-old boy. He had seen a GI who looked like Hurt near the quarry but could not identify Hurt in a lineup. Yoshiko Kamimura, a waitress, testified about bloodstains on Hurt's pants. Hair samples were lifted from the door handle and seat cover in the sergeant's rusted-out green-and-white Ford, but none matched the girl or tied Hurt to the slaying. The best a Japanese professor could say was that the hairs "could be" hers. Even on death row, Hurt still fixated about the hair residue. "He swore they never really proved it on him," recalled social worker Thompson. "He was always talking about hair samples."

The trial wore on for two weeks. In December 1955, Sergeant Hurt was convicted and sentenced to die. He barely blinked. But his lawyer, Captain Carrick, immediately asked for a reconsideration and leniency. He presented letters and petitions from Hurt's hometown of Lothair in the coal-mining country of southeast Kentucky. They described him as "honest" and "law abiding." Prosecutors countered with an affidavit showing the thirty-one-year-old officer earlier had served eleven months in prison for assault and attempted rape in Detroit.

In a private session with the staff judge advocate, Hurt insisted he was innocent. He charged that witnesses had lied or based their testimony on press accounts. He leaned into the judge and claimed, "I didn't do it."

He said little on death row. "He was very intoxicated over there and couldn't remember much about his crime," recalled Sergeant Peterson. He never received mail from home.

"Once they had a flood in Kentucky and he said maybe the damned place washed away," remembered Sergeant Ray. "He said that was why he never heard anything from his people."

His military appeals failed, but Hurt and his relatives in Kentucky managed to gain the ear of Kentucky politicians. Representative Carl D. Perkins, a Kentucky Democrat and World War II army veteran, wrote the White House. He described the growing concerns from his district where Hurt "comes from" that "something could be done about" commuting the sentence.

In the Senate, Thruston B. Morton, a Kentucky Republican, personally forwarded a Kentucky VFW resolution to the Eisenhower administration, urging a commutation. "The conviction rests upon circumstantial evidence and there exists some doubt concerning the guilt or innocence of the accused," the VFW warned.

Senator John Sherman Cooper, another Kentucky Republican, pressed the White House on the hair samples. "Give this matter your deepest consideration," he urged the president. "The death sentence is one that should be very carefully meted out; it is so irrevocable."

Senate Majority Leader Lyndon Johnson and Senator Ralph Yarborough, Texas Democrats, asked a law firm to pursue Hurt's appeals. Texas lawyer Robert J. Hearon Jr. warned White House assistant counselor Phillip Areeda that executing Hurt "might very well constitute a manifest miscarriage of justice."

A brace of political muscle from powerful office holders from two Southern states united to support this otherwise nondescript Kentucky native. He was a local boy, one of theirs, and once protests over the

Okinawan slaying erupted into international anti-American outcries, they rushed to defend this white American sergeant.

But in May 1959, Army Secretary Wilber Brucker recommended death. "I have studied this case carefully," Brucker said. "And I am convinced of the guilt of the accused." He also was disgusted that Hurt had falsified his enlistment papers by not mentioning the earlier assault case in Detroit.

Hurt's supporters kept pushing, though. Judge S. M. Ward of Hazard, Kentucky, worked with Hurt's parents for a commutation. "The father of this serviceman is eighty-eight years of age and his mother is seventy-seven," Kentucky Republican representative Eugene Siler told Eisenhower. "They have not seen their son for more than six years."

Homer Davis tried to win a new trial. At a federal court hearing in Kansas, he brought up the outrage in Okinawa and the failed defense attempts to move the court-martial off the island. "This was a sham, a pretense of a fair trial," Davis argued. But the judge was unimpressed and rejected the appeal. Prison guards who brought Hurt to the Kansas City, Kansas, courthouse in a six-jeep convoy returned him to death row at Fort Leavenworth on what now seemed the end of the road.

The Eisenhower White House was beginning to buckle under the weight of Hurt's influential supporters. Hurt had never truly confessed. No eyewitness placed him with the girl. His whereabouts that night was unexplained; even the drunken Hurt could not remember. And the hair samples did not match. The attorney general began to feel the death penalty was "inappropriate" and called instead for a long prison sentence. Such a circumstantial case, he suggested, would seem to "justify" executive clemency. Areeda in the White House gnawed at his own doubts. "One can hold Hurt guilty only with reservations," he reasoned.

On June 1, 1960, Eisenhower struck down the death sentence and gave Hurt forty-five years in prison, with no parole. Hurt was moved upstairs and, in the years ahead, served as an administrative trustee at the Fort Leavenworth prison. Later transferred to the federal penitentiary next door, he suffered a stroke in 1969 while playing handball. Hurt lost the use of his right arm and leg and hobbled with a cane around the prison yard, but still kept challenging his forty-five-year sentence.

"The way things are there is nothing to hope for me," he wrote the warden. He wrote to the pardon attorney, the Senate, and President Ford's attorney general, pleading for dismissal of his case or at least parole. "I can only believe that I was sacrificed to appease the dissident political elements who were demanding an end to American mil. Occupation," he wrote, still haunted by the anger of the Okinawa protests surrounding the murder.

In January 1977, President Ford made Hurt parole eligible. Hurt limped out of prison, and by November, he began vocational training at the Goodwill center in Cincinnati. He worked as a night watchman, and in 1981, he married. A year later, his bride, Lura, a kitchen helper, mailed papers to Washington trying to win him a full presidential pardon. He was still waiting for word when he died in August 1984 at the VA hospital.

★　★　★

The ferry pushed off across the elegant Main, southern Germany's longest river, carrying businessmen bustling to work, shoppers headed to market, and tourists out for a summer cruise. The waters glistened crystal blue that June 1956, when suddenly a cry rose up aboard ship. Several men tackled army Private Ralph T. McFarlane and hauled the young soldier off the boat, but not before he had robbed the cabin master, slashed a passenger, and stabbed the ferry conductor to death.

McFarlane confessed almost immediately. He admitted to army investigators that he purchased the six-inch German-made hunting blade ten days before for a souvenir when he visited his family in Wyoming and Colorado. He claimed he stole the money to help his ailing mother.

Before he was sent to trial, McFarlane's unit, in a goodwill gesture a decade after World War II, raised 1,670 German marks, or the sizable amount of four hundred American dollars, and presented it to the ferry operator's widow. Colonel James R. Winn penned an open letter to the German press, apologizing and calling the slaying "regrettable." He would do everything, he said, to assure a just sentence for the eighteen-year-old soldier. He also promised it would never happen again.

The court-martial convened within ten days, the courtroom and galleries jammed with three hundred German citizens and American soldiers.

The evidence was clear, and McFarlane was found guilty of wounding German housemaid Hildrud Wagner, nineteen, and killing the boat operator, forty-five-year-old Joseph Ostrowski, on the Kreuz-Wertheim ferry.

But the Court of Military Appeals was troubled by the speediness of his trial. His attorney had been given little time to review the evidence, interview his client, or line up witnesses. He rarely interrupted or objected to prosecutors; he never examined his client's mental state. He did not even present a closing argument. And before the death sentence was pronounced, the defense lawyer called just two officers who briefly testified that McFarlane was a "good soldier" and well liked, hardly enough to spare a man's life.

"Defense counsel here," the Court of Military Appeals lectured, "conceded everything, explored nothing, was unprepared on every issue, and made the least of what he had."

The judges said McFarlane's lawyer should have been given more time and resources to interview McFarlane's family and friends, his army superiors, and fellow soldiers: "When a life is at stake great care should be exercised. When a crime is committed overseas ten days' time is inadequate to prepare the defense of a capital case."

The appellate court resentenced McFarlane to life in prison with the possibility of parole. He disappeared so quickly off death row that few could recall much about his short stay, other than fleeting images of a "skinny, scrawny" young recruit, "a laughable character." He sometimes tried to talk or act tough but more often cowered on the floor in the back of his cell. As one prisoner remembered, "He didn't deny what happened coming off that river boat." Soon it no longer mattered. Ralph McFarlane, one of the lucky ones, vanished from army death row. They handed him over to the federal prison system, and there he remained until September 1975. He was paroled from a US penitentiary at Terre Haute, Indiana, and released to his home state of Wyoming.

But he was far from rehabilitated. McFarlane cycled in and out of the Wyoming criminal justice system for crimes ranging from drunk driving to soliciting sex from a minor. Not until February 1989 was he at last set free from the Wyoming state penitentiary. By then, the system had had about enough of Ralph McFarlane. Once he had been an army soldier who beat a death sentence. Upon his final release, they attached an admonition to his state prison records: "According to the Defendant's record he has spent approximately twenty-six years in prison. This is half of his life."

*   *   *

Private Edward Heilman hailed from an east Texas railroad town called Terrell, home to a sparkling new military college and an infantry regiment of the Texas Army National Guard. At the time of his crime, he was twenty-two years old, blond, muscular, and tattooed.

During basic training, he became obsessed with a pair of fellow recruits. Upon transfer to West Germany, he began harassing those two soldiers. One June morning in 1959, he broke into a supply room and stole a .45-caliber automatic pistol. In a sudden burst of barracks gunfire, Heilman killed Private Charles Ehrstein and gravely wounded Private James L. Hahn. Shot four times, his leg badly hit, Hahn testified from his hospital bed.

Heilman was convicted in West Germany in October 1959 of premeditated murder, attempted premeditated murder, and larceny, and given the death penalty. But his case never reached Eisenhower's Oval Office in Washington. In November 1960, the army board of review struck down the death penalty for this Texas soldier, ruling he was mentally disturbed and had not purposely planned the attack. The board believed the shootings were not in truth "premeditated." The board imposed instead a reduced sentence of fifty years in prison. The Court of Military Appeals separately agreed that Heilman's life should be spared.

What saved Heilman were concerns about his sanity and suspicions about his sexual orientation. At his court-martial, a private identified only as Gaines insisted Heilman was unfit. "I think he's insane," Gaines said. "Things he's done, like breaking windows with his hand, cutting himself with the razor."

He described a night in the enlisted men's club when Heilman and another soldier were drinking and "just hitting each other." Heilman also once smashed his fist through a double-glass window. Said Private Gaines, "I think he's mentally unbalanced, anyone who acts queer like that."

There was the rub: many in the army suspected Heilman was a homo-sexual; few had any tolerance for that, in army uniform or prison overalls.

Once he left death row and transferred to the federal prison system, he petitioned for an even shorter prison sentence. The secretary of the army reduced it to thirty-nine years.

As late as 1969, Heilman was still angling for a way out the door of the penitentiary in Terre Haute, Indiana. From behind bars, he mailed savings bonds to Private Hahn's parents in Oklahoma, hoping to win their forgiveness for wounding their son. But Hahn's family never cashed the checks. "Mom and Dad wouldn't accept the money," recalled Hahn's brother, Roy Hahn of Midwest City, Oklahoma. "Our parents didn't want anything to do with the man who went crazy and caused all this. He never should have been sent to Germany."

As a result of Heilman's attack, army doctors in Texas amputated Hahn's leg below the knee. The injury ended his military service. He re-turned home to El Reno, Oklahoma, and worked in prosthetics, building artificial limbs for others. Hahn died at fifty-nine, never fully recovering from his wounds. And his widow, Sue Hahn, never forgave the army. Heilman, she insisted, should have been hanged long ago. "The man de-served to die."

But Heilman lived on. Released in December 1972, he settled in the rural Ozarks around Harrison, Arkansas. There he died in March 2007 at the age of sixty-nine.

Chapter Six

★ ★ ★ ★ ★ ★ ★ ★

EISENHOWER

Private Leroy Henry had been assigned to an army gasoline supply company. Now he was ordered "hanged by the neck until dead." When he heard the jury's decision, the soldier shook his head and wept. Police stood him on his feet in the US Army courtroom in England and ushered him to a "condemned cell" in Somerset's Shepton Mallet Prison. A new gallows had been built, ready for the black soldier from St. Louis, court-martialed for raping a white woman in the Bath region of England.

In May 1944, tens of thousands of American soldiers were preparing for the D-Day invasion of France. For months, London and the English countryside were draped in Yankee uniforms, young wide-eyed men called to help liberate Europe. Henry, thirty years old, insisted that the woman, married to a local truck driver and a mother of two, was a known prostitute he had paid for sex. But Irene testified he threatened to cut her throat. "I am a housewife and don't know the accused," she told the army jurors. Henry countered, "I have never had a knife in all my life."

The judge announced the death sentence ten days before the great Allied armada launched for Normandy. The harsh punishment sparked an instant outrage in Bath and throughout southwest England, and on the Thames in London, too. More than thirty-three thousand signatures were hastily gathered, names scrawled on the backs of bank ledgers, hotel registries, snack and tea bar sales records, even school and exercise books. Some came from guests and employees at the posh St. Ellens Villa, and many were pasted with red stickers. "Matter of Urgency!" they shouted. "Coloured Soldier Appeal!" Alderman Sam Day and a local baker, Jack Allen, helped deliver the signatures to General Dwight D. Eisenhower.

Separately to his door surged hundreds of handwritten letters. "My neighbors and I have had no peace since we first read of this case . . . ," wrote
Mrs. B. Jones of Parkstone Place. "I am disgusted at the difference made
between black & white men here. God made us all." Albert Gregory of
Bath warned the general that "to hang any man, white or black" for such
an alleged offense "is the greater crime."

British newspapers fumed too. "A put-up job," protested the London
Daily Mirror.

The timing could not have been worse for Eisenhower. He was consumed with finalizing logistics for the sweeping attack across the English
Channel. Were his men ready? Would the weather hold? Would the English people support him? This last-minute public outcry threatened his
plans. The army ordered a fresh review, though Irene still contended that
he flashed a knife and threatened her if she "shouted or screamed." She was
terrified as he pushed her over a wall near Firs Field, she said.

Henry had been drafted in January 1943. He had no prior criminal
record, and his tour of duty was to run "for the duration of the war, plus
six months." He was legally separated from his wife. In St. Louis, he drove
trucks for twenty-five dollars a week. In the army, he was a trucker and
mechanic, and was well liked by his command.

In a statement to army police, Henry admitted helping Irene over the
three-foot high wall. But he stressed, "She did not resist in any manner."

At his court-martial, he testified that he had signed the statement only
after army agents deprived of him sleep and food and kicked him from
behind. He was forced to stand at attention until he keeled over on the
floor. "They started off rough from the very beginning," he said.

He testified he and Irene had had sex twice before. He paid her an English pound for each tryst. He made a third date, and afterward "she asked
me for two Pounds and I did not have two Pounds. I said I had well over
a Pound. She said, 'I will get you in trouble.'"

"Did you have a knife?" his army lawyer asked.

"No, sir."

"Did you ever borrow a knife?"

"No, sir."

"Did you ever own a knife?"

"No, sir."

When Irene, thirty-three years old, settled into the witness chair, First Lieutenant John A. Pullins, the sole black juror, asked her about other encounters with the army private. Had they met before at the nearby King William public house?

"I do not go out," she fired back.

Henry's chain of command initially defended the verdict and sentence of death. Major Theo F. Cangelosi made much of Lieutenant Pullins being allowed to sit with white officers in the jury box.

"This colored officer voted in favor of the death penalty," the major proudly noted, "because the vote of the members of the court imposing the death penalty was unanimous." Lieutenant Colonel H. M. Peyton affirmed the death sentence, finding no doubt that Henry and the woman had had "carnal knowledge." But he added a personal caveat: "Inasmuch as this is not an aggravated case of rape, it is believed the sentence *should* be commuted to life imprisonment."

Captain Frederick J. Bertolet, assistant staff judge advocate, wanted the "confession" thrown out. Henry's statement, he concluded, was signed by "an ignorant soldier" with just seven years of grammar school and low scores on army tests. He too recommended life in prison. The captain also attached the signatures of two hundred local residents to the official court record. Stacks of petitions with thirty-three thousand more signatures cluttered Captain Bertolet's office.

In London, Howard Bucknell, a minister-counselor, demanded a racial breakdown of American soldiers sentenced to die during the US military buildup in England. "How many," he asked, "were colored and white respectively?" The army balked. "There is no discrimination on grounds of race or color," the command staff replied, noting that Parliament had permitted the Americans to punish their "delinquents" in Britain as they saw fit. "The whole matter is entirely within the competence of the United States authorities."

The *Daily Mirror* was indignant. "In America which has a color problem peculiar to herself, clemency might not be possible," the paper editorialized. "Here [in England] it may not be impossible as an act of grace to take a different view."

The *Tribune* in London published the court-martial transcript nearly in full, declaring "at this critical stage of the war one of the principles for which our men are fighting is the defense or restoration of dignity and equality for all individuals whatever their color, race or creed."

Newspaper readers condemned the US courts-martial system; some blamed Irene and "not the Negro." Suggested one reader, "If he is good enough to fight for us then he is good enough for a square deal."

Mail poured into army headquarters in England.

"If this man is hung it will be an injustice for this particular offence," Alderman Day of Bath wrote Eisenhower. Elizabeth Spencer Warwick of Bathwick Hill believed Irene should be punished.

"Spare the negro's life," she begged the general. "The woman is a well-known bad lot; she ought to have been charged with perjury and flogged. Surely his life is of FAR more value."

Thomas Bunker, a shop steward in Chippenham, collected signatures at his Westinghouse Brake and Signal plant. Sid Pritchard, manager of a Bath winery, tapped his employees to help win the "reprieve of the US negro soldier who," he told Eisenhower, was "convicted in what we consider to be a grave case of injustice."

In the United States, Clara Clayman, executive secretary of the Lynn Committee to Abolish Segregation in the Armed Forces, asked the Judge Advocate General's headquarters for clarity. "The harshness of the sentence hardly seemed to be justified," she wrote. "It would seem this sentence was imposed purely on a basis of racial prejudice."

Colonel R. E. Kunkel, chief of the military justice division in the nation's capital, responded by singling out that sole black juror. "A thorough examination of the record of trial by this office revealed nothing whatsoever indicating 'racial prejudice,'" the colonel persisted.

Nevertheless, Thurgood Marshall, NAACP legal counsel in New York, who in ten years would help win the *Brown v. Board of Education* ruling in Kansas and in ten years more become the first justice of color on the US Supreme Court, hurried an urgent cable to Eisenhower's SHAEF headquarters in England. Regarding the "American Negro soldier sentenced death for rape," Marshall advised, "we request stay execution and opportunity review Court Martial record this case."

The outcry from both sides of the Atlantic, the mounting petitions, and the overwhelming publicity hit home. Army spokesman Colonel Jock Lawrence complained the British papers "constantly make us look as if we are some uncivilized nation, having come here to invade them, to rape their women." The newspaper stories, the editorials, and the criticism, he believed, "do more harm than Mr. Goebles [sic] himself"—referring to the Nazi propaganda minister.

However, the fury could not go ignored. On June 2, four days before the invasion boats pushed off for Normandy, Major General Charles H. Corlett, nicknamed "Cowboy Pete," recommended striking the death sentence and replacing it with "hard labor" for the rest of Henry's life.

The ultimate decision was Eisenhower's, and only after the Allies gained a foothold in France did the supreme commander respond. On June 17 he threw out the death sentence, released the soldier from the Somerset prison, expunged the court record, and returned Henry to his truck supply company. Eisenhower felt "the evidence was insufficient to sustain the conviction."

W. J. Wenham, a solicitor and parliamentary agent in London, was ecstatic. "Your decision," he thanked Eisenhower, "lifts you at once into the front rank of the greatest and noblest of the American names."

The *Tribune* declared that "[t]he Negro community feel that they are no longer unprotected and exposed to the racial prejudice of a court-martial."

In the United States, the African American press hailed the decision, saying it will "send the morale of the Negro soldiers soaring."

The rejoicing would not last. By war's end, a year later, six other American soldiers, five blacks and one Hispanic, all of them court-martialed for rape, were hanged at Somerset's Shepton Mallet Prison. No white soldiers were executed for rape.

However, it must be noted that Eisenhower only intervened in the Henry case once his hand was forced. On issues of race and justice, as an army general and president of the United States, he often made decisions only when mounting circumstances required it. Even at the dawn of the civil rights era during his presidency, he never publicly embraced integration, calling instead for a "gradual" change in race relations. He sent troops to Little Rock, Arkansas, because he had taken an oath to enforce the law, but privately opposed the Supreme Court decision integrating the nation's schools. The public's impatience over civil rights would erupt after his presidency, and by then Dwight Eisenhower was viewed by many as a relic of a bygone time, the last president born in the last century, long ago molded in the segregated caste system of the US Army. He had returned from a devastated Europe a victorious war hero, smiling, with arms outstretched in a momentous Manhattan ticker-tape parade. He left the White House during a gray winter snowstorm in 1961, to many, the faded image of an old man whose time had passed.

For eight years, President Eisenhower had led the nation, serving as commander in chief and ultimate judge over all of those soldiers, black and white, imprisoned on death row at Fort Leavenworth. The tone he set began as far back as November 1952, two months before he took office, in a White House meeting with Harry Truman. The outgoing president strongly encouraged the former army general, the nation's champion against Nazi tyranny, to create a "minority group" of presidential assistants to address "complaints" and "hurt feelings" from America's blacks, Latinos, and immigrant groups. But, Truman lamented in his diary, "I think all this went into one ear and out the other."

It was how he was promoted up the army ranks and into presidential politics that molded the man. Born in Texas in 1890, raised in a central Kansas farm town, and schooled in a white-run US Army, Eisenhower was inclined to let the country change on its own terms, at its own time. His public support for integration was often weak, and he rarely acted alone on racial issues. He freed Leroy Henry at a time when he desperately needed England's crucial backing in the Normandy invasion. He seldom spoke from his heart against Southern atrocities and held his tongue after the brutal, racially motivated murder of teenager Emmett Till in 1955.

"I the mother of Emmett Louis Till am pleading that you personally see that justice is meted out to all persons involved in the beastly lynching of my son in Money Miss," Mamie E. Bradley telegrammed Eisenhower from Chicago. "Awaiting a direct reply from you."

Eisenhower did not respond.

The Till slaying did enrage one of his few black White House aides, a young, hopeful, and very-low-level assistant named E. Frederic Morrow.

He fired off a memo calling on immediate federal leadership because the racial tensions in America seemed about to explode.

"The warning signs in the South are all too clear," Morrow warned. "The harassed Negro is sullen, bitter, and talking strongly of retaliation." The memo was largely ignored. As it happened, in the Lyndon Johnson years, riots of disenfranchised black Americans would erupt in cities across the country.

In 1959, Morrow heard from a black private, Henry Nevin, imprisoned for five months at Fort Leavenworth for injuring a man in what he called self-defense. "How unjustice [sic] can one get? I really did not expect that from the army," Nevin wrote to Morrow. "I could see out in civilian life and deep down South. . . . But this is the U.S. Army. One would expect a little justice."

All that Morrow, a former NAACP field secretary and army veteran, could offer was to suggest Nevin seek parole. By then, the Eisenhower presidency was winding down, his second term coming to a close, and Morrow went away deeply frustrated. "President Eisenhower's lukewarm stand on civil rights made me heartsick," he would write in his diaries. "His failure to clearly and forthrightly respond to the Negro's plea for a strong position on civil rights was the greatest cross I had to bear in my eight years in Washington."

Eisenhower did help push through legislation creating a civil rights division in the Department of Justice and an independent commission on civil rights with subpoena powers. In addition to Morrow, the president also appointed a smattering of blacks to other minor posts in his administration. But they often felt locked out of his White House, with little influence. Derrick Bell, a former air force officer, served briefly as one of the few black attorneys in Eisenhower's new civil rights division. He quit rather than bow to demands that he cancel his membership in the NAACP.

"I was moved to a desk set up in the hall," Bell recalled. "I was barred from doing any race-related work and instead was given a series of non-race-related research projects. It was busy work. I took the hint and resigned."

Upstairs in the White House or out on a golf course, Eisenhower often revealed in private conversation his stubborn refusal to change with the times. His clunky, awkward language was a vestige of his upbringing in Abilene, Kansas, and his young manhood on the drill fields of the US Army.

His son, John S. D. Eisenhower, described the complexities of the father he affectionately called the Boss. "First of all, the social upheavals of the 1960s had not yet arrived," he wrote in his memoir of his father, *Strictly Personal*. And "it is true that the Boss, having been poor himself as a boy, was not instinctively an avid social reformer. But he believed deeply in the equal rights of every individual, as witness his sending the 101st Airborne Division in 1957 to enforce integration at Little Rock and the passage in that year of the first civil rights bill in nearly a century after the end of the Civil War." He added, "Dad achieved best results by doing things his own way." The president's grandson, David Eisenhower, cherished stories the old man shared of his West Point colleague John Markoe, who later headed an all-black unit patrolling the southwest border. After a barroom brawl defending black recruits, Markoe was discharged from the service. "He was ahead of his time," Granddad Eisenhower conceded to David. "He stood up for his Negro soldiers." But he also stressed the downside of such heroics, warning his grandson that it cost the man his career. "There but for the grace of God go I," he said.

The 1954 *Brown* decision first tested Eisenhower's leadership on racial equality. "I am convinced that the Supreme Court decision has set back progress in the South at least fifteen years . . . ," he privately told a White House aide. "We can't demand perfection in these moral questions. All you can do is keep working toward a goal and keep it high. And the fellow who tries to tell me that you can do these things by force is just plain nuts."

Yet he was the president who had nominated Earl Warren as chief justice. "Biggest damn fool mistake I ever made," Eisenhower privately lamented. Once when Warren attended a White House function, Eisenhower took him aside and in a confidential chat spoke highly of John W. Davis, a lawyer and longtime friend of the president, who was representing some of the Southern states opposed to integration. Mentioning white Southerners in general, Eisenhower quipped: "These are not bad people. All they are concerned about is to see that their sweet little girls are not required to sit in schools alongside some big black bucks."

In another private session, Eisenhower counseled his chief of staff Sherman Adams that even with court orders like *Brown*, "you cannot change the hearts of people by law." A week after he sent troops to guard the Little Rock high school, Eisenhower was already expressing a desire to withdraw the soldiers. White House aide Arthur Larson remembered Eisenhower was determined to stay within the bounds of his legal powers and not choose sides in the *Brown* ruling, despite his personal views on the issue.

He sent troops only because the law required it.

"The only assurance I can give you," Eisenhower warned Arkansas governor Orval Faubus during the height of the school standoff, "is that the federal Constitution will be upheld by me by every legal means at my command."

Hinting that, in his heart, he opposed forced school desegregation, he told four moderate Southern governors, "I have never said what I thought about the Supreme Court decision. I have never told a soul."

William O. Douglas, a Franklin Roosevelt appointee to the Supreme Court, faulted Eisenhower for not making an effort to think outside of his long-ingrained, comfortable, white world. "He had played golf too long with the 'wrong' people, those who preferred a caste system," Associate Justice Douglas said in his autobiography, *The Court Years*. Had he gone on radio or television and spoken out against discrimination, Douglas believed, the nation would have healed much sooner. Instead, Douglas maintained, Eisenhower's "silence" on the *Brown* ruling "gave courage to the racists who decided to resist the decision ward by ward, precinct by precinct, town by town, and county by county."

The president did speak on national television to explain his decision for dispatching troops to Arkansas, but mainly stressed that the Constitution was what mattered, that the court's order came first. "The fact is that is the law and as president of the United States I have the responsibility of seeing to it that it is enforced."

Eisenhower's go-slow policy continually frustrated many black civil rights leaders.

"I was sitting in the audience at the Summit Meeting of Negro Leaders yesterday when you said we must have patience," baseball legend Jackie

Robinson wrote Eisenhower in May 1958. "On hearing you say this, I felt like standing up and saying, 'Oh no! Not again'. . . . 17 million Negroes cannot do as you suggest and wait for the hearts of men to change. We want to enjoy now the rights that we feel we are entitled to as Americans."

Eisenhower responded to Robinson a month later. "I am firmly on record as believing that every citizen—of every race and creed—deserves to enjoy equal civil rights and liberties," he wrote. "For there can be no such citizen in a democracy as a half-free citizen."

Chapter Seven

★ ★ ★ ★ ★ ★ ★

BLACK DEATH ROW

Shortly before midnight on March 1, 1955, the first of three military convoys rolled out of the Castle at Fort Leavenworth. Seven army vehicles carried high-ranking army officers, official witnesses, and one condemned soldier. They followed the old river road high on the bluffs, to Eisenhower Road and then a warehouse at the state penitentiary—a twenty-minute drive under the lantern moon.

At 11:55 p.m., they escorted their first man, twenty-five-year-old Private Chastine Beverly of Balty, Virginia, into the storehouse on the prison grounds. The high-ceilinged stone structure had been leased that night under a federal-state contract because the army at Fort Leavenworth had yet to build a new hanging platform. The US Army would deliver the soldier; the state would hang him. Beverly, dressed in a regulation army uniform sans decoration or insignia, stood silent as guards removed his handcuffs. They wrapped a leather-and-chain "hanging harness" over his shoulders and a strap across his legs, then led him a few paces to the foot of the gallows. Colonel James W. Davis, commandant of the military prison, asked for any final words, anything left to say after three and a half years on death row. Beverly looked squarely into the eyes of the colonel. He moistened his lips with his tongue, seeming to hold back his tears.

"Nothing at all, sir," he managed. A Kansas prison deputy warden led him up the thirteen steps. On the high platform, Kansas prison guards lowered a black hood over his head and strung a heavy noose around his neck, fashioned from a new hemp cord. They yanked it tight behind his left ear, following the army execution guidelines. Major Milton E. Berg, a Protestant army chaplain, recited from his prayer book. "God take away the sin of the world . . ." Few caught his words, but all jolted at two minutes after midnight with the slap of the heavy metal trapdoor.

Medical officers slit open the front of Beverly's shirt. Armed with stethoscopes, they searched for a fading heartbeat. At 12:14 a.m., an army captain approached Colonel Davis and saluted. "He is dead," the captain reported. Litter bearers removed the harness, rope, and straps, and cut the body down. A guard reached for a portable phone and radioed post head-quarters back at Fort Leavenworth. Bring the next one, he said.

So it went, twice more that night, the three men hanged in alphabetical order. James L. Riggins, twenty-six, of Birmingham, Alabama, was said to be the ringleader of the army trio that beat a taxi driver to death in a rob-bery in rural Missouri. He had been a boxer at one time and was regarded by many as the "bad boy" of the outfit.

The second summoned to the warehouse, Riggins stood composed but angry. "No," he barked at Colonel Davis. He had nothing to say. So the chaplain completed his benediction—"Oh Christ," he intoned.

Riggins took longest to die. The fall did not break his neck. For eighteen minutes and forty seconds, the former army private, six feet, two inches tall, 205 pounds, slowly suffocated. He raised his strapped legs up to his twisting torso. It was, the soldiers thought, a final show of indignation.

The last to die that night was Louis M. Suttles, twenty-six, of Chat-tanooga, Tennessee. He merely shook his head; what more was there to say? From atop the scaffold, his eyes darted around the room, finally fixing on someone in the crowd standing with others at parade rest below. Then came the hood and a prayer and the trapdoor. He was dead in three and a half minutes.

Joseph A. Thompson, the black prison social worker, always believed it was his face that Suttles desperately sought in his final seconds. "He nod-ded to me and the next minute he's hanging there like a sack of potatoes," Thompson recalled. "I saw it as so fruitless, so meaningless."

Their bodies were shipped home in freight cars, back to the American South. Army details gathered up their tools and returned to their billets. For days, army officials at the fort refused to talk about the triple hanging. In Topeka, the state was so disgusted it announced it would no longer contract with the army to carry out its executions.

Helping the military hang three men in a single night seemed far too distasteful, and certainly "not in the best interests of the state," wrote Martin M. Kiger, chairman of the Kansas Board of Penal Institutions. The US Army had its own massive Castle prison and towering turrets; let it build its own gallows, the state declared; let the army hang its own.

Sergeant Elgie Maiden of the army execution detail was struck by how courageously, and quietly, the three black privates had gone to their deaths. Earlier that night, he had watched them devour final meals of fried chicken, a T-bone, and barbequed spare ribs. Riggins offered a final goodbye. "Looks like I'm going to have to leave you," Riggins called out. Like they were old combat buddies, Maiden thought, like they had shared a foxhole, a foxhole called the United States Disciplinary Barracks.

"They were all perfectly calm," he remembered. "They'd been in here so long with so many appeals and so many legal actions. You could see them over a period of time losing all hope. It got to the point it seemed like they were ready. When Suttles came in, he had hair as black as his face. When they hung him, his hair was gray and it wasn't from worrying about when or if he was going to die. It was worrying if he had been the one who struck that fatal blow. He couldn't live with the fact of not knowing if he was the one who killed that man or not."

★   ★   ★

In September 1951, cab driver Harry Langley, fifty-one years old, staggered out of a patch of trees in Pulaski County, home to an army engineer training post at Fort Leonard Wood in the Missouri Ozarks. He was deep in shock, suffering from pneumonia, and limping along Route 66.

"They beat me," Langley muttered, sinking in and out of consciousness as police rushed him to a hospital.

"Who beat you?" demanded a patrolman.

"Three niggers," he said.

He was dead on arrival at a hospital in Springfield, Missouri, suffering a skull fracture and chest injuries. In the woods, army police recovered dried blood on rocks, an empty billfold, and the driver's chauffeur cap. A little over $155 was missing. The three soldiers were arrested in a stolen car near Rolla, Missouri.

Fearing he would be lynched, Beverly broke first. He had never made it past the sixth grade in rural Virginia; what scared him now was an investigator mentioning "a guy in Waynesville who'll make me talk a plenty." For four days, they kept Riggins locked inside the "black box," an underground bunker at Fort Leonard Wood with no light, heat, or furniture. A solitary window was nailed shut, and the glass painted over. The cell was cold and damp; puddles of stale rainwater slicked the cement floor. Riggins suffered from asthma; he could not breathe well. After two days, army officers hauled him out and showed him written statements from Beverly and Suttles, blaming him for the murder.

Riggins first claimed self-defense. They were shooting dice under the cab's headlights, he began. "We started to arguin' . . . and that's how the fight started." Then an exasperated Riggins decided to tell the truth, to get this "monkey off my back." He told army police, "Get your pencil, and start writing."

All of them talked. Beverly said he tried to run away when the others stoned the driver. Suttles said he threw only two rocks, insisting it was not enough to kill Langley. Riggins claimed one of the rocks hit him.

"I didn't hit that guy nary time, nary time," he insisted. He said he yelled for the others to stop, saying they should summon a doctor. They stole a brand-new Chevrolet, but state troopers, searching for Langley's assailants, chased the sedan off the road. The troopers delivered the three soldiers back to Fort Leonard Wood.

Army police paraded Suttles in front of thirty armed and angry farmers and townspeople. He was told he better cooperate.

"You'll come out light if you make a statement," an army criminal investigator whispered in his ear. Some in the crowd carried rifles and handguns; a woman sliced her thin finger across her throat.

The editor of the Pulaski County *Democrat* warned against anyone taking out their frustrations. "I am happy to say no race riot occurred," wrote the editor, John H. McMillin. "It is a tragedy when someone's life is taken by others to satisfy greed or whatever terms one might choose to call it. But it's a double tragedy when the criminals are of the colored race."

McMillin worried that "race prejudice" was "apt to flare up." He was concerned the army under the new Truman army desegregation rules was accepting too many black recruits. "The military installation at Fort Leonard Wood has more than its share of colored troops," he wrote, "which is a condition that is very bad for the people of this area, as well as the colored people themselves."

The trio was court-martialed together, and all three were found guilty. Their khaki pants and shirts were spotted with bloodstains, and Langley's $155.23, mostly in twenties, was stuffed inside Beverly's front pocket. Up to ninety people—thirty civilians and sixty in uniform—elbowed into courtroom pews, and after six days and fifty-five witnesses, all three were sentenced to hang. Once assigned to tank battalions, the privates were driven the next morning to Fort Leavenworth. Before nightfall, they were deposited on death row.

They never imagined that Langley would die. Riggins remained especially bitter about that.

"He just never expected things to end up like they did," recounted death row's Master Sergeant Thompson Biggar. Staff Sergeant Richard Curtsinger said that after three and a half years on Seven Base, all three resolved to die with their heads held high. "They were going to try to escort the guards," he recalled. "No one was escorting them anywhere." But all three were frightened.

"They were afraid their bodies would be mutilated," remembered social worker Thompson. "They'd heard stories of people executed and then their hands cut off or the organs used for experiments. Maybe it was old pirate tales; I don't know. But they wanted a friend there to make sure they died with dignity."

Richard Hagelberger, one of the white death row prisoners, heard the commandant descending the stairs and three times reading the death warrant.

"It scared me," he recalled. "But you have to get it out of your mind."

At every turn, their three appeals came up empty.

"The sentences are legal," concluded the army board of review.

"Affirmed," agreed a Court of Military Appeals.

Two local attorneys, Homer Davis of Leavenworth and civil rights advocate Elisha Scott in Topeka, took up their case.

Davis was small, stout, and bald-headed. He sported several bright rings on his fingers and wore thick eyeglasses. He dreamed of attending West Point but came up two inches short. He did serve as a lieutenant commander in the navy's legal and intelligence corps during World War II, handling simple court-martial cases in the Brooklyn Navy Yard. The son of a Leavenworth newspaperman, husband to a school teacher at Fort Leavenworth, Davis passed the bar in 1929. He served as a police judge, and as an assistant federal prosecutor in 1938, he convicted two men for killing an FBI agent and watched them hang. "In those days I didn't know anything about capital punishment, but I wouldn't want to go through that again," he admitted years later.

In time, he deeply opposed the death penalty, believing even the worst offenders should be given a chance at "mental rehabilitation." The best way to prevent crime, Davis was convinced, was not to end a man's life on a high platform but to start him out with a good home and a religious upbringing. An FDR Democrat, he switched to criminal defense work and opened an office in the two-story red-brick Manufacturers Bank Building in Leavenworth, what was once a freighting warehouse for wagon trains pushing west.

"My name got tossed around a lot," he said, among inmates in Leavenworth County, at the army Castle, the federal penitentiary nicknamed the "Big Top" next door, and the state prison at Lansing.

"This was my hometown," he recalled years later, reflecting on his advocacy work for death row soldiers in the 1950s. "And here were these people up there to be hung. I knew they had no money to get a lawyer," he remembered. "I walked into the basement of that prison, in my hometown, and saw these men who were bound to die. I felt it was my duty to help them."

Elisha Scott was born in 1890 to a Topeka day laborer who herded cattle and sold coal, and a mother who took in laundry when her husband died young. He was schooled at Washburn University and practiced law at the state capital. He worked closely with the NAACP's legal committee and, for several terms, served as president of its Topeka branch. He argued civil rights and school desegregation cases across Kansas and Missouri, and his mail often arrived at his office addressed simply to "Colored Lawyer, Topeka."

He never made much money either, defending bootleggers and unrepentant prostitutes, though once he did well successfully handling black and Native American clients driven off their Oklahoma and Texas land rich in oil. He often could be operatic in court, his voice thundering over the jury box like a prairie preacher. He often filled courtrooms—with blacks and whites alike—craftily picking his juries and quoting scripture. He wore heavy double-breasted suits, but was none too proud to drop to a knee on the courtroom tiles and cry for mercy. He once defended a former, elderly slave charged with murder. Scott begged the jurors, "Do not send this poor old man who did only what he thought was right to spend his last years in the bondage of a jailhouse as he spent his early years in the bondage of the plantation."

In the 1920s and 1930s, Scott set off on a tear around the Midwest. He won a case in Kansas of a black man accused of assaulting a white woman by showing the "victim" had lied under cross-examination. In Duluth, Minnesota, he helped calm the black community when a white mob of five thousand pulled three black men from the local jail and lynched them. In Tulsa, Oklahoma, he counseled black residents when white officials refused to let them rebuild their homes after race riots there.

School desegregation cases were his forte, his passion, and bringing those challenges his *casus belli*. Elisha Scott learned early in life how to find strength in championing lost causes. To keep him motivated, he liked to say, he carried an empty Listerine bottle that he secretly filled with Old Crow, an 80-proof sour mash Kentucky whiskey.

When he died of cancer at seventy-two, he was representing a group of black parents demanding their children be allowed into schools in Wyandotte County, Kansas. The local newspaper, the Kansas City *Kansan*, buried his obituary on page two. The one-column headline did not come close to capturing the man: "Noted Negro Elisha Scott Dies Here."

Davis and Scott teamed up and managed to get a hearing for the three Fort Leonard Wood soldiers before a federal judge in Kansas, only to have him rule against them. They warned the federal Court of Appeals that the confessions were forced; the appellate court turned them down. They appealed to the US Supreme Court, contending the army privates were not provided "effective" defense counsel, and again brought up the "psychological" coercion.

"The petitioners are colored," Davis and Scott pointed out. But the high court would not accept the case. So Davis and Scott urged President Eisenhower to reduce the death sentences. "The justice of the case entitles the three condemned American soldiers to be heard," Scott implored the president in December 1954. Noting the men were "of African descent and color," he called their request for leniency "our last earthly hope."

He wrote again two weeks later. The cab driver's slaying was not premeditated, Scott insisted; manslaughter should have been the proper charge. "All I am asking is for a commutation of the death sentence to life or a period of years," he wrote. The Eisenhower White House was unmoved.

"The soldiers were given the benefit of the doubt and every possible consideration," replied Bernard M. Shanley, special counsel to the president. "We all wish that the facts could be otherwise."

The soldiers' families tried, too. Beverly was regarded as "a good boy in bad company." He was single; his army paychecks helped support his ailing parents. His mother, Cassie Beverly, typed a two-page letter. "I am a poor negro woman, 61 years old, living with my husband in the rural section of Caroline County, Virginia," she told Eisenhower. "Five of my sons have served in the United States Army, and four of them received honorable discharges." She begged for Chastine's life. "Mr. President, we have no money to hire lawyers, or to find out exactly what was happening to my son." She pleaded, "My son should be punished, but not with the supreme penalty of death."

As death grew near, she wrote Eisenhower again, in February 1955: "Only the Lord has kept me to be living to-day." The army, she said, was Chastine's downfall. "He was always kind and humble hearted when he was home."

Riggins was born in Florida. He dropped out after a year of high school and trained as a professional boxer. He once was hit especially hard in the head, what he called "the punch" or being "punched drunk." Sometimes his memory failed him, he said; sometimes he could remember little. He too never married and had been in uniform just six months when they were arrested for murder. His mother, May Lee Jones, in Birmingham, Alabama, sent a few short lines to Washington, hand-scribbled in pencil. "I am begging you in the name of the Good Lord," she wrote in December 1954. "Please be liency [sic] with my child and spare his life."

Suttles came from Tennessee; he would leave behind a wife and two young girls. He once worked in construction but enlisted in 1950; his family depended on his army salary. Sarabelle H. Eldridge of Chattanooga wrote Eisenhower in January 1955, describing herself "as a white citizen of this city, and one who has known the negro boy, Louis Suttle [sic]. His mother is [a] maid in my home, having been so for about seven years. Louis was always a good boy, working at various grocery stores, and as are all of the children of this family, very obedient to his mother. . . . Please give this boy a sentence other than death. . . . Have mercy on this poor negro boy."

Six weeks later, all three were dead.

★   ★   ★

Soon after the night of the triple execution, the army set to work on a new gallows, this one inside the Castle walls. Neal Harrison, the prison's civilian executive assistant, freshened up a formal army execution protocol. Thirteen witnesses and thirteen steps, and for each midnight hanging, all the prison inmates would be placed on lockdown. To make things even smoother, they later added a ramp to ease prisoners onto the platform.

"They'd had a small riot at the Kansas State Penitentiary after those other three were hung," Harrison recalled many years later, in his nineties by then. "That's what stopped the civilian executions. They got a real good price for doing it [with Kansas], but they just couldn't control it anymore. So I wrote our standard operations procedure for executions for military personnel. We did it inside the old power plant. I went over to the command college and found some old 1923 material and I used it to set it all up. My job was to be on the telephone between Washington and Leavenworth in case of a commutation. Of course it never rang."

What the army wanted was army efficiency. The men down on death row could only sense the commotion up above.

"I can guarantee you none were much asleep," said Private Robert Dresden, back then a prison tower guard.

"If they were next, they'd want to know everything about a hanging, as much as they could learn," remembered Master Sergeant Biggar. "They'd hang on to every rumor, every word they could pick up. They'd re-argue a man's case amongst themselves, but once that man was gone they didn't display any sorrow. They displayed anger that they might be next." Then the death cycle spun again.

"They were real curious about the whole procedure," Sergeant Biggar continued. "How it happened, how it felt, did it hurt? But not so much concern for the man who was hung. They just wanted details. They were anxious for details. How it went, what were his last words? But they never found out. They never knew and we didn't tell them. And the man gone over to the power plant, he wasn't around anymore to fill them in."

A skilled carpenter, Master Sergeant Orvill Lawson ran the prison woodworking shop. He also had assisted in the Japanese hangings. Now Lawson and two other guards set to work at night in the abandoned power plant, sweeping away spider webs from the stone walls and raising a high wooden platform. "It was built of solid oak, collapsible and removable, if needed," he recalled.

"We built it in our spare time, in the evenings, working over the course of a month to finish the job." As the army carpenters sawed and planed and sanded, Lawson ruminated over the spectacle lifting higher toward the ceiling. "We'd be building this and I'd be thinking how hanging would have to be the worst way to go. Even if you immediately break your neck and go unconscious, you're still going to suffocate to death. The mind doesn't die that quickly."

When they were done, Lawson recalled, he carved a special wooden knot—like a hangman's loop—from a throw-away chunk of hedge and presented it to his old friend Bill Maddox, the new official army hangman. Of course, Lawson told no one at the prison; that, they kept a secret.

★   ★   ★

The guards locked the doors and shuttered the windows on the power plant. Sergeant Maddox sat at his desk at Fort Riley waiting for his phone to ring. But hanging a man was nothing new. The British had introduced it in the fifth century, though they also experimented with blinding and castration. Other methods were burning, boiling, or beheading. But hangings generally were clean and efficient, remarkable for their finality and how effectively they cut short a man's life.

Yet, by the 1950s, much of Europe and Central and South America had outlawed the death penalty. In the United States, Maine, Michigan, Minnesota, and Wisconsin banned it as well, though it largely remained popular among county sheriffs and prison wardens in the rest of the country. The US Army perfected the art after the war crime trials in Japan following World War II. Chief hangman in Germany was a burly Kansas-born master sergeant named John C. Woods. "I wasn't nervous," he once declared. "A fellow can't afford to have nerves in this business."

At Fort Leavenworth, two years passed before the army tested its new boards. On the night of February 14, 1957, two young black privates, court-martialed in 1953 for separate murders, were hanged in alphabetical order over the same midnight hour. Both were twenty-three years old.

The brass brought in two military doctors and a pair of army chaplains. Any last words on the hanging platform "will speak for itself," the army announced, though there were none. And most importantly, the new protocol stipulated, "the executioner will be a member of the military; his identity must remain anonymous." At Fort Riley, Sergeant Maddox received his temporary duty orders for Fort Leavenworth—"In connection with military activities more advantageous to the Govt," it said in army code. Sergeant Maddox quietly understood. He loaded his trunk and backseat with his ropes and straps, handcuffs and tape, and headed east on the new Eisenhower Highway, Interstate 70. In his spiral notebook he jotted down the heights, weights, ages, and "overall drops" of the two condemned soldiers. He clipped out a brief item from his Junction City, Kansas, *Union* newspaper about the soldiers' legal appeals and pasted it in his binder.

In the prison power plant, the unvarnished, unpainted gallows awaited, but it could only accommodate one man. So Private Thomas J. Edwards from Ardmore, Oklahoma, once assigned to an overseas engineering battalion, was taken first, though he did not initially go quietly.

"We went down to see what size clothes he wore for the hanging and he said, 'If you sons of bitches think you're going to murder me tonight, I've got news for you,'" recounted Master Sergeant Tom Dunham. "He was mad as hell."

Edwards on death row wrote poetry and song lyrics, and often sang loudly and disturbed the other men in their cells. Several prisoners begged to be let out, if just for the chance to clobber him.

"He was the kind of guy nobody liked," remembered Sergeant Curtsinger. "He had no personality. But he wouldn't hurt you. You could put a 10-year-old girl in that cell with him and he wouldn't hurt her."

Sergeant Elmer Peterson thought him gifted. "He was going to be a songwriter," the sergeant recalled. "We'd send his lyrics though channels to a song company and they'd put it to music, make a record of it. He didn't make any money out of it, and none of them ever made it on the market. They'd send him back a copy of the sheet music but he never heard it. We didn't have a record player, and of course no piano down there."

One of the black prisoners, Frank Harris, thought Edwards insane and, for that alone, should have been spared. "He'd lost his marbles," Harris remembered. "We watched this happen on the row. We watched him go crazy. He thought he was a girl. His voice changed. He wasn't swishy but he'd put his hands on his hips and we knew, looking at him, that we'd lost him."

For hours, Edwards would stand and stare through his bars, or sit and blow on a harmonica, making a lot of racket.

"He let his hair go," Harris said. "We couldn't reach him anymore. We called him Tom-Tom but nothing got through to him."

Edwards twice tried to kill himself, first wrapping sheets around his neck. "The guards heard the thud and cut him down. Then he broke the light bulb in his cell and cut himself on the wrist."

When he was nineteen, he had beaten a German woman to death in a rage over racial epithets after a sexual encounter in the Bavarian town of Kitzingen, in March 1953. He smashed her head into a stone wall and twisted a band of torn fabric around her neck. He left, assuming she was still alive, walked to a taxi stand, and returned to camp.

An army jury convicted him of the premeditated murder of Maria Stowasser; they ordered him put to death. Two army appellate courts upheld the findings. One ruled that at the time of the murder and during his trial "the accused was sane." Another psychiatric evaluation found him suffering an "aggressive character disorder . . . easily provoked."

Still, the army judged him sane and shipped Edwards out to Fort Leavenworth. His wife, Charlie Mae Edwards, asked Eisenhower to save her husband, if only so their young daughter would remember her father. "We would not want her life to be an unhappy one due to this misfortune," she wrote the president in June 1955. She also asked for help to pay her college tuition, now that she no long could count on his army salary. "If there is anything you can do to spare my husband's life, I beg you also to do that."

The White House showed little interest. Attorney General Herbert Brownell believed Edwards was mentally balanced. He cited a diagnosis that concluded: "We realize the presence of a twilight zone between sanity and insanity, but this record shows the accused as possessing a mental condition of such capacity to place him in the category of those persons who are sane."

J. William Barba, assistant special counsel in the White House, brushed off assertions that Edwards had temporarily lost his mind. He was "obviously a sick person," Barba conceded, but he knew what he was doing along that footpath that night. "Forgiveness is difficult," he decided, as Edwards did not show "the slightest bit of control."

A week before he died, Edwards wrote long letters to the president. Over two consecutive days, he insisted he must have been briefly insane when the twenty-one-year-old woman was slain.

"This is not a plea for mercy, but a plea for impartial American justice, which I, as an American, deserved," he declared. He felt he should have been given a lighter sentence and examined at length by an impartial board of medical officers. Before his trial, he claimed, he was only seen for an hour. "The question now in my mind is, why?" He dismissed his army trial as a sham; the court picked as chief prosecutor the army lawyer Edwards had rejected for his defense attorney.

"It appears to me to be more of a scheme than anything else," Edwards believed. He claimed self-defense, contending, "I was forced to defend not only my life but my race as well." Capital punishment, he suggested, was meaningless. "No one will profit by my death." Instead, "the five-year-old daughter of mine will lose something which no one else can replace."

Yet Edwards seemed resigned to the scaffold.

"Before I go to the gallows on the 14th of this month," he told the president, "you will prove you practice what you preach (justice) by considering these unselfish facts. Is that asking too much of the man who holds my present life in his hands? Justice will not be accomplished by my death." He ended with a bitter prediction. "Life to most people these days is the cheapest thing in existence. . . . Will I be put to death for a crime in which I was mentally irresponsible for?"

The day before he died, Edwards learned by telegram that the White House rejected his pleas. The night he was hanged, he sat alone listening to the prison radio headset.

Shortly before midnight, Colonel Davis appeared at his cell door and read the Order of Execution. Guards marched him across the moonlit yard and into the power plant. He wore a bare, olive uniform. They tied his wrists, arms, knees, and ankles. Colonel Davis whispered, "May the Lord have mercy on your soul."

On the gallows, Edwards offered not a word as Sergeant Maddox squared his feet atop the trap door and placed a black cap over his head. The hangman pulled the lever at 12:01 a.m.

As the body was cut down and thrust into the back of an idling hearse, more guards hurried toward the power plant with Private Winfred D. Moore. He would hang for killing a cab driver in North Carolina and wounding a passenger. They led him to the foot of the gallows at 12:30 a.m., and two minutes later, Sergeant Maddox again sprung the trapdoor. For fourteen minutes, they waited in silence, to make sure he was gone too.

An Eighty-Second Army Airborne Division soldier at Fort Bragg, North Carolina, Moore had been locked up since the summer of 1953. He joined the army at seventeen. Moore insisted he only meant to rob the cabbie and the other passenger, a fellow black soldier. His .45-caliber pistol misfired in an act of self-defense, he maintained. Afterward he returned to his billet and slept. The next morning, he visited the army barbershop and boarded a bus into town. By then, the driver Charles W. Pettit had been found dead in his taxi, shot through the throat in his new blue-and-cream Ford sedan.

The other passenger, army Private Othello H. Smith, was wounded in the neck and shoulder, and left for dead. Moore was arrested a few days later, on July 3. All he had collected was some spare change from Smith's right hip pocket and a couple of loose coins that fell out when he pulled Pettit's body from the taxi. "I got into all this trouble for a couple of half dollars."

The army put him on trial six weeks later. His jurors were all army officers; none were enlisted men like Moore. From a wheelchair, the wounded private fingered the defendant. No one had threatened Moore, he said; he just suddenly fired. He said he had begged for help, but Moore told him, "You just have to lay there and die."

At dawn, two other GIs happened upon the victims and the abandoned cab.

Moore told it differently. At first, however, he refused to cooperate. So guards isolated him in a Fort Bragg stockade segregated from other prisoners, and at last Moore relented. Over four days, he gave army police three separate statements.

"It came to me that I would rob both the taxicab driver and the Negro soldier," he admitted. He pulled the pistol from under his shirt, and when he demanded money, the driver suddenly flashed a small, black-handled jackknife.

"Ain't no young black punk is going take my money," Pettit warned. Moore was frightened. "I fired," he confessed.

Despite an army evidence team recovering that cabbie's knife near the driver's body, the jury sentenced Moore to die just the same. Moved to death row at Fort Leavenworth, the small, thin-built soldier sat quietly in his cell, marking time. He rarely showed emotion, although on the day he boarded the army bus to Fort Leavenworth, grim, resigned, and shackled, he knew his life had ended.

"Never said a word. I never knew he had a voice," marveled Sergeant Peterson. "He'd nod his head to you, but he wasn't too talkative."

Only once did he surprise the guard detail. They began giving flu shots to condemned prisoners, and Moore resisted, afraid it was some kind of experimental drug. Four officers had to hold the prisoner down. And then he was quiet again.

"He squealed more about that than he did about the whipping he got for being hard to handle," remembered Sergeant Maiden, describing the struggle to subdue Moore On the night they came to hang him, he was silent then too.

Moore's wife, Patricia, lived with their daughter in Columbus, Georgia; his mother, Frances, in Virginia. But the Eisenhower presidential files include only a single letter on his behalf, from a funeral home director in Virginia Beach, Virginia. W. Francis Taylor Jr. wrote to the president in July 1954; by then, Moore had sat silently on death row for nearly a year. Taylor described himself as a "very dear friend and neighbor" of Moore's mother.

"If possible, you would do his most devoted, loyal, and Christian mother a very great favor to commute his sentence," Taylor pleaded with the president. "Since this has happened, she has been suffering both physically and mentally, and is in a pityful [sic] state." Taylor conceded he knew "nothing" about the case and that he was only interceding "for the sake of the son's mother, Mrs. Frances Moore."

He begged the president, "Please sir do what you can for her."

The Eisenhower White House did little.

"I find nothing in the record that warrants disturbance of the maximum penalty imposed," Attorney General Brownell advised the president. White House Assistant Special Counsel Barba noted Moore's record was largely clean. Only once had he been cited for disobeying a command. In civilian life, he had been arrested for stealing a truck "on impulse," and his father paid for the damages to the fender. Moore completed eleven years of school and then enlisted. What may have led to his problems at Fort Bragg, his final downfall, was suddenly finding himself in some financial trouble. "He apparently lost half of his pay gambling on the day of the crime," Barba wrote.

Eisenhower ordered the hanging, and Winfred Moore went to his death without a word. The fall from the rafters broke his neck. His body was shipped to his wife in Georgia, just as Edwards was returned to Oklahoma. The commandant, staff, and prison guards locked the power plant again. As Sergeant Maddox remembered it, he drove home with few worries, settling comfortably into bed well before sunrise.

But First Lieutenant John J. Bateman long struggled over his role in the two hangings that night. An army doctor, Bateman also was training in psychiatry. He later would sit on an army clemency board that urged the government to spare the life of Private John Bennett.

"He didn't enjoy the army particularly," remembered his widow, Joan Bateman. "No, no. He wasn't one who particularly enjoyed that kind of thing. He was from Logan, Utah. When he started his residency he went down to the draft board, and they said, 'Don't worry about that. We won't call you before you finish your residency, and maybe never.' And he got called up anyway. He wasn't very happy about that." Now he found himself in a dual role, a doctor and an army lieutenant, standing beneath the gallows with his stethoscope in hand, listening for flickering, fading heartbeats at the toll of midnight.

"It was very troubling for him," Joan said. "He couldn't sleep for several nights because he had to pronounce them dead. That was his job. And he was very upset. He didn't sleep for two nights. I didn't sleep either."

★   ★   ★

Sergeant Peterson played poker with Ernest Ransom in his final hours that April night of 1957. He secretly dealt him aces and wild cards off the bottom of deck, letting the prisoner win. But Ransom seldom smiled.

"He was a colored boy, another cold one," the sergeant recalled. "He was pretty sure of himself, the Gary Cooper–type. He'd look at you, stare at you and not say too much. If he said something, every word counted."

First Sergeant Kenneth Kramer remembered Ransom as "cocky, a wise guy. He was sarcastic, a chip on his shoulder. He didn't like himself. He didn't respect anybody else."

On hanging day, Sergeant Dunham struggled to prepare Ransom for the gallows.

"We had a bulldozer of a time dressing him," he recounted. "His trousers were 30–29, but we put a 16 shirt on him and we couldn't think of buttoning that. So we put a 17-inch neck shirt on him, but just barely. He wasn't tall but all his bigness was in his shoulders and neck. And he had bad discipline. He didn't care for nothing or nobody. He kept telling us, 'I hope the good Lord knows how I feel.' But who knew how he felt?" He snarled at the execution detail, "I'm going to take you with me." Escorted through the green door, he cursed, "Bury me face down and kiss my ass."

His family in North Carolina never claimed his body, so they buried Ransom in the little hillside cemetery outside the prison walls, in a clearing along the windy river bluffs.

"I remember thinking how this man must have been so poor, so poor his family couldn't pay to bury him proper," recalled Tech Sergeant Harold L. Baldwin, part of the six-man burial team. No flag covered the casket or flew at the services. No soldiers saluted, and no honor guard played taps.

"I remember it was right after lunch," the sergeant said. "The detail went out and met the hearse at the gravesite. We lifted the coffin out of the hearse and carried it over. The hole was already dug when we got there. The chaplain said a few words, nothing special, and we lowered him into the ground. That was it. We turned around and left."

Etched into his white marble tombstone was the barest of epitaphs. It listed neither his rank nor serial number, nor noted that here lay a combat veteran from the Korean War who had fought through the brutal winter of 1952–1953 and the budding summer and fall that followed. Nor did it praise him for winning two Bronze Stars and the United Nations and Korean service medals. No cross was engraved into the headstone. Just his name, the date of his birth, the date of his death. A life in three lines.

He was born in Jackson, North Carolina, but his large family soon fanned out, his father, Lester, moving to Northampton County, North Carolina; his mother, Malinda, to Garysburg, North Carolina; an older sister, Blannie Underdue, to the Bronx in New York. Nine other siblings spread out around North Carolina and Virginia. In January 1952, Ernest went down to Raleigh and enlisted.

In April 1953, four years before he was hanged, Private Ransom downed a fifth of whiskey, stole two .30-caliber carbines and a rack of ammunition from his company quarters at Inchon and killed a Korean guard. Chae Seung Man was shot against a factory wall, four spent casings and

Private First Class John Arthur Bennett shortly after his December 1954 arrest for rape and attempted murder in the waning months of the Allied Occupation in Austria.

The eleven-year-old girl was attacked at nightfall along the snow-dusted Muehl-bach creek in an Austrian village near the US Army's Camp Roeder.

An Austrian gendarme helps patrol the crime scene at dawn. The US military police and local authorities recovered the girl's missing brown shoe and her calendar.

Known to all as the "Castle," the army's maximum-security prison soared above the Missouri River. Along with Bennett, sixteen other soldiers—eight white and eight black—shared death row.

The main entrance to the stone fortress promised hope for soldiers held inside. "Our Mission–Your Future," proclaimed the motto over the front gate. But on death row, white and black prisoners were not always treated the same.

Killed a Lieutenant

"I'M GOING to get me an officer," was the reported remark of Pvt. Michael F. Kunak, 19 (above), Baltimore, Md., just before he walked up to a group of officers and reporters and fired a fatal shot into Lt. Howard Williamson during "Exercise Longhorn" maneuvers at Fort Hood, Tex. Later Kunak reportedly said, "I know I was wrong. I expect to be hanged. It was cold, deliberate murder." Kunak is a cook's helper in 82nd airborne. (International)

A news article from the Wilmington, Ohio, *News-Journal*, April 2, 1952. Private Michael Kunak wanted out of the service in the worst way. To make that happen, he shot and killed an army lieutenant. Eventually removed from death row and then paroled, Kunak got his wish.

Left: National Archives. Right: US Army, courtesy of the Ike Skelton Combined Arms Research Library.

Master Sergeant Maurice Schick drowned the young daughter of an army colonel in Japan. On death row, he was often boastful, but a legal defense team unearthed his dark past. He returned home.

Army carpenters built a scaffold in an old power plant off the prison yard. The work was supervised by Master Sergeant Orvill Lawson, who thought, "Hanging would have to be the worst way to go."

US Army

Private Thomas Edwards killed a woman in Germany. Though he largely kept to himself on death row, he did not go quietly to the gallows. "No one will profit by my death," he warned President Dwight Eisenhower.

US Army

Private Ernest Ransom won a chest full of medals in the Korean War. But in an alcoholic rage, he killed a Korean guard and raped a local teenage girl. At Fort Leavenworth, authorities misspelled his name.

Left: Photo courtesy of author. Right: US Army.

No one claimed Ernest Ransom's body, so the army buried him in a small hillside cemetery just outside the prison walls. Few liked him. "He was a colored boy, another cold one," grumbled a sergeant who worked death row.

Private Abraham Thomas suffered a debilitating stroke at Fort Leavenworth, but the army soon considered him "entirely normal and healthy." A few months later, they hanged him.

Rapist Will Be Hanged

FT. LEAVENWORTH —(P)— Ernest L. Ransom, a soldier convicted of murder and rape while stationed in Korea, will be hanged for the crime April 3, the Ft. Leavenworth information office said Thursday.

Ransom, who will be 26 March 29, has been imprisoned at the U. S. Disciplinary Barracks here. He is a native of Jackson, N. C. His parents, Mr. and Mrs. Lester Ransom, now live at Garysburg, N. C.

A court martial convicted him at Inchon, Korea, in June 1953 of shooting to death a Korean guard then raping a 14-year-old Korean girl. Ransom was assigned to the 933rd Anti-aircraft artillery Automatic Weapons Battalion at the time, April 19, 1953.

His sentence was reviewed and approved by President Eisenhower, the information office said.

Former Soldier Is Executed for Murder and Rape

FT. LEAVENWORTH (P) — Ernest L. Ransom, 26, was hanged ealy today for murder and rape committed while he was a soldier in Korea.

The hanging was in the power plant building of the U. S. disciplinary barracks, site of two other recent military executions Feb. 14. He was pronounced dead at 12:17 a.m.

Ransom, a Negro from Garysburg, N. C., was convicted in June 1953 by a general court-martial at Inchon, Korea, of shooting to death a Korean guard and raping a 14-year-old Korean girl.

Ransom in a regulation olive drab uniform devoid of insignia, showed no emotion as he was led down a ramp from the second floor of the building to the gallows.

Doctors listened for a heartbeat 15 minutes before pronouncing him dead.

No family members were present.

MAY 57

3 APRIL 1957
NO# 60

Fort Riley Kansas.

2. MSGT WILLIAM H MADDOX JR RA6262111 207th MP Co this sta WP Ft Leavenworth Kans o/a 1 April 57 TDY for aprx 5 days in connection with military activities per request of Col James W Davis, Commandant Fort Leavenworth TPA as being more advantageous to the Govt TPA charge to Ft Leavenworth Kans Funds TDN 2172020 755-2028 P3000-02 S14-021 (3042) (CN1050) Upon completion TDY EM will rtn proper orgn this sta

FOR THE COMMANDER:

M. R. NELSON
CWO, USA
Asst Adj General

NAME	Wt	Hight	AGE	OVERALL DROP	DATE
RANSOM	172	66½"	26	9.7"	3 APR 57

Master Sergeant William Maddox served as the army hangman. He learned the trade during the Japanese executions after World War II. In Kansas, he detailed his work in this spiral notebook.

Colonel Weldon Cox was the last prison commandant during the final hangings. Whenever another execution drew near, it was his boots that were heard clomping down the stairs to death row.

Colonel Leonard Becicka fought on D-Day in France and in the Korean and Vietnam Wars. But it was witnessing one of the hangings that bothered him most. "It was very traumatic for me," he would recall.

> In the foregoing case of Private First Class John A. Bennett, US 52 342 347, United States Army, Headquarters and Headquarters Battery, 11th Anti-Aircraft Artillery Battalion (Automatic Weapons)(Self Propelled), the sentence is approved and will be carried into execution under the orders of the Secretary of the Army.
>
> The White House
>
> JUL 2 1957 , 19___
>
> *Dwight D. Eisenhower*

On July 2, 1957, after Bennett had been on death row for two years, President Eisenhower officially approved his execution. It set in motion a desperate effort to save the soldier's life.

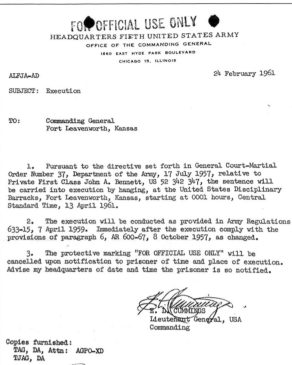

FOR OFFICIAL USE ONLY

HEADQUARTERS FIFTH UNITED STATES ARMY
OFFICE OF THE COMMANDING GENERAL
1660 EAST HYDE PARK BOULEVARD
CHICAGO 15, ILLINOIS

ALFJA-AD   24 February 1961

SUBJECT: Execution

TO: Commanding General
          Fort Leavenworth, Kansas

    1.   Pursuant to the directive set forth in General Court-Martial
Order Number 37, Department of the Army, 17 July 1957, relative to
Private First Class John A. Bennett, US 52 342 347, the sentence will
be carried into execution by hanging, at the United States Disciplinary
Barracks, Fort Leavenworth, Kansas, starting at 0001 hours, Central
Standard Time, 13 April 1961.

    2.   The execution will be conducted as provided in Army Regulations
633-15, 7 April 1959. Immediately after the execution comply with the
provisions of paragraph 6, AR 600-67, 8 October 1957, as changed.

    3.   The protective marking "FOR OFFICIAL USE ONLY" will be
cancelled upon notification to prisoner of time and place of execution.
Advise my headquarters of date and time the prisoner is so notified.

                              E. L. CUMMINGS
                              Lieutenant General, USA
                              Commanding

Copies furnished:
   TAG, DA, Attn: AGPO-XD
   TJAG, DA

The third time Bennett was ordered to die came in the early weeks of the John F. Kennedy presidency. The new White House staff scrambled to decide the fate of the young soldier, by then the last man on death row.

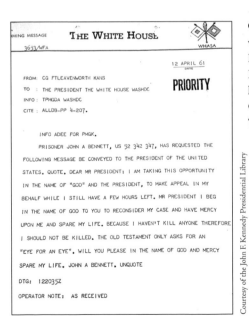

INCOMING MESSAGE   THE WHITE HOUSE
3633/WFA   WHASA

                                    12 APRIL 61
                                    DATE

FROM: CG FTLEAVENWORTH KANS
TO : THE PRESIDENT THE WHITE HOUSE WASHDC   PRIORITY
INFO: TPMGDA WASHDC
CITE : ALLDB-PP 4-207.

     INFO ADEE FOR PMGK.

     PRISONER JOHN A BENNETT, US 52 342 347, HAS REQUESTED THE

FOLLOWING MESSAGE BE CONVEYED TO THE PRESIDENT OF THE UNITED

STATES. QUOTE. DEAR MR PRESIDENT: I AM TAKING THIS OPPORTUNITY

IN THE NAME OF "GOD" AND THE PRESIDENT, TO MAKE APPEAL IN MY

BEHALF WHILE I STILL HAVE A FEW HOURS LEFT. MR PRESIDENT I BEG

IN THE NAME OF GOD TO YOU TO RECONSIDER MY CASE AND HAVE MERCY

UPON ME AND SPARE MY LIFE. BECAUSE I HAVEN'T KILL ANYONE THEREFORE

I SHOULD NOT BE KILLED. THE OLD TESTAMENT ONLY ASKS FOR AN

"EYE FOR AN EYE". WILL YOU PLEASE IN THE NAME OF GOD AND MERCY

SPARE MY LIFE. JOHN A BENNETT. UNQUOTE

DTG: 122035Z

OPERATOR NOTE: AS RECEIVED

On what the army insisted would be his last day alive, Bennett implored President Kennedy to save him. He had killed no one, he stressed. "The Old Testament only asks for 'an eye for an eye.'"

eight empty cartridges littered around his body. According to his confession, Ransom broke into a private home and raped a teenage girl. Police arrested him at dawn.

Horribly hung over, he described to army interrogators what little he could remember. Each page of the confession was read back to him; he signed each one. A few small changes were edited into the text, and he initialed them as well.

"I got back from chow and about 1815 hrs I goes down and got a fifth of whiskey and set [sic] in the hut and drank about two thirds of the whiskey," the statement read.

"Then I takes the rest of it over to C-14 and I stayed over there about 30 minutes and [drank] the rest of it." He described stealing the carbines and ammo, tossing the weapons over a wooden army fence, and happening upon the Korean guard.

"I turned loose on him and kept going. I was standing by the wall and fired into the alley where he was."

How, the police asked him? Why?

"I had it on automatic. I don't know . . . He kept saying something to me and I was already angry and confused and I shot at him."

Inside a nearby home, he tied a man's hands and assaulted his daughter.

"Was gonna shoot them but I went to sleep or blanked out and the next thing I knew the MP was there and had me."

An army doctor concluded Ransom suffered from "acute alcoholism." An army captain testified that Ransom's gait that morning was "unsteady," his breath "alcoholic," his speech "disoriented," and his memory "gone for recent events."

He was twenty-two years old, and with nearly a year of combat behind him, he chose not to testify. The jury found him guilty of premeditated murder, rape, assault, and robbery and sentenced him to die. The army boarded Ransom onto a train for Pusan, but en route, he snuck past two guards and leaped from the locomotive. Bruised and filthy, he slogged for an hour through three miles of rice paddies until the engineer could pull the brakes and send a search party into the muddied fields. When they found him, his clothes were drenched through.

His next stop was the Disciplinary Barracks at Fort Leavenworth. The board of review affirmed the conviction and death sentence; the Court of Military Appeals concurred. In Washington, reports to the Eisenhower administration showed that while Ransom suffered no psychological disorders, "his intelligence level is below normal [and] he has a mental age of ten years, nine months."

His mother said that when he was younger, "he was jailed several times for being drunk and disorderly." He had quit high school and moved to New York, worked for a year and a half, returned to North Carolina, and enlisted. Within a year, he was shouldering a rifle in the snow banks of Korea, assigned to the 933rd Antiaircraft Artillery Automatic Weapons Battalion.

"He had one previous military conviction—being drunk in uniform in a public place," his military records disclosed. "Otherwise his Army ratings were satisfactory."

The US Pardon Attorney and John Lindsay, executive assistant to the attorney general, recommended no clemency. Lindsay believed most men would have passed out before reaching the bottom of that fifth of liquor.

Barba, assistant special counsel, lamented, "As in a majority of these cases, the crime was committed overseas by a young soldier who, psychiatrically, is considered immature and below normal in intelligence. Added to his case is a high degree of intoxication combined with seemingly aimless violence."

With Ransom two days away from dying, a Catholic priest wrote the president from Poughkeepsie, New York. Capital punishment, Father Harold Livingston Thomas implored, "is both revolting and unjustifiable." He begged for the soldier's life. "For this I pray and for this I thank your Excellency, knowing that like your illustrious predecessor, Lincoln, you have a heart full of compassion toward those condemned to die."

It is the only letter on Ransom's behalf in the Eisenhower White House files.

On April 3, 1957, the army prepared for another hanging.

"No mental disease. Intoxication issue considered. Guilt conclusive," the final army execution planning report stated.

Only two reporters, both wire service stringers, deemed the hanging newsworthy enough to attend.

High atop the gallows waited the stoic Sergeant Maddox. He already had taken Ransom's measurements, though he misspelled some of it in his spiral ledger: "Ransom, weight 172, hight, 5 ½ sub hight less 6, [and] 9 7 ½ over all drop." The prisoner died without any last words.

"He went out tough," remembered the prisoner Maurice Schick. "He was a machine, no conscience, no regrets, no nothing."

Earlier in the week, Ransom had fallen behind in that poker game, owing Sergeant Peterson "a couple of million dollars in IOUs." As they played that final night, he desperately tried to break even. For a while, they played High Card to speed things up, the sergeant dealing him more wild cards and aces from the bottom of the deck. When the chaplain stopped by to visit, Ransom shooed him away.

"You couldn't do me any good before," he muttered. "You can't do me any good now. I've got to get even here." Just before they escorted Ransom away, Sergeant Peterson recalled, "He didn't owe me anything."

★　★　★

All the dreary summer of 1958, Abraham Thomas begged for his life.

June 25:

"God will look into things," he wired Eisenhower. "I never have been in no trouble before not even in jail."

July 1:

"Me and my mother just on the wrong [black] side of the line, that's all," he wired again. "If we was on your [white] side, then we would be OK."

July 3:

"I would have getting my sentence reduce like the other fellow did that was on your [white] side," he wrote the president. "But since I am on the [black] side that you hate the most I have to die."

In a lover's quarrel four years earlier, Thomas had killed two fellow soldiers and two women during a rampage in a German apartment, what some knew as a neighborhood brothel. He was swiftly convicted in an army court-martial and condemned to die. A. C. Felton III, a lawyer and mayor in Thomas's small hometown of Montezuma, Georgia, tried to save him.

But Felton, a World War II veteran, was woefully unprepared to handle a death penalty case. "This is my first experience in a federal matter," he conceded to the White House, pleading for guidance on executive clemency.

He tried to show that while Thomas stalked his lover's apartment for two hours, he did not mean to kill anyone. Only when he caught her in bed with another soldier did he explode in a "blind passion."

"My client is understandably anxious in view of the fact that his execution is next in line," he said in lobbying Walter F. George, a special presidential assistant and ardent segregationist. He asked to see Eisenhower during a golfing trip in Thomasville, Georgia, but "an appointment could not be arranged."

By then, it was too late. Army Secretary Wilber M. Brucker agreed with the decision to hang Thomas. Attorney General Brownell believed he should pay for killing the others.

"The overall circumstances do not, in my judgment, mitigate in any way his taking of four lives," Brownell advised. In the White House, assistant counsel Barba did not buy the argument of blind passion.

"I have no doubt that he intended to kill," Barba concluded.

In Leavenworth, the attorney Homer Davis attempted to bring Thomas's case before the Supreme Court, seeking a stay of execution for this "illiterate Negro soldier" who when arrested was waiting an army discharge because of his low IQ. Thomas confessed only after harsh questioning by army police in a detention cell in Augsburg, Germany, Davis argued. He was driven back to the apartment "where the investigators pointed out to him pools of blood and gore . . . on the walls, the ceiling and where the bodies had lain."

Then "he was questioned for most of three days and part of two nights without food or blankets." He was given only eggs for his single daily meal, denied requests to see a doctor, and "was subjected to having his statement recorded on a tape recorder, without his knowing it, [and] then at his trial the tape was played to the court."

When Thomas declined to testify in court, the prosecutor pushed the play button and the soldier's account filled the army courtroom. "You heard in Thomas' own words, as he related how he killed these four people," the prosecutor coached the jury. "According to his own testimony he had blood in his eyes."

Davis cited other court-martial confessions that were improperly obtained, including John Bennett's. "The interest of the United States in a criminal case is not that it should win a case," maintained Davis, "but that Justice shall be done."

Government lawyers led by US Solicitor General J. Lee Rankin countered that Thomas had been advised of his rights and was never coerced. "He wasn't mad at anyone, had no hard feelings, and had been well treated," they advised the Supreme Court. Army police offered him no promises, they said, even though Thomas "was uneducated, having completed only the third grade, but not stupid."

A mattress and blankets were not initially furnished him, they conceded, "but his cell was heated, it was lighted and constructed so as not to work hardship on him. He was not deprived of anything that other prisoners had." The Supreme Court declined to hear the matter.

In November 1957, Thomas suffered a stroke. He collapsed playing table tennis during a brief recreation session. He fell to the ground, vomiting. His head pounded, and he was unconscious for at least a half hour until he "gradually awakened."

"He was found unconscious by the guards," remembered inmate Schick. Another prisoner, Frank Harris, would never forget seeing Thomas, with his high cheek bones, long chin, and short legs, lying prone atop a gurney, headed for the prison infirmary. He looked "cross-eyed," many remembered, one of his eyes rolling around in the socket.

"We called him Chuckles," Harris continued, recalling how he would flip backward over his bed, landing on his feet. "But underneath him was a violent bitterness and we came to realize that he used this court jester thing when things got him down." Thomas was one for tricks. On occasion, he would play a prank on the guards. Using blankets and pieces of clothing, he would construct a dummy and hang it from the prison radio earphones.

Sergeant Curtsinger and other guards raided his cell every time he hung a dummy with his pillow and earphone cords. As they turned the big iron lock, Thomas burst from under his bed or behind his locker.

"He just got the biggest bang out of that," Sergeant Peterson laughed. None of the guards thought Abraham Thomas made much sense, even before the stroke.

"In today's army, he wouldn't have even been in," predicted Sergeant Curtsinger. For no apparent reason, he rooted passionately for the Cleveland Indians, the northern Ohio baseball team far from his home in Georgia, closely following the games on his radio headset. On death row, he wove rugs and constructed model airplanes. "He was very carefree and cheerful and was especially interested in baseball," his medical records stated. His world seemed far away.

"I used to tell him, towards the end, 'When you get there, mention me to God,'" Harris recalled. "He'd shake his head and say he didn't believe in God because God wouldn't have let this happen to him."

Every Sunday morning, he passed on attending Mass with the other prisoners in the small room off death row. "Next Sunday," he always promised.

After the stroke, Thomas was driven to an army hospital in Denver. Captain Lawrence S. Sonkin soon thought the soldier with six years in the army, most of it on death row, had improved enough to return to Seven Base. Though he rated the odds of another stroke "about fifty-fifty," the doctor said, "If he has no recurrence he will be entirely normal and healthy."

Back in Fort Leavenworth, medics again appraised his mental state: "Thomas was a husky Negro wearing glasses and appearing unusual because he used only one eye to look at you and the other one is directed off to the side. He was alert, cooperative, and displayed no gross evidence of depression or anxiety. He spoke up clearly. . . . There was no looseness of associations, delusions or hallucinations. He was well oriented as to time, place and person."

"It doesn't feel good to have to go for an offense you didn't commit," he told the Castle doctors. "But I'm willing." He insisted someone else carried out those murders in Germany, warning "the guilty person is getting away with something."

But the records said he also realized "the Supreme Court has refused to hear his case and that his only remaining chance is an appeal to the President."

Homer Davis could offer Thomas little hope; the White House would not budge. "They got him so he was as normal as he could ever be at the army hospital. When he could function a little bit, and get back on his feet, they brought him back and hung him." Davis visited him once more near the end. "I could get answers from him but I knew damn well he was ill. . . . You had to take time to explain things to him."

His Georgia attorney Felton seized upon the stroke in a final bid for mercy. He warned White House officials that Thomas had been "unconscious for a considerable period of time" and was "partially paralyzed" at the Denver hospital. He called for a delay in the execution until they could obtain "a more accurate diagnosis of the condition existing in the prisoner's head."

But army headquarters was satisfied with a medical board analysis that Thomas had "recovered." Secretary Brucker notified Felton the hanging would proceed. The date would hold, midnight July 23.

Two weeks before the scheduled hanging, Felton frantically wired White House Special Counsel Gerald Morgan. "Family of Abraham Thomas reluctant to give up. Have I any avenue to obtain commutation?"

His mother, Missouri Thomas, of rural Montezuma, twice wrote Eisenhower in 1958, as death approached. "Please spare my child please have mercy on me," she pleaded. "Don't kill me please I am just worry to death. I done work my self to death right hear in Georgia and Abraham aint never been in jail until now. his father is dead been dead 12 years. He has no body but me and the good lord." She added, "I don't want no mony. I want my child. We can suffer right hear together."

In her second letter to the president she said she hoped "my sick child" would live a long life. "Let him die a national death," she wrote, meaning from natural causes. "He said he didn't do that so what you want to kill him for . . . have mercy please on poor me."

The White House turned them down. "I am indeed sorry that it is not possible to send you a more favorable reply," Morgan told the mother.

Those final days, Thomas hurried more letters to Eisenhower, more telegrams too.

July 3:

"I don't know what I will haven to do to convance you that I am not guilty of that crime. i didn't even think that your heart was that hard!"

July 10:

"Dear Mr President . . . It ain't no doubt that you don't have any heart at all, because if you did, you would reduce my sentence. But you don't, well God will have to pay you, and will because you are taking an innocent mans life. Hope whoever he was who committed this crime what I am about to die for will come to you and tell you that he done it."

July 17:

"Dear Mr President am making a last appeal to you on behalf of my 66 year old mother to reduce my sentence. . . . Somewhere in your heart you have some mercy in there because I am sure you had a mother too thank you."

The army prepared again for an execution. Four witnesses would be present, two doctors and two chaplains, Father Dudek and a new Protestant minister, Captain Thomas Carter.

The morning of the execution, Joseph Thompson paid a final visit. "I could hear him as I approached," the prison social worker recalled. "Thomas hated Eisenhower and that day he was so loud. He was mouthy and profane, his arms folded, moving around. He was hollering at everybody."

Thompson tried to quiet him. "But I couldn't. He yelled that the president didn't give a damn about him, didn't know what he was going through, didn't care about common people."

When evening descended over the Castle walls, Father Dudek visited. Staff Sergeant Ted Ray marveled at how the priest managed to calm the doomed soldier. "Abraham told Father Dudek he had to listen to the evening ballgame," Sergeant Ray remembered. "He didn't have time to talk to him. He loved the Cleveland Indians and he was more involved in that damn ballgame than he was in dying." Father Dudek nodded; he knew just what to say. "You can listen to all the ballgames you want in heaven."

★ ★ ★

Of all of them, black or white, poor or blessed, Private John E. Day Jr. endured death row the longest—from his December 1950 arrest in Korea until his execution nine years later. Military and civilian courts repeatedly turned down his appeals. Eisenhower twice affirmed the death sentence, although the president of South Korea urged mercy in honor of all the US soldiers "who came and fought with our men in defense of freedom." Even the Supreme Court would not consider his case. He was twenty-one years old when he committed murder and sexual assault, and thirty by the time he was hanged at the Fort Leavenworth gallows.

Day shot and killed a Korean national and sexually assaulted the man's wife as Seoul was being evacuated and the capital was falling to invaders from the North. The woman's infant daughter also died, yet she forgave him. "I would be sorry to see another death when I know that it will bring only unhappiness," she wrote Eisenhower. "It will not help me or anyone else."

Day served in an army transportation heavy truck company. Tall and muscular, he had deep-set eyes, a gold tooth, and a sandpaper mustache. On his last night of freedom, he drank so much Korean whiskey, sake, and wine that the next morning, terribly hung over but still cocky, he told investigators he could not remember much of the night before. He asked to speak to an army warrant officer and gave the agent a one-paragraph statement.

> I came downstairs to look for the house boys. I went down to the basement. While I was down there I saw this woman and I started to talk to her. After I started to talk to her this man jumped up and tried to keep me from talking to her. He started talking loud but I couldn't understand that he was trying to get me to leave the woman alone. The woman wasn't putting up a squaak [sic] and then he was pulling on me so I shot him.

After I shot him he fell and the broad ran up the outside stairs and I went up behind her. I caught her out by the trucks. She was scared and I took the baby off her and took the baby back inside. I don't remember what I did with the baby. After that I went up and went to bed.

Witnesses testified that Day threatened them all.

"The colored American soldier pointed his carbine at me and ordered me to go with him to the basement," said Duk Il Whang. "The soldier told me he would kill everybody in the room if the woman did not give into him."

At his court-martial, which lasted just a single day, the star witness was the dead man's wife; their infant daughter had also died in all the commotion. She cried as she struggled to describe how Day grabbed her baby.

The judge ordered a short break, and when the court-martial resumed, defense lawyers suggested that Day did not treat the child "in a rough manner" but simply placed her in the front seat of a truck.

"What happened to your baby?" the army defense lawyer asked.

"She was dead," the mother replied.

The jury found Day guilty. The judge announced he would "be put to death in such manner as proper authority may direct"—the rope or a firing squad. The board of review upheld the conviction and punishment, as did the Military Court of Appeals. The secretary of the army recommended hanging. Eisenhower agreed.

Day had been raised by his mother in Washington, DC, along with four brothers and two sisters. After minor arrests for drunkenness, he joined the army in 1949, war came to Korea, and so did the hurried evacuation from Seoul.

"Crime committed under stress of war conditions," noted Barba, assistant special counsel to Eisenhower. "Seoul fell to the Chinese a week after the crime was committed."

He cited a letter from Korean president Syngman Rhee urging clemency in gratitude for America's help defending their homeland. Barba acknowledged that Day's army lawyer "could have been better prepared." He was given just three weeks to ready himself, while prosecutors had nine months before Day was court-martialed on October 1, 1951. Nevertheless,

Barba added, "Generally, the record indicates that he received a fair trial although it could have been more thorough and accurate." He concluded, "Nothing in the record is sufficiently extraordinary to warrant clemency in view of the atrociousness of the crime."

The NAACP, the Catholic bishop in Washington, and the American Justice Association tried to intervene. Most heartfelt was the prayer from the woman who had been sexually assaulted and had lost her husband and little girl. "Pvt. Day was young when he committed the offense," she wrote Eisenhower in August 1954. "He did not know what harm he was doing. He has been in jail for three years now and has had time to repent this offense. I am sure that he is sorry."

She added, "I do not wish to see Pvt. Day's mother hurt, as I was hurt three years ago, by the death of her son. As you surely know, those were difficult times in December 1950. What may have seemed just for those times seems far too severe now that we have peace again."

Lawyer Homer Davis asked a federal court in Topeka to postpone the execution because Day's constitutional rights had been violated by that short statement while he was still intoxicated. In November 1955, Judge Arthur J. Mellott ruled against him. Davis turned to a federal appellate court in Denver; he lost there, too. In the fall of 1956, the Supreme Court declined to hear the case.

Martha A. Day believed her son had never been fairly tried. "He has been under this sentence for a long time," she wrote the president. Helping her in Washington, attorney Harry E. Wood hoped to find a sympathetic ear in the White House. By then, Day had written his lawyers, showing that even on death row, he was rehabilitating himself through books, correspondence classes, and other do-it-yourself efforts after a childhood on "the jungle" streets of a Washington ghetto.

"There are other worlds than these I have known," Day told them.

Wood, a World War II army veteran, forwarded the letter to Eisenhower. "Despite his wish that the letter not disturb me, it has done so, and I feel compelled to bring it to your attention," Wood told the president. He praised Day's attempts at turning his life around. "Life is sometimes cheap. But even the momentary emergence of a human being into a new and better world is priceless."

Day himself pleaded with the army's high command. "I realize now that the chance for a decent, constructive life begins inside of a person," he confided to Army Secretary Brucker. "That is one truth to become ingraved [sic] in my heart. . . . Before now, sir, I have had very little self-pride or respect for others because I felt a stranger in a world I could never understand. . . . And though it has been far from easy to carry this sentence, this pales in the realization of what I have done. A lasting sorrow has come to me over the years."

In July 1959, Eisenhower approved the death sentence for a second time. The execution would proceed the night of September 23. Wood wrote the president again.

"For nearly eight years, he has lived with an interminable and unimaginable burden," the lawyer implored. "Day is a product of the society out of which he grew. Required by circumstances to grow to young manhood in what he now recognizes as a jungle world, he was then given a gun and sent to Korea. . . . He now faces death without fear but with sorrow and repentance for what he has done. No one could pay a greater price, even with his life."

Homer Davis wrote Eisenhower, too. "How many deaths Day has died in these last eight years only he can tell. He comes from a very sordid background of poverty, city slums, and a drunken father who deserted the family at an early age. Surely, Society is responsible to some degree in this matter."

Private Day was not done either, not yet. In a July 20 letter, he spoke soldier-to-soldier to his commander in chief, recalling the burdens of war as the northern armies swept south down the Korean peninsula. "I often thought of running away and becoming purposely lost in the confusion of battle," he told the president.

Now these long years in a solitary death cell had deepened his fears. "My wordless cries of remorse have kept me awake overnight for many of the two thousand and seven hundred days and nights I have waited under this sentence."

His days were numbered, even as, in August, You Chan Yang, South Korean ambassador to the United States, reiterated President Rhee's plea for mercy "in this young man's behalf." A few more lawyers' letters filtered in, but the president would not reconsider.

On death row, where he had changed so much, the prisoner still could not reconcile dying. "All this time he kept saying, 'I wonder why now?' He wondered why now they were doing this to him," recalled Thompson. "Because he wasn't the same man that eight or nine years ago was firing an AR rifle."

On Seven Base, Day read constantly and largely ignored the blather from the television at the end of the tier. Trustees wheeled carts of library books and magazines down the hallway, and he chose history and fiction. He composed his own prose and verse. He taught himself Spanish and converted to Catholicism. He wore his hair clipped army-short, his hands clean, and his cell spotless. If a guard slammed his cell door shut, Day admonished that if their roles were reversed, "I would respect an inmate's humanity."

Sergeant R. W. Pinson, who had worked in a graves registration unit processing American bodies in Korea, came to admire Day. "He would have made it on the outside," the sergeant was certain. "He educated himself. He took courses by mail. He didn't sit there like a lot of them and just gripe . . . He was still writing letters down there, hoping to get out. I told him I hated to see him wind up like this."

On his last morning, he wired President Eisenhower, including not his death row cell number but rather his army ID dog tag. "Informed of your decision. Humbly ask reconsider with attention to previous letters. Attention respectively drawn to Readers Digest page 180, plus new facts in case. Sincerely Pvt John E Day RA13233886."

Dr. Karl Menninger, the Topeka psychiatrist and staunch death penalty opponent, had written the Reader's Digest article, "Verdict Guilty—Now What?" stressing compassion for the condemned. "Playing God has no conceivable moral or scientific justification," the doctor declared. Day had stumbled upon the article a few days earlier and put in a collect call to Menninger.

"People won't listen," he told the psychiatrist. "They won't do anything about it. Nothing will happen to change the present system until they realize how futile it is." He asked him to appeal to Eisenhower on his be-half. So Menninger phoned the White House, only to hear that this "was a matter for the army."

Menninger called the secretary of the army; "It's a matter for the courts," they told him. A federal judge told him the legal appeals had run their course. The psychiatrist came away disheartened. "I reflected on how many hundreds of thousands of dollars it had cost the people of the United States to try to decide whether or not we could officially kill this young man with a clear legal conscience," he lamented. "But we did."

With only a few hours left, Homer Davis visited John Day a final time on death row. "He had an old *Liberty* magazine thrown on his bed and that was all that was in that damned cell," Davis remembered. "I sat down and talked to him for quite a while. I was trying to find out anything new. I'd exhausted all my remedies and didn't know what else to do. And as I left it struck me as a damned poignant thing about that magazine. How forlorn it was that that was all he had in there and yet even to the end, he was still trying to better himself."

Davis later heard that his colleague Harry Wood was even more dis-traught. "He walked the streets of Washington all night. He couldn't keep from taking it to heart."

Day shared a brief visit at the prison with his mother and then sent her home on the afternoon train to Washington. He did not want her to see him die such an ignoble death.

"There was a little crying, hugging and carrying on," remembered Ser-geant Ray. "He had an hour with her and they cried."

In the power plant at midnight, Day scanned the army uniforms cir-cled below him. He watched as the hangman approached, his long thin fingers reaching out.

John Day spoke, his voice low and even.

To everyone there that night, at 12:02 a.m., he said, "Thank you all for your consideration."

Chapter Eight

* * * * * * * *

A GREAT TROUBLE

For weeks, Percy Bennett could not bring himself to tell his wife that their son had been arrested. But once John was sentenced to death in Austria, he broke down. Then they set out for the Red Cross office in Chatham, Virginia. They were a poor, confused, and frightened farm couple. With their daughter Katherine, they passed the courthouse square and its cold marble Confederate statue standing sentry.

Inside the Red Cross office on April 1, 1955, they huddled with executive secretary Delma M. Easley. The family unburdened their fears that John might have been framed by the army or mistaken by the girl. They worried he was being harshly punished because he was black. His mother, Ollie Bennett, wondered if she should write her son's commanding officer. He could have a violent temper, she conceded. But their daughter thought John was never any trouble. "He never did anything bad," Katherine told the Red Cross.

He was the fourth of eight children, and after three miscarriages, his mother recounted how she "nearly died" giving birth to him in April 1936. The next day she fell into "a fit," Ollie said, and lay unconscious "for a long time." She did not rise out of bed until autumn.

John had wet his bed until he was five. As a child he would "hear voices in his sleep," his mother went on. He was deeply, deathly afraid of thunder and lightning and would hide himself away. He frequently climbed trees and fell from them. Once he toppled off a cherry tree branch. For days, he slumped around the house and "seemed to feel bad." He failed the fifth grade and quit school after the seventh to help his father with farm chores and repairing homes and barns around Pittsylvania County.

And there was his temper.

"He was always different," Ollie told the Red Cross. "He would get very mad with the others, and then they would let him alone."

John often drank too much and kicked up trouble. By then, liquor had run deep through several branches of the Bennett tree. His maternal grandfather drank heavily and died in the state hospital. His mother's uncle took to the bottle and was hospitalized for a "mental disturbance." A first cousin fell sick and could not work; he killed himself. The army discharged one of John's brothers for "continued nose bleeding" and "head trouble." And John, soon after he left home for the army in August 1953, told his mother he suffered "a bad fall." She said the army considered discharging him, too.

Years later, Katherine remembered how the family struggled to help her younger brother. "We didn't have money, and we didn't have a high education enough to really know what was going on," she recalled. Before he left, his girlfriend, pregnant with their daughter, sued him for child support, and he sent her $30 a month from his army pay, until he was arrested.

Managing a small farm with a horse and lovely creek meandering near the fields, her parents could not afford modern equipment. They planted corn and cut tobacco. John played softball. "He was good," Katherine remembered. "They had organized teams, community teams. The people in the community, boys and girls, played together."

Once John was sentenced to die, their parents could no longer cope. Katherine continued, "My daddy was a sweetie-pie and just ideal, but he just couldn't at first tell mother. He was so hurt, just so hurt."

"My father took this bad because that was his son," recalled John's older brother, Ira, a career army officer. "And my poor mother took it very hard. She never went to see him. She had heart trouble, and she couldn't bear it."

★   ★   ★

Pittsylvania County, Virginia, served briefly as the capital of the dying Confederacy. Nearly a century later, well into the 1950s, schools, restaurants, and water fountains were still segregated by race. White Southern pride was rooted into the community, where some of the county's bright-leaf tobacco barns had long ago housed Yankee prisoners.

Robert Gilbert's father, the Reverend R. G. Gilbert, a black preacher, restaurateur, and early civil rights leader, wrote to Washington in support of the imprisoned John Bennett. And Robert remembered well those trying times in Chatham, the county seat, as "like a third world country." Black residents kept largely to their own neighborhoods, streets without sidewalks, playgrounds without grass, and homes far from the center of town.

Growing up, Robert said, "I often wondered why I couldn't go places. Always you knew something was wrong in life. My friends and I would go into the drug store and order milk shakes but we couldn't sit down. At the movies we always had to sit upstairs. I had to order a hot dog waiting outside. And there was an unwritten law: You knew where not to go, especially after ten at night. And there were rumors about what cops had done, that some folks were buried behind the jail."

Once, as teenagers, he and friends ordered hamburgers at a nearby drive-in restaurant. The white cook, a fat man in a grease-stained apron, frightened them off. "We don't serve niggers," he growled.

Robert and his friends protested. "We didn't order niggers," they jeered. "We ordered hamburgers."

But Gilbert's father cautioned tolerance. Someday, things would change, he preached. For now, he hung a sign in front of his restaurant-hotel in the city's black community: "For Coloreds."

Much of Chatham and the surrounding farm country, black and white alike, soon heard of John Bennett, his army trial in Austria, and the pending death sentence in Kansas. The local papers reported many of the legal developments in the case, and the radio followed it as well. Of equally deep concern to the local community, and the Gilbert and Bennett families as well, was what had happened to another neighbor, Odell Waller, a black sharecropper jailed for killing his white landlord in a pay dispute in July 1940. Waller insisted he fired in self-defense; white witnesses called it cold-hearted murder. John Bennett was just four years old then, but his parents and older siblings understood its frightening consequences, and its consequences ricocheted for years around the town square and outlying farms.

Waller stood trial in the courthouse in Chatham. That September, an all-white jury deliberated just under an hour and convicted him of first-degree murder. Twenty-three years old, he was ordered to die in Virginia's electric chair. The death sentence prompted a national campaign to save Waller's life. Organizers connected to labor unions and the NAACP as far away as New York raised funds for legal appeals. At stake, they said, was "the badly shaken faith of our Negro minority in American democracy." First Lady Eleanor Roosevelt tried to get her husband to intervene, but the president did not want to upset his white Southern base.

Waller went to his death early one morning in July 1942, two years after the murder. His body was returned to Pittsylvania County, where Reverend R. G. Gilbert preached at the funeral. "Trouble draws men to God," he intoned. But Waller had the last word. He left behind his own handwritten epitaph, several pages long, what became known as his "Dying Statement." Whispering from the grave, Odell Waller warned, "The penitentiary all over the United states are full of people ho [who] was pore. . . . They are in prison for life that's what happens to the poor people."

Odell Waller could not have been far from the Bennett family's worries when they left the Red Cross office, unsure where to turn next. For now, they could only trust the military, the courts, and the Eisenhower administration. The army should never have taken him, they felt; surely the army would save him. "The whole family would be happy for him to come home," Katherine told the Red Cross as they departed.

★   ★   ★

Bennett awoke his first morning in his death row cell, his pillow bitten apart and his sheets damp in tears. For weeks, he kept to himself, following orders on the tier and drifting around the rear of the prison yard at rec time. As the weather warmed to spring, he began tossing a baseball at the brick and concrete prison walls. By summer, he was throwing with fury. He imagined pitching for the general prison population's baseball team, even though the squad was off-limits to death row soldiers.

High in a guard tower, Private Robert Dresden scanned the yard below and marveled at Bennett. "The best submarine pitcher I've ever seen," he later declared. "I had the best seat in the house and he could steam that ball. He'd pitch underhand hardball, a kind of sidearm submarine."

Other guards crowded around windowpanes or crept onto the yard once Bennett was twenty minutes into throwing at those walls. "The guys would call out certain pitches," Dresden remembered, "and John Bennett would oblige." Staff Sergeant Marvin Jacobsen, responsible for yard maintenance, watched him stuff a sheet of torn tablet paper into a crack in the wall, tie his long sleeves around his waist, arch his back, and fire from forty-five to fifty feet, aiming perfectly for that target. "The ball would bounce back to him; he wouldn't have to move," the sergeant remembered. "When you're locked up all day, there have to be frustrations. When you enjoy baseball, you're darn well going to get those frustrations out."

Sergeant Walter Beckerjeck managed the prison team. A veteran of World War II, Korea, and later Vietnam, his season stretched from April 15 through August 15, four months of "big time" baseball in lush fields and dirt lots around Kansas and Missouri. Soon, he too was stopping in the prison yard. "I saw how good he could throw and he wanted to play ball like mad, real bad," Beckerjeck remembered. "He wanted that more than anything."

Beckerjeck lobbied his superiors and the director of custody to make an exception and give the death row soldier John Bennett a chance on the prison team. Could they find a slot for this one condemned man? Very little chance, he was told. Next to none, they said.

"And I didn't push it," the ball team manager remembered. "I'd been in jails long enough to know you live by the rules." He carried the bad news down to Bennett on death row. "I said we were both wasting our time because he was never going to get out. I told him there was no chance he was going anywhere. I told him that if he ever did get out of there though, then we could talk. And there he was, more or less thinking he would. I don't know where he got that idea, because the policies were so cut and dry. But he thought he had a chance and that he'd get out. That's what he said."

Many were certain he would make it out alive.

"He always thought he was going to get a reprieve," insisted Staff Sergeant Curtsinger. "Deep down, he thought it. Hell, we all thought it."

Sergeant Peterson calculated the odds in Bennett's favor. "All the rest of them were murderers. If anyone could beat it, John had a chance."

"He was the youngest of us, the one we all expected to live," remembered inmate Frank Harris. "We saw life in him."

Bennett did not study law books or compose long letters to attorneys or Washington lawmakers. He did adopt a pet rat and read the Leavenworth *Times*, enrolled by mail in a Moody Bible course, and cried a lot, often until his eyes burned red. Sometimes, he lay in bed pretending to catch flies. He would giggle at nothing, laughing until his eyes watered. Or he would clutch his pillow for hours and jerk his feet, "like you'd kick a ball," remembered one guard. He kept his cell spotless and shaved daily, though that was not required. Bennett smoked unfiltered Camels and chewed on his prison overalls. He dug black blues on the prison radio headset, soul and gospel, too—Muddy Waters and Curtis Mayfield, the Roosters and the Impressions. He sometimes sang along, thin and plaintive like a caged canary. If his arm tired out in the yard, he sat alone on the grass, his back against that wall, lifting his face to the sun. Back in his cell, he played solitaire for hours. He would cling to his cell bars, then drop to the floor, and knock out dozens of push-ups. "We could hear him panting," an inmate two doors down recalled.

Death frightened him. "They're going to kill me!" he would sometimes shout. For hours, he stared at pictures of his mother and sister Katherine, beautiful on her graduation day. The guards had housed him in the last cell at the end of the row, and inmates who did not see him much noticed he "aged fifteen years in fifteen days."

Rarely did he mention the rape in Austria. If he did, he insisted all the GIs were having sex. Sometimes he alleged someone else assaulted the girl and when he sought help, he was the one arrested. "I was the black man," he complained. "I was the goat."

Sergeant Jacobsen thought Bennett sounded like some kind of black Southern caricature. "Backwoods," the guard said. "What you think of from the 1940s and '50s. He spoke slowly in incomplete sentences, real Southern slang, a lot of 'dis' and 'dat.' He didn't want to look at you when he was talking. He'd look away. He'd look up."

Some inmates urged him to hire a white lawyer. But Joseph Thompson, the prison's black social worker, disagreed. Not in the 1950s. "Whether it was rape or murder, they were all in the soup together," Thompson judged. "He might have hoped he had a little more leverage. But there wasn't anyone in that prison that was black and didn't feel prejudice."

Many of the white inmates guessed he would beat the hangman, just like all of them did. Maurice Schick, who had killed a child, put it this way: "He was skinny, young, light complexioned, kind of a coffee complexion with a lot of cream in it. In some ways he had a lot of white in him. He was going to get off."

Angenette Pompey believed it, too. She had moved to Kansas City, Missouri, to be near her son, Frank Harris, on death row at Fort Leavenworth. When he was a child, they lived in segregated Mobile, Alabama. She worked as a maid; he ran a paper route. Together they shared a one-room house with a porch and an outside toilet. When he was transferred to the Castle prison for killing a fellow soldier, his small, frail mother rode the bus there every Sunday, a $2 round trip over the big river bridge if the brakes and the winter weather held up.

Over time, she evolved into a sort of "den mother" for many of the black soldiers on death row; after her own son, John Bennett was her favorite. Bennett would write her letters on notebook paper, typically a page and a half long, always sounding upbeat at the start. "How's the weather, Hot Shot?" he would begin. For years, she stored the letters in her attic.

"He sounded like a boy who was confused to me," she reminisced many years later. "He seemed to be of good standing, brought up well. He would tell about his people, his family, about prison."

He also could turn nervous, doubtful and frightened. "He'd get edgy and erratic. . . . Like he was crying or trying to talk but couldn't. As if he was sorry," Pompey said, "I got a lot of sad letters in those days. There seemed to be a tremble in his handwriting." She encouraged him: where there's life, there's hope.

She knew that most all of the death row soldiers missed their mothers, and that broke Pompey's heart. "In one letter he said what a wasteful life he had had. Because he felt he hadn't begun to live. He would wonder what would have happened if he was a white man, or if the girl over there in Austria hadn't been white." In another, he asked, "I know God will forgive me, but will they?" Who "they" was, he never said.

Captain Thomas Carter, the Baptist prison chaplain, ministered to Bennett. He was thirty years old when he arrived in 1958. His first hanging was the night John Day was marched to the gallows. "I went home feeling nasty about this business," he remembered. "Now I had to do the best I could to help any of the others prepare to die."

For Bennett, "I attempted to show him what having faith was all about. He realized he had messed up his life. He wanted to make whatever remained of it better." Bennett grew in his faith. If he were hanged, "he wanted to make it a testimony to God just by the way he died," the chaplain recalled, "even when he stuck his head in the noose."

Guards had built a large water tank on wheels and rolled it to a second-floor chapel. Bennett changed into khaki shorts, and Carter baptized him on March 9, 1960, channeling John the Baptist and reciting prayers of thanksgiving. The prisoners often asked to return to the chapel for Sunday services, and guards always had Bennett sit in the rear. As a death row soldier, he was the last one there and the first escorted out. Sometimes he sang along or read scripture responses with other prisoners. "Mostly though he was quiet," remembered Chaplain Carter. "But everyone knew he was there."

Also studying Bennett were the prison command staff, the Pentagon, and the Eisenhower White House. A new "Personal History" was added to his file at the Castle; here was a soldier who "got along well in basic training and was never involved in any disciplinary difficulties."

It was clear, however, that despite his competency as a soldier, Bennett had brought to the army his childhood troubles. His father was too permissive, too "lax with his children," the history maintained. His mother was "an aggressive strict person afflicted with chronic hypertension."

Also attached to his file was another letter from Elise Demus Moran, the Austrian general's widow who led the protest against Bennett's death sentence. His victim, Moran wrote, "is back at school for some time already and she is worried in her mind and Heart that someone should be put to death on her account."

After nearly a year on death row, Bennett underwent a fresh battery of tests and interviews with army mental health experts. He offered some details about the assault, saying he had "wanted to remain in quarters" that morning, but his first sergeant insisted all soldiers not on duty should visit Salzburg and the countryside. Bennett said he went Christmas shopping and then stopped in at the gasthaus, Francis's Place. When he later met the other soldier in the Siezenheim fields, he said, they drank and Bennett smoked two marijuana cigarettes. They discussed "a game of chicken," daring each other to find a female. But he denied raping Gertie. "He insists that he was innocent of 'touching' the girl," the report stated, "but believes the other soldier 'must have used her.'"

He spoke of his difficult childhood and his father's sharecropping. Though now just shy of twenty, Bennett still suffered horrible nightmares. The dreams were similar to when he had spent "a long time in bed" with "head trouble" at the age of ten. He had never been treated by a physician at home. Instead, his mother "doctored" him.

"He has been rather quiet, thoughtful, and cooperative," the report summarized. "He reads quite a bit and chain smokes at times. He has no somatic complaints, except for the infrequent seizures. He corresponds with his family but does not want them to visit him here. He feels that he deserves clemency since he did not commit the actual rape or assault but was merely an accessory."

The prison psychiatrist, First Lieutenant John J. Bateman, reviewed the test results, interviewed Bennett, and recommended a commutation. "I had epileptic fits since the age of five," Bennett told the doctor. "I'm hot natured," too, he said. He enlisted because friends nagged him about his pregnant girlfriend.

"It was enough to drive a man crazy," Bennett said.

His stories about the assault in Austria often changed.

"I only put one hand on her shoulder and my other hand between her legs," he said another time.

"I don't know what happened to the other guy. He wasn't even at the trial. I don't think he was even caught. They didn't tell me why they were holding me for investigation until 2:30 a.m. the next morning."

Lieutenant Bateman diagnosed Bennett with "chronic" emotional instability, poor judgment, and "psychiatric disability." In recommending a commutation, the psychiatrist advised: "I do not feel that death is a suitable method for the disposition of a person who is mentally ill." Considering his poverty-ridden childhood, his "subculture (Negro)" background, and his difficulty controlling urges, the lieutenant urged the prison to transfer Bennett from death row to a "long range rehabilitative program."

However, army judges sitting on the board of review did not consider death for rape "excessive"; it was permitted then under military law. Even after examining Bennett's age, his low intelligence, and drunkenness, and discounting that Austria had no death penalty, the board ruled Bennett should die.

"All of these matters, in a proper case, might furnish an appropriate basis for clemency," the board decided. "However, we do not believe this is such a case." Though the board had studied numerous murder cases, it nevertheless concluded that, with Bennett, "seldom, if ever, have we been faced with a record which revealed a more vicious offense, or an accused who had less to entitle him to any consideration."

The US Court of Military Appeals was equally unforgiving. It championed the army investigation and court-martial as models of American jurisprudence. "This record can be considered as showing a good example of the level of due process ... in the Uniform Code of Military Justice," the appellate court determined.

In June 1956, Bennett's mother pleaded with President Eisenhower. She had yet to hear anything directly from the army, only rumors circulating around Chatham that her son's appeals had been denied. "We found this out by radio broadcasts and by the newspapers," she wrote. "Friends and kinfolk brought the word to me because they know I do not any more read the papers or listen to radio for fear of what I will hear about my son."

"I am writing to ask your help in a great trouble," Ollie Bennett added. "Help me," she begged the president. "We have not been to see him because he did not want any of us to come. However, we have written regularly and he writes to us. He knows that we love him. We had begun to hope by the long delay that he might have his punishment lightened."

★ ★ ★

The Bennett family also rallied their neighbors to press the White House. A teacher, Bertha Banks, described John as "well behaved and well mannered; I found him to be honest and truthful." Now that he sat behind bars, she said, "I find it is very hard to believe that he is guilty of the crime."

Carrie Shelton stressed that he was a teenager the night of the attack, and intoxicated. "The fact that the government does little or nothing to protect our boys from access to alcohol and that drinking is too popular among our service men is certainly a good reason for clemency," Shelton warned Eisenhower. "I know you are a hard-boiled general but can't you show mercy on this poor boy and his mother?"

Even Bennett's supervisor in Austria, Captain William M. Fuller, with four battle stars from Korea and now assigned to a headquarters battalion in New York, echoed his earlier strong support for his former soldier.

"Private Bennett is neither inherently criminal in instincts nor vicious by nature," Captain Fuller pleaded with Eisenhower. "I believe his crime was unpremeditated and directly traceable to an immature mentality and alcohol-inflamed passion." He recommended neither death nor life in prison, but a fixed number of years.

In Washington, Army Secretary Brucker reviewed Bennett's statements and the girl's age, and recommended death. Attorney General Brownell did not believe Bennett was mentally impaired; rather he simply had a "poorly organized personality structure." He suggested Eisenhower ignore the clemency petitions from Austrian citizens, dismissing them as "based generally, if not entirely, on opposition to capital punishment." He also advised the president to disregard Bennett's mother.

"I recognize the concern which she naturally must have in the welfare of her child and to that extent I have sympathy for her," he counseled. "But I cannot conscientiously accept her plea as justification for a lightening of the sentence."

Not until early 1957 did Assistant Special Counsel Barba inform his superior, White House counsel Morgan, that he felt death was appropriate."This was a brutal crime," Barba wrote, "devoid of mitigating factors for which punishment by death is certainly warranted." Morgan sent the Bennett file into the Oval Office, and on July 2, 1957, Dwight Eisenhower signed the death warrant.

"The sentence is approved," the president ordered, "and will be carried into execution under the orders of the Secretary of the Army."

Bennett heard nothing that day. Social worker Joseph Thompson interviewed him on death row though, and Bennett felt confident in the possibility of a commutation.

"The inmate appears to be well oriented," Thompson noted. "He speaks in a coherently relevant manner. There appears to be no delusions or hallucinations. His memory does not appear to be impaired. There is no evidence of an affective disorder at this time."

In Chatham, word that Eisenhower approved the death sentence led the news. His parents and Katherine were horrified. On July 30, they hurried to nearby Danville, Virginia, and crowded into the offices of local civil rights and criminal defense attorney Jerry Williams. His two-story brick "Southern Aid Building" sat just off Danville's downtown. From there, he had worked on earlier cases of black men accused of sexually assaulting white females. Despite his best efforts, he had lost those clients to the state executioner. Nonetheless, Williams was the best-known black lawyer in Pittsylvania County. An army veteran himself, he had befriended Thurgood Marshall. When the Bennett family gathered around his desk, he asked his associate Andrew Muse to telephone Washington.

Muse reached Lieutenant Colonel Harold E. Parker, a chief in the military justice division. "I was calling to find out what the procedure is to initiate a possible commutation," Muse began.

Colonel Parker asked if Muse was a lawyer. He told him yes, but that Williams would "be handling the case but he is tied up and he wanted to get the call through on his behalf. The question is, what is the procedure for possible commutation?"

"The president is the only one who has the power to commute a death sentence."

"Do you know who on the staff of the White House would handle that kind of thing?" Muse persisted.

Colonel Parker mentioned Morgan and the presidential counsel's office. "I think they have several lawyers. I am not sure whether they entertain such a request at any time before the execution."

Muse asked, "If, on a trip to Washington, I wanted to review the file, could I come to your office?" He explained that their client "is in Leavenworth and his parents live out here and they have none of the papers."

"What is the present status of the case as far as the parents know?" the colonel asked.

"They don't know of any date being set. They have been informed that it had been approved but not when he would be executed."

Secretary Brucker promptly scheduled Bennett to die at 0001 hours military time on August 29. On August 14, prison commandant Colonel James Davis showed Bennett the order. Now it was official, now he had been told. Within an hour, Bennett phoned Jerry Williams, who told Bennett that he must immediately write the president. Bennett spread three pieces of lined notebook paper across his bunk and clenched his fingers around a pencil. Slowly his hopes slid over those pages.

"Dear Mr. President," he began. He described growing up in Virginia where "I have caused no trouble and have never been in any trouble." He enlisted to "work hard to represent and defend my country as a soldier at home and abroad." He praised Austria, but "I feel that during the trial the court that tried me was under pressure from the Austrian public and the Press." It was wrong to have the girl testify during his trial. "Her appearance in her low physical condition was an additional pressure and aggravation to the court." He quoted the Old Testament—"an eye for an eye." He declared, "If the girl was not killed, neither should I be." But his death sentence was the result of "public pressure and prejudices against me." Bennett asked for a delay, and more consideration. "I am a poor boy from a poor family who has always done the right thing. But we are so poor that we are having trouble paying for lawyers." He insisted that "equal justice . . . should be available to all under the law of the United States." He ended with a prayer. "Mr. President, I beg you, please don't kill me."

Washington instructed the army to prepare for another hanging. "The President has considered this case carefully and finds no circumstances which would warrant the exercise of executive clemency," Morgan advised Colonel Davis at Fort Leavenworth.

When news reached Percy and Ollie Bennett, they frantically wrote a short letter to the president. So distraught, they did not even understand the army's method of execution. "Dear President . . . ," they began. "Please in the name of God and the heartfelt sympathy . . . save my son John A. Bennett from the chair. Please give him a chance. I have prayed to God for mercy."

Though their new lawyer, Williams, was certainly a fighter and would become a civil rights leader in his town, he was no miracle worker. But if Private Bennett were to be saved, it would take more than a figurehead in a small Southern community. He knew next to nothing about military law, and his record defending other black men in rape cases was abysmal.

A decade earlier, in the summer of 1947, Williams had defended Buford Russell Morton, thirty-one, charged with raping a twenty-seven-year-old local woman. The white mother of two claimed that Morton, a black man, forced her into a wood thicket behind the North Danville bus station at knifepoint. He threatened to stab or shoot her if she talked, she alleged, snarling that she "knew too much."

At the trial, Williams demonstrated how the woman and Morton actually were longtime friends. They had shared drinks together, and "there had been other compliant, clandestine meetings." The white newspapers mocked the black defendant in the courtroom, degrading him as a "bullet-headed stocky negro dressed in seedy clothes." They ridiculed him for taking the stand and acting "philosophic, his eyes constantly roving over the jury box."

The jurors believed the woman. She had been hospitalized and what happened in the woods was largely based on her word alone. There was little to no physical evidence. The jury sentenced Morton to the state electric chair in Richmond. The Danville *Bee* delighted that "the ends of justice have been met in what stands out as one of the most brutal and bestial crimes perpetrated in this city for a long time."

Three months later, Buford Morton was strapped into the electric chair at 7:30 in the morning. He was dead within ten minutes.

"An unpleasant duty," announced the state prosecutor, who also praised the jury's verdict. The *Bee* though had the final word. It noted there had been "no public outburst" by the white community, even alleging that "many colored people were of the opinion that justice had been done." The paper offered no proof of that assertion; it seemed meant to ward off any revenge, maybe even to ease some white guilt.

Williams had also assisted in legal appeals for the Martinsville Seven, a group of black men who were accused of raping a white woman in 1949. In short trials over the course of just eleven days, all seven were found guilty and handed the death penalty. Many whites applauded the verdicts as state-endorsed lynching.

Williams helped persuade the NAACP to mount the legal appeals, and he joined the team arguing before the state Supreme Court of Appeals. But the local press hounded these efforts, too, alleging they were a Communist front. The Danville *Register* called the black lawyers "scum who have changed their loyalty from Uncle Sam to Uncle Joe." The appeals failed; all seven men were executed over two days in February 1951.

A midsized man, slightly overweight, Williams had grown up in Danville, where his father drove a car for the Danville mills and his mother taught school. Jerry took forever to get through school—eight years of college undergraduate work and three years of law school in Washington, DC. He kept taking breaks to raise tuition money. He worked as a bellman at fashionable apartment buildings on Washington's Connecticut Avenue. Sometimes he drove the radio celebrity Arthur Godfrey to his broadcast station; Jerry got a kick out of that. Then came the war and the draft, and the army scooped him up in 1942. Williams was assigned undercover work in Philadelphia and on the West Coast. He helped chase Communist agitators, too. When cases went to trial in San Francisco, he would slide into a back bench and study closely how the lawyers built their arguments, persuaded the juries, and snuck by with some occasional courthouse theatrics.

When the war ended, Williams returned to his native Danville and in 1946 started practicing law. He married his wife, Ida, a schoolteacher like his mother. His family was growing, but he rarely missed his Saturday night poker game. He smoked too many Lucky Strikes (a pack a day for fifty years, until lung cancer finally got him), and he demanded the best of his five children. His rules at home were simple: none were ever to patronize a white establishment. They all were to see black doctors and black dentists, and visit only black restaurants and black stores. He laid down that law around the dinner table. Never give in to segregation, he warned. "We didn't use the water fountains," remembered his lawyer son Robert Williams. "We'd get a whipping for that."

Williams was a descendent of tobacco plantation slaves. The children and grandchildren of these slaves grew up to train as doctors, lawyers, and teachers, and made up new generations of professional men and women.

And he led by example. He lobbied to open the Danville library to black residents and to desegregate the parks. He worked with the NAACP and came to know some of the giants, including Thurgood Marshall, who once stayed at their house because Jim Crow did not allow black hotels in Danville. He helped found a bar association for black attorneys, as more around southern Virginia were following his lead. He was not an exceptionally elegant legal writer, but he held his own in a courtroom. Nor did he tire of raising money for the NAACP's Legal Defense Fund. Character was power, he instructed his children. "That was his passion," his son Robert recalled.

Williams shouldered the Bennett case with the memory of those two lost cases heavy in his heart. He was forty-five years old by then, cautious but well spoken. By the time of his death in 1988, at the age of seventy-five, he had served as the finance officer for the local American Legion "colored" chapter, as president of the Danville NAACP, and as one of the city's first black city council members.

"Dad first ran for City Council in Danville and had no chance in the 1950s," recalled another son, a lawyer also named Jerry Williams. "He knew he couldn't win. He was just trying to engage the black community to come out and get involved."

*   *   *

Williams agreed to defend Bennett, Robert remembered, mostly "because he was impressed with the Bennett family. That's why he invested so much time to try to get the young man off. I remember how upset my father was."

With Bennett's execution date looming just nine days away, Williams filed an emergency petition in federal court in Kansas. He returned to the argument that, under international law and US treaties, Bennett should have been tried by the Austrian courts. Federal Judge Delmas C. "Buzz" Hill postponed the August 29 execution until he could hear the matter. It marked a significant victory but came with a troubling catch. Judge Hill was the son of a country doctor from Wamego, Kansas. He served in the army JAG corps during World War II. As a captain, he helped prosecute a Japanese officer for the Bataan Death March. After he was elevated to the federal bench, Hill sat on a three-judge panel that ruled against desegregating Topeka's public school—a ruling later overturned in the landmark *Brown v. Board of Education* case.

Yet a court hearing was certainly promising, and Bennett's father and older sister, Katherine, drove to Leavenworth. They first stayed with relatives in Kansas City, Kansas, and the next morning followed the road signs toward the prison rising above the west river bluffs. They parked in the gravel driveway and nervously approached the center archway that for half a century had loudly proclaimed "Our Mission—Your Future," a promise clearly not meant for death row men. The gray limestone blocks that made up the walls matched the chillness of the air that grim fall day.

Katherine and her father had not seen John since he shipped out for Europe. He still looked thin and handsome, but more muscular; his face was lighter, signs of prison pallor. He wore a drab uniform to match that gray sky. They were so happy to see him though, she recalled, and sad his mother had not joined them. "It was just too much for her to bear," Katherine explained. The visit, however, felt antiseptic. Two white prison guards stood nearby, their arms crossed.

What did impress her was how John tried to be courageous. "If he was scared there he didn't show it, or had got used to it," Katherine remembered. "He was like my mother, he just toughed it out." She continued, "But sure he was scared. But he said he got used to it. He knew he wasn't going to get out. And we knew that he was concerned and it was hard on him and it was hard all of us and we couldn't be alone with him."

He described his new pet, which slithered through a hole in his cell room floor: "I'm acquainted with a rat!" he joked. "But this rat don't know where we are."

The hearing opened in Topeka the morning of October 29, 1957. Katherine and Percy Bennett leaned forward from back row seats as John, in his prison uniform, testified. His lawyer told him to speak louder; the judge told him to slow down. It seemed they were having a difficult time understanding his rough, Southern dialect. Bennett settled into the chair, breathed deep, and folded his trembling hands.

Williams's hope was to convince this judge that the US Army should never have had such a hold over Bennett after he was arrested. The girl was raped near her home, on Austrian soil, not at the army camp. He was off duty; he was not at that moment representing the US Armed Forces. He should have been turned over to Austrian authorities. Williams asked if other GIs had been tried by the Austrian courts. Bennett mentioned a drunken soldier who rammed his car into a gasthaus wall. "The Austrian gendarme caught him and they held him in custody until they could try him," Bennett recounted. "And when they tried him he didn't pull no time. They just fined him for damage of the gasthaus and for drunk driving."

Another soldier named Kibbidue, Bennett's battalion ammunition sergeant, was arrested with a minor and held briefly in an Austrian jail. "He stayed 45 days and he was fined, and when he was released he came back to his outfit," Bennett testified. "And after he got to his outfit the onliest thing he did was, the government sent him out of the Austrian territory back to the United States."

No US Army prosecution? "They released him to the military custody to see whatever action they wanted to take," Bennett said. "And at that time the military, they refused to court-martial him."

When asked about the protests around Salzburg after his arrest, and the Austrian government's demand for civilian justice, Bennett said his post commander, Colonel Frederic C. Cook, "stated that the army would try me and make an example out of me for the benefit of the rest of the troops in Austria, to show that they could not overrun the Austrian population and get away with it."

While in custody, Bennett said he heard *Stars and Stripes* newsmen roaming the police squad hallways, hoping to interview him. "The reporters was trying to get in to see me," Bennett testified. A top army police agent "was afraid if I get to see the reporters myself that I would make him out a liar and that it would not look good in the records."

At dawn, police released him for "lack of evidence," and for a few blissful hours, it seemed the entire episode would be over with, Bennett said. However, later that night, Bennett's company commander, Captain Fuller, summoned him to his office and informed him that the army was going to prosecute him after all. "Bennett," the captain told him, "don't feel bad about me doing it because I don't want to do it. I am just carrying out my orders."

Re-arrested, Bennett told the police he had been seeing a movie at the Camp Roeder theater when the girl was attacked. But, as he now testified, the officers held a gun to his head and forced him to sign a confession. (At his trial, the lead army police investigator did admit that he was armed during the interrogation, but never said he brandished the weapon.)

Lieutenant Colonel Peter S. Wondolowski of the Washington JAG office cross-examined Bennett. He was middle-aged and stocky, with a tight army crew cut. Later, as an army judge, he presided over one of the My Lai murder cases from the Vietnam War. He asked Bennett about the girl. This was an appeal hearing, and the army lawyer wanted to emphasize that the victim had identified him in open court during the court-martial trial. That could seal things with this judge in Kansas.

"Did she point to you as the man who raped her?"

"She did not point to me as the man that actually attacked her," Bennett insisted. "She referred to me as my complexion."

"She didn't indicate that you were the man that grabbed her?"

"Yes, from my complexion."

Wondolowski tried again. "She pointed to you as the man that did it?"

"Yes," Bennett conceded, "on that ground."

Bennett stepped down from the stand. Throughout his life, he was always being hauled away somewhere—to rural black-only schools or to bed with blinding headaches, to the army, to prison, and now this federal courthouse. He had barely known his army attorney overseas. He never heard from the army lawyers who handled his failed military appeals. He only had just met Jerry Williams. Bennett was arrested, freed, and then re-arrested. He initially was moved to a stockade five miles from Camp Roeder because the army was worried about the Austrian protest. In the swirl of events, and the slow lonely months on death row, it was nearly impossible for this poor, barely educated son of segregated southern Virginia to understand where his life was headed next. In all, he had been locked up in Austria, Germany, Pennsylvania, and now Kansas. The hearing ended, and he was driven back to death row.

Judge Hill took his time. For three months, they all waited. After much consideration, at the end of January 1958, he denied Bennett's petition. "Austria had no jurisdiction over personnel of the military forces of the United States," the judge ruled. Bennett's court-martial, he found, was "properly constituted and within its lawful powers." The judge's one gift was to continue delaying the trial until Williams could appeal.

To the Tenth Circuit US Court of Appeals, Williams cited a series of Allied agreements—Yalta, Potsdam, and a Moscow Summit. Austria, Williams argued, "had the court facilities to try this type of offense." He added, "There is a wide disparity in the punishment under the Austrian Law and the Uniform Code of Military Justice for the same offense." The court ruled against him in May 1959, adding that "[i]n occupied countries, members of United States Armed Forces are subject to military law and within exclusive jurisdiction of constituted military tribunals."

The door that had opened so briefly to the possibility of a retrial or lighter sentence was quickly swinging shut. Williams's petition to the US Supreme Court and attempt to file a new appeal in a federal court in Washington failed. They were running out of time. On December 11, Judge Hill canceled the stay of execution. Six weeks later, on January 28, 1960, the army rescheduled Bennett's execution for 0001 hours, Thursday, March 10, 1960. When told of his new execution date, the doctors said, Bennett collapsed into "storms of crying and biting his bed sheets."

★   ★   ★

The army ordered more evaluations. Military doctors reassessed Bennett's "blind stuppers" and childhood headaches. They prescribed drugs to calm his nerves and help him sleep, but after two weeks found "no change."

Neurologist Dr. Bernard Foster saw Bennett on February 8, 1960, at the Menninger Clinic in Topeka. He determined the soldier suffered up to two epileptic seizures a day. Three more army doctors convened a board of medical examiners, and while they could not "convincingly correlate" Bennett's epilepsy with the rape in Siezenheim, they warned of that "significant possibility."

The board stressed that "[h]ad this man received a diagnosis of epilepsy at the time of his trial, it may have had a significant effect on the deliberations and decisions of the court." It concluded, "It does not appear appropriate to execute this man." It urged life.

That same day, the second official order came down: "Execution by hanging," on March 10.

In Washington, the surgeon general of the army had reviewed Bennett's medical files. He found no mental disease, rather just a "dull, apathetic, frightened, young Negro soldier." He saw no reason to delay the hanging any longer. Hangman Sergeant Maddox was ordered to prepare his gear.

On March 2, Bennett's sister Katherine notified the legal office at Fort Leavenworth that Williams "was in the process of preparing a last-minute appeal for clemency," she told them. The army was determined to proceed regardless.

On March 7, Secretary Brucker reminded Eisenhower he had approved the death sentence in 1957. "I adhere to my previous recommendation that the sentence of death be executed."

Desperate, Williams filed yet another petition to another federal court in Kansas. He asked for another emergency stay of execution, emphasizing the question of Bennett's mental fitness.

Bennett now was a mere two days away from death. Guards escorted him to a special basement holding cell called Eight Base, what prisoners referred to as "the dungeon." Thus began a forty-eight-hour death watch. From there, Bennett sent a final telegram to Eisenhower. It was brief. "I am now writing asking for clemency in my behalf . . . I pray to God and to you that my life be spared."

Dawn broke on March 9, John Bennett's last day. Chaplain Carter began a series of visits as Bennett awaited his last meal—fried shrimp. "He seemed resigned to dying," the minister said.

By early morning Sergeant Maddox was at the wheel of his car, rumbling down the Eisenhower freeway, his ropes, straps, and belts tangled in the backseat.

Late in the morning, Bennett asked to call his sister. They spoke briefly, and when they hung up, Katherine bent over in grief. "They're just trying to prove something," she cried to their mother. "Momma, they're just trying to prove to Mr. Eisenhower they can nail somebody."

Bennett was allowed one more phone call. He remembered John Day, the last soldier executed, just six months earlier, had reached out to Dr. Menninger in his last hours. So Bennett asked the guards to dial the Topeka clinic.

"It's a little uncanny when you get a phone call from an inmate," the doctor remembered years later. "But I'd visited a lot of jails—Lansing, Leavenworth, New York City. Prisoners knew about me."

Bennett pleaded. Could he help?

"I tried everything I could," Menninger recalled. "Being a doctor, people appeal to you for help and you can't turn them down."

Several in the office offered their thoughts, but Menninger waved them off.

"My opinion of Eisenhower was never all that high anyway," he announced. "It went straight to the bottom after that phone call."

His telegram to the president hit the wire at 1:56 p.m.

"A call just came from the United States Disciplinary Barracks at Fort Leavenworth asking me if I would be willing to talk to John Bennett, a prisoner who is to be executed tonight," it said. "I am told that he was officially found by an Army Medical Board to be afflicted with epilepsy. I agreed to talk with him. He requested I petition you for executive clemency. I do so with fervor not only because I am opposed to capital punishment, but because, as a physician, I think it is particularly immoral and medieval to execute a man known to be suffering from a brain disease for which he is in no way responsible."

Secretary Brucker phoned Menninger and told him earlier studies confirmed Bennett was sane. Menninger's heart dropped. "I think I understand your position, and I believe you understand mine," he replied.

Night fell. The prison went still. In Virginia, Williams had yet to hear on his latest legal petition. On Eight Base, the fried shrimp arrived, already a little cold, on a prison tray. In Washington, Eisenhower was handling a final round of phone calls. A UN resolution on South Africa was stalled because of a "race problem" in the United States. Arms talks were underway in Geneva. The Nixon for President campaign had geared up. And Secretary Brucker was briefing the president "re clemency for condemned individual."

According to White House notes, Eisenhower phoned Brucker. He asked "about some case involving a man named Bennett." Five years had passed since the soldier was condemned to die—far too many for Eisenhower. In his mind, the death penalty was necessary for cases like Bennett's. He needed to send a strong message about the importance of discipline in the army ranks. But John Bennett's case had lost its importance, and it was likely few from Austria remembered it much anymore.

"The case has dragged on so long all those people are now out of the army and that is now lost," Eisenhower complained to Brucker.

Brucker mentioned to Eisenhower that "apparently, also, some doctors have recommended clemency." They continued to chat, when Brucker suddenly interrupted the president. "Um," he stuttered. "A judge has just granted a stay . . ."

Bennett's life had been spared—once again.

Down on Eight Base, the phone rang "like crazy," recalled Sergeant R. W. Pinson. The time was 9:30 p.m. Two and a half hours left in Bennett's life, and army boots again thundered down the stairs. Colonel Cox announced that a federal judge had acted on Williams's petition and granted a short stay of execution, maybe another week, maybe a little longer. Smiles flashed all around. Bennett looked back at the untouched shrimp. Everyone seemed so pleased that several guards dug in, and Sergeant Pinson and Chaplain Carter returned the prisoner to death row.

"We put him back in his old cell," Pinson recalled. But before they could shut the bars and turn the lock, Bennett raised his arms and beamed, "I beat the rope!" The chaplain remembered it differently. He said Bennett proclaimed with a big broad smile, "Man, it's great to be home again!"

★   ★   ★

He was relieved but not saved, spared but not redeemed. Once again, he would be tested in court, now before Judge Arthur J. Stanley Jr. And like Judge Hill, Stanley also knew the army well. He had ridden with the famed Seventh Cavalry and helped push Pancho Villa's rebels back into Mexico. He ended the fight a lieutenant colonel and returned to Kansas. He loved the old fort on the river heights and authored a history of his favorite army post. "Fort Leavenworth flourishes, alive and well," he proclaimed. Stanley had helped establish the Fort Leavenworth Hall of Fame and in death would be buried at the Fort Leavenworth National Cemetery.

The lawyer Williams had amended his petition to include the new medical board findings. He contended that Bennett "is now and remains mentally incompetent." When the hearing began the morning of March 23, 1960, in Kansas City, Kansas, four psychiatrists gathered to testify for the defense. Chief among them was Dr. Menninger.

Menninger fretted over the impossibility of demonstrating a conclusive link between Bennett's epilepsy and his crime. But it also would be impossible to prove there was no tie. "I don't know you can prove there's no connection," he recalled years later, when he spoke of his testimony for Private Bennett. Beyond Bennett's case, and beyond the possibility of his epilepsy triggering the crime, Menninger had a greater issue on his mind. "Capital punishment is a piece of savagery we ought to get over . . . The death penalty is a simple fix solution, a kind of fanciful and operatic spectacle with a grand finale, loud but holier. But it doesn't fix anything. And they can't execute all those people. What could they do? Put them all on a boat and sink it?"

The doctor's war against legal executions sprang from a cautionary tale in his 1938 book, *Man Against Himself*. Menninger relayed the story of a longtime state executioner in New York. Over the course of his career, the man helped execute 141 prisoners in the electric chair. One day, he descended to the basement of his home and shot himself in the head. Here was a government official, Menninger wrote, "[w]ho had made a business of killing others who finally turned his professional skill upon himself."

Menninger's position against the death penalty was widely known and spread further as his star rose around the country as a medical professional. For a time, he believed executions should be broadcast on the small screen. "Put it on television and see if the people don't see how dirty, how inhumane, how nasty a business it is and they will make you stop it," he once declared. In mass mailings to legislators, senators, and governors, he argued, "State killing is terribly expensive. And this is to say nothing of the torture of waiting." He felt the courts only prolonged the agony.

"The chances of any particular murderer being hanged are about one in two hundred and he knows it and everyone else knows it," the psychiatrist wrote. "Why should the courts go on with this ridiculous game of Russian roulette?"

"No one is sane enough to be executed," he warned his peers. "Most are just poor, black or Mexican and uneducated." He continued, "Wardens loathe it, and so does everyone else in a prison."

Called to testify for Bennett, Menninger discussed the phone call from Fort Leavenworth. "This man wanted to say something on the last day of his life to me," the psychiatrist told Judge Stanley. "He knew of my opposition to capital punishment and I agreed to listen." Bennett urged him to lobby President Eisenhower. "I told him that I would do that, that I would do it on principle, because I would do that for anyone who asked me to. I have very strong convictions on the matter of capital punishment, as it affects the control of crime, the administration of justice in respect to offenders and on a moral basis."

Menninger only knew that Bennett had been diagnosed with epilepsy. Though he never examined Bennett, he spoke from experience. "A man who has epileptic seizures doesn't know anything about the outside world at the time he has the seizures." And seizures, he warned, are "aggravated" by alcohol or marijuana, a reference to Bennett's drinking and drug use. "Any damaged brain is more susceptible to any toxin."

Williams also questioned Dr. Foster, the Menninger Clinic neurologist who concluded Bennett was epileptic. By his estimation, the seizures typically lasted for up to forty seconds, the doctor testified, leaving Bennett unable to recall a thing. An electroencephalogram "clearly showed the patterns" for epilepsy, "with a very high percentage frequency."

To counter that testimony, Colonel Wondolowski read from Bennett's signed confession in Austria; he said it showed full well the soldier knew what he had done.

Under cross-examination, Captain Marshall Edelson, an army doctor and psychiatrist assigned to the Fort Leavenworth prison, acknowledged the army medical board could not directly connect the epilepsy to the encounter along the stream in Austria. "I did not find any evidence indicating that he was having a discrete epileptic seizure at the time he committed this act," the captain conceded.

It was late by the time Bennett was sworn in. He had arrived in army handcuffs and again spoke in his low, Southern drawl.

Williams asked about his family history. The soldier started with his maternal grandfather, Lewis Coleman, who was born into slavery and died in the Virginia state hospital. "I don't know for sure, Lawyer Williams," Bennett began. "I think it was either in '50 or '51. He had epilepsy."

A cousin killed himself. "He was described, for two or three days, before he committed suicide, as having been in a daze, seemed to be unaware of himself," Bennett testified. "On the third or the fourth morning he was found hanging from his upstairs ceiling."

Growing up, Bennett said little felt right around the family farm. "Lawyer Williams, on one occasion, I think, the first occasion following—it was in the spring when I had the fall and in that same year I was accused of attacking one of my brothers."

"You don't know anything, don't remember anything about it?" Williams asked.

"I remember—he was laying on the bed and that I come up the steps and attacked him. But I remember going through the door but I don't remember doing nothing to him. And I remember when I come to myself I was in the kitchen."

The trouble persisted through his teens, right up until boot camp in Maryland.

"I had a fall . . . and it seems we had, I had a little headache and confusion out of that." He was seen at the camp hospital.

"Now these attacks that you had, Bennett, how long during your life did they last, where you had things like that that might happen to you?" asked Williams.

"All my life," he replied.

"Can you recall the attack in Austria?"

"No," Bennett said. "I have no knowledge of it whatsoever."

Williams sat down, and Colonel Wondolowski took over. In his clipped army cadence, he asked Bennett to describe what his seizures felt like.

"They are subject to coming at any time," Bennett told him. "They might last a little while, they might last a long time, or else they might be repeating themselves five or six times or more, see. They can repeat, or they will repeat, or have repeated."

The colonel asked if army specialists from Washington ever examined him.

No, Bennett said. "I was waiting for them. They sent me out here to Leavenworth and I had been out at Leavenworth for a good four or five months and still no one said nothing to me about it."

Judge Stanley indicated he was unimpressed with Bennett's case. Indeed, the judge's mind seemed already made up. He thought it cruel to string Bennett along like this when he was so close to dying. "I question the real kindness of holding out hope to a man in the situation in which Mr. Bennett now finds himself," the judge admonished. He said he was "inclined now" to dismiss the appeal and set a new execution date. But he agreed to study the legal briefs and to continue the stay of execution.

Judge Stanley did not formally rule against until June 28. He concluded that Bennett's army trial lawyer should have brought up "the issue of insanity" during the court-martial five years earlier in Austria. Now the issue was moot.

Washington and the army were elated. Colonel Robert J. O'Connor, chief of the JAG's Litigation Division, already had boasted in a private memo that "the Army is humane. It does not seek to punish people not responsible for their acts." He added that fourteen army doctors examined

Bennett over the years, "and he was found legally sane." The colonel further suggested that Bennett had whipped up some poor Southern attitude to gain sympathy from the judge. "His testimony was given in short halting statements and he well portrayed himself as an individual of low intelligence."

Back on the army's death row, time wore on dismally.

Last winter and spring "his overseers noted that his morale was rather poor, due to the uncertainty of his status. [But] in the last three months his morale has been better," reported Fort Leavenworth psychiatrist Captain George J. Berry, after examining Bennett on Seven Base.

Bennett wove rugs, pounded on a speed bag, and lifted weights. Seldom did he sleep well, even with new medicine to block the headaches and seizures. Despite the lack of sleep and low morale, Captain Berry found, "There is no evidence of psychosis as manifested by delusions, hallucinations or a thinking disorder." And while "he is somewhat optimistic about his case, he has considerable anxiety over his appeals pending in the courts." Yet Captain Berry concluded in September 1960 that Private Bennett actually "remains somewhat cheerful."

Bennett cherished the dwindling late autumn afternoons and his hour under the slanting sun to fire a baseball at the prison walls. The speed bag and the weights built his upper-body strength, and he was weaning himself off the Camel cigarettes to increase his lung power. From the high turrets, tower guards followed the rhythmic patterns of each pitch—the stillness, the windup, the sudden release, and the slap against the wall. The death row soldier who twice had beaten the army hangman continued to endure.

"When we took him to the exercise yard, he reached down and took a handful of dirt and ate it. Just one handful; no more," recalled Master Sergeant Holsey K. Mills. "He worried about not seeing the World Series, about the new baseball season next year and afraid of missing it. He told me more than anything else he didn't want to miss that."

On death row in 1960, the last of the white soldiers were spared. Maurice Schick left in April, Isaac Hurt departed in June, and Ed Heilman in November. Soon Bennett had the place all to himself. And by year's end, the country had a new president.

Chapter Nine

* * * * * * * *

KENNEDY

A new White House dawned in the middle of the night. As the last precincts closed on Election Day 1960, the Democratic candidate slipped slightly ahead of Eisenhower's vice president. It was, media critics agreed, the "most suspenseful evening anyone ever spent in front of a TV set."

The victor, however, missed the finale. Exhausted, he retired to bed. Only when the morning light fanned over Cape Cod did he learn he had been elected president of the United States. After eight years under Dwight Eisenhower, youth and vigor glamorized official Washington. "A new generation of Americans," Kennedy promised, would lead the country now.

In the year leading up to the election, campaign fever swept through the death row hallway. Guards and convicts followed primary battles, convention speeches, radio reports and televised debates. That election year, the last of the condemned men devoured the Leavenworth *Times*, hushed one another to tune into radio broadcasts, and strained their necks toward the black-and-white screen at the end of the tier.

"They wanted to know all about a candidate's politics and how it would affect *them*," stressed Master Sergeant Thompson Biggar. As night shift supervisor, he would switch off the TV and hear the prisoners still stirring in the dark, whispering about the latest twists in the marathon political year. "Presidential politics were pretty close up there with baseball and sports," Biggar said. "They'd talk about it, read newspapers, listen to radio news. Whatever they could get their hands on."

Guards joined in the cheering for a new administration, too. "They all rooted for Kennedy," said Sergeant R. W. Pinson. "They didn't like

Eisenhower. We considered him nothing much for the enlisted man. Morale went way up when Kennedy won."

The new president was everything Eisenhower was not. Young, handsome, a Democrat, a liberal, and a Catholic, Kennedy inspired new confidence and vitality in a nation worn down by the Cold War. In his thousand-day presidency, he would challenge America to leave footprints on the moon, escort civil rights beyond the schoolhouse door, and at the brink of nuclear annihilation, confront the Soviets over missile sites in Cuba. His lofty rhetoric, charming First Lady, and their style and resilience banished the old Washington of the 1950s to what felt like a distant memory.

As the army and its death row project at Fort Leavenworth prepared for the new commander in chief, they worried how it would affect Bennett, their remaining death row soldier. On January 12, 1961, a week before the inauguration, an internal Pentagon memo asked, "What can Bennett do now, as a last resort?" Only Bennett remained on the basement cell block. "There are no other cases involving the death sentence pending at this time," the memo cautioned.

Three days before the inauguration, the US Court of Appeals tossed out Jerry Williams's latest petition on Bennett's behalf. The court did not rule on the merits. Rather, it brusquely dismissed the case because Williams and the Bennett family had fallen behind on court costs. Even so, with one eye on the emerging Kennedy administration, Williams reconsidered his legal options. He would not surrender to the courts nor stand idly by as Judge Stanley in Kansas prepared to lift the stay of execution.

On February 4, with Kennedy now in office, the Virginia attorney wired his Kansas counterpart Elisha Scott, the "Colored Lawyer" in Topeka. "John A Bennetts parents brothers and sisters, are unable to raise any more funds for his defence, and this condition has slowed me in his defence. Please file motion to reinstate the appeal, and appear before Judge Stanley February 8th on motion to dissolve stay."

Scott pleaded with the Denver appellate court for additional time to raise more money. "Please keep in mind that you are being asked to help in a worthy cause," Scott implored the court clerk. "A human life is involved and the God of Heaven will be pleased and the interested party relieved of extended worry and the young man will have an opportunity at least to prosecute his appeal." Their petition, Scott emphasized, "[i]s just and meritorious."

"Poverty is the sole reason" they had fallen behind in court fees. And yet Bennett, Scott and Williams maintained, "may lose his life for crimes of which he stands convicted and of which there are serious doubts that he was mentally responsible." The court though rejected their pleas for mercy. In Topeka, Judge Stanley lifted the stay of execution.

Now the army moved swiftly. For the first time, the Pentagon briefed the still-settling-in Kennedy staff on the Bennett case. In a memo hand-carried to the new secretary of the army's office, Major General Charles L. Decker, the Judge Advocate General, advised them on February 16 of Ei-senhower's approval of the death sentence and the six years of psychiatric assessments and legal wrangling. Decker though carefully omitted Ben-nett's epilepsy and the conflict between the army and the Austrian justice system at the time of Bennett's arrest. He added, as if it were a relief for the new administration about to consider such a grave matter, "This is the only court-martial case in which a death sentence has been adjudged that is pending at this time."

Army Secretary Elvis J. Stahr Jr. agreed it was time for Bennett to pay with his life. That same day, he wrote Kennedy summarizing the assault in Austria, the long death row confinement, and the prior court battles. "Ger-trude," he advised the president, suffered "excruciating pain." Bennett had long ago admitted the sexual attack and even "reconstructed the crimes for the investigators." But the new army secretary did not bring up Bennett's history with epilepsy and other mental defects, nor did he mention that rape in Austria was punished by no more than twenty years. He directed Fifth Army Headquarters in Chicago to set a third execution date.

In a wire communiqué, the Fifth Army promptly ordered Fort Leav-enworth to "notify prisoner immed [immediately]" that the stay had been lifted. Colonel Weldon W. Cox, the prison commandant, along with six officers on his top staff, Chaplain Thomas Carter, and a prison psychia-trist assembled in front of Bennett's cell just before 4:30 the afternoon of

February 17. The commandant informed his prisoner he would die at a "time and place" yet to be designated by army superiors. For now, Colonel Cox only asked Bennett if he had enough paper and pencils in his cell to contact his lawyer.

Lieutenant Colonel Thomas W. Birch, assistant chief of the army JAG office in Washington, immediately wrote to Bennett's father in rural Chatham, Virginia. "Your son's sentence will now be carried into execution," the JAG officer told the Virginia farmer. "I regret that my letter must contain such distressing information," he added, "but you are assured that every aspect of your son's case has received careful consideration." In a separate memo to his public affairs unit, Colonel Birch separately summarized the Bennett case for a press release. The memo covered the crime and the years-long legal battle, but omitted many of the complications that shaped his experience: the epilepsy diagnosis, the possibility of justice in Austria.

The formal Order of Execution came down on February 20. He was to die at a single tick past midnight, just after 12 a.m. on April 13. Colonel Cox would officiate, assisted by two Fort Leavenworth medical officers, three chaplains, and four high-ranking army witnesses. The commandant did not immediately notify Bennett, but word quickly spread through the prison corridors above Seven Base.

Two chaplains hastily fired off letters on his behalf to their chain of command. Bennett had received little religious training during his Virginia boyhood, wrote Captain Carter, and yet "he has participated in the worship services here on an active basis since his arrival in 1955." The chaplain had baptized him in the mobile water tank, and Bennett "has confessed his sins to God and feels that he has been forgiven." Major Joseph E. X. Frain, a Catholic priest, felt the prisoner's "adjustment under close confinement and steady surveillance has been excellent . . . He has never been a disciplinary problem. He has tried, according to his talent, to do his best while here . . . He has become more the man."

At 1:10 in the afternoon, February 27, Colonel Cox led another contingent down to death row. The commandant read the Order of Execution and reminded Bennett that "all officers of the USDB staff" would help if he needed to reach his lawyer. Back in his office, the colonel handled one more task. He telephoned the hangman Master Sergeant William Maddox to inform him that the army once again required his services.

From Virginia, Katherine and Ira Bennett, his older brother, hurried to Fort Leavenworth and, again with white prison guards standing nearby, spoke to him through a phone and plate glass window. "He was scared but he had gotten used to it," she remembered of John. "He worried he wasn't going to get out. He knew what his situation was, what he was up against. He knew these people and knew what they were going to do. He accepted that." She remembered John leaning into the glass and whispering over the phone, "I never realized the girl was that young. I thought she was older. If I had known she wasn't older."

Before they left, the guards allowed them to gather privately for a moment in a nearby alcove, a room so small, Ira recalled, "we couldn't move around much, just sit there and talk." John, he remembered, "wasn't angry. He told us his troubles, a little bit about them bringing him back to the States and how they treated him. He was very happy to see us. I mean very happy. It meant the world for us to see each other. And he said they told him they wouldn't let him leave until they hung him. That's how he felt. He told me every living person, everything that's living, is born to die. And that's why he wasn't afraid."

When the hour grew late, guards led John away. But he stopped first near that window again and slapped his hand on the glass. Ira, a career army officer, promptly saluted his brother back, pressing his palm against the other side. The two army brothers shared what both assumed would be a final farewell. Later, as he and Katherine drove home, nearing Virginia and the old South, Ira felt all the more convinced John would not make it. "I didn't think they'd get him off," he reflected. "I didn't think he had a prayer. Blacks in the army didn't have that kind of opportunity. We didn't have nothing."

Ira Bennett had worn the uniform for too long not to feel otherwise— twenty-seven years, from 1952 until his retirement as a sergeant major. To him, racial discrimination was embedded into army life. He always suspected that many of the white officers looked down on black recruits as second-class soldiers. And the smallest slights often hurt the worst. In all those six years John had lingered on death row, waiting to learn if he would live or die, with the Bennett family worried back home, Ira had received just one letter from him. "But it was six months before I got it." And seeing those white prison guards hulking around them in the Fort Leavenworth visiting area crawled under Ira's skin, too. "I was nervous when I went in there. I was nervous for him and being in prison. Because I knew the way they treated prisoners at that time. If you were white, you had better opportunities."

In the White House, the family's hopes landed on the desk of Lee C. White, a new assistant special counsel to President Kennedy. Born into the Jewish faith, he was personally opposed to capital punishment, and he struggled over the case of John Bennett. He had been a Kennedy loyalist throughout the 1950s, working as an aide to the future president's father and a legislative assistant when John Kennedy represented Massachusetts in the Senate. Now, as a New Frontiersman, his tasks and assignments were constantly shuffled in those first hundred days, and White typically read the newspapers at home "or on the way in to try to figure out what I was going to work on that day." If you want to serve a president, White would lecture, "you've gotta be his guy. Put yourself in his shoes."

White was personally and morally opposed to capital punishment, and yet unsure how to proceed with John Bennett. Seeking guidance, he first asked the president's brother, Attorney General Robert F. Kennedy, for his thoughts on executive clemency. Robert Kennedy would make civil rights a "considerable part" of his focus. He once noted how two tourist guidebooks provided only one hotel for blacks in Montgomery, Alabama, and none in Jerry Williams's hometown of Danville, Virginia. "But a dog," Kennedy continued, "provided he is traveling with a white man, is welcome to spend the night in at least five establishments in Montgomery and in four in Danville."

On February 27, the attorney general sent White a list of prior federal death row cases. "If clemency is to be granted," he underscored, "the President must take affirmative action." Once the courts had spoken, he alone could halt an execution. If Kennedy did nothing, Bennett would hang. It came down to a single question: Would President Kennedy be willing to overrule President Eisenhower?

In Virginia, the Bennett family considered the Kennedy administration their best chance and last hope. Eisenhower had gotten them nowhere. "Being a general like he was and the time he came up and all the way things were, he was just against it," Katherine remarked years later.

Williams expected much from the new president, too, convinced he would step in. "My father was very supportive of Kennedy and the election and was active in working for him in our community and our politics here," recalled his son Robert Williams. "Kennedy had the power to commute [Bennett]."

In those early weeks of 1961, Bennett's lawyer opted to forgo more legal appeals. Their luck had run thin, and the family could no longer afford the mounting legal costs. Instead, he opened the Uniform Code of Military Justice. With the lamp burning late on his desk in Danville's Southern Aid Building, Williams researched the army's legal system, the federal government, and how to compose a plea for presidential clemency.

In Washington, Lee White came across the earlier army board findings of epilepsy and clemency recommendation. He invited top army officials to his West Wing office at the White House at noon on March 3, including Brigadier General Alan B. Todd, Assistant Judge Advocate General. According to Todd's notes attached to the Bennett file, White "expressed interest" in the board's conclusions. He "inquired into the mental status of Prisoner Bennett," and the general countered that the army's surgeon general had reviewed the findings but adhered to earlier reports that determined Bennett was sound of mind. General Todd further cautioned White that "[n]o action was taken by the President [Eisenhower] to change his approval of the death sentence as a result of this consideration." With some relief, General Todd noted, "Discussion of the case apparently satisfied Mr. White."

Before they could leave though, White pulled General Todd aside. He asked him, "Would clemency pleas be addressed to the President?" He wanted to know if the White House should expect a formal petition for clemency soon. Likely, the general replied, by Bennett or his lawyer, "or both."

General Todd returned to JAG headquarters and ordered Colonel Birch to phone the prison. He was anxious to learn how Bennett was holding up. Fort Leavenworth reported back at three in the afternoon, saying they were following "Standard Operating Procedures" with Bennett. "Psychiatric consultations" would be conducted daily, they promised, with regular visits by Chaplain Carter. "On the day prior to execution, the prisoner will be under constant observation."

By now, letters were arriving at the White House entrance. On March 3, Gertrude H. Wilkinson of Richmond, Virginia, urged Kennedy to "reverse this decision and save this boy . . . Please temper Mercy with Justice." She felt the army in part was to blame. "My heart goes out to this Mother as it does to the Soldier boy. They are taken so far away from home and such evil temptations are thrown about the camps, along with strong drink etc, it is sometimes a wonder that so few of these tragedies occur."

White prepared a memo on March 4 for the president. In "points to be considered," he advised that President Truman, the last Democrat in the White House, did not permit executions. He contended, incorrectly, that "NAACP lawyers represented Bennett in his civilian court review efforts—so the civil rights question is present in some degree." (Williams and Elisha Scott were members of the NAACP, but the organization declined to intervene.) Another "point worth noting," White wrote, was comparison of the Bennett case with that of a four-year-old girl seized the previous month from a Manhattan playground. In late February, Edith Kiecorius was found sexually assaulted and murdered in a disheveled Chelsea neighborhood rooming house. A fifty-nine-year-old drifter had just been arrested; the public was clamoring for his trial and execution.

White further advised Kennedy that "since President Eisenhower already refused to grant clemency, the possibility of an unpleasant comparison should be noted." Here he was speaking politically again and warning Kennedy that he risked a public backlash if he overturned Eisenhower. (In truth, Eisenhower never "refused to grant clemency"; he approved the death sentence but never was formally presented with a petition for clemency.) White also said he believed the army surgeon general had "answered satisfactorily" that no psychiatric link existed between Bennett and the assault in Austria.

"Bennett has been at death's doorstep for six years," he wrote. "This is not a case of a life for a life—the victim survived. But the crime was a heinous one." He concluded with a personal note: "Unless one is opposed to capital punishment [and I am], this is a case in which the man's life should be taken."

In handwritten notes on a legal pad, White separately jotted down a set of "additional points" for the president. It remains unclear whether he added them to a second memo, presented them orally to the president, or ended up doing anything at all with them. In these notes, White wrote that under the new military justice code, "Bennett is the first and only serviceman to have been sentenced to death for rape without accompanying murder." He stressed that, historically, soldiers accused of rape in peacetime are "tried in civilian courts both here and abroad."

Of Gertie, the girl in Austria, he said, "The victim in this case was back in school 3 weeks after the crime, is healthy and the many Austrians join those who have petitioned for clemency in sparing Bennett's life. It is my recommendation that the sentence be commuted to life imprisonment. Although originally I recommended that there was no reason for upsetting the death sentence [assuming you (Kennedy) would ever approve execution], in view of these considerations I recommend commutation to life imprisonment."

White brought the president's top military aide, Major General Chester "Ted" Clifton, with him to the Oval Office. As White recalled years later, the briefing lasted an hour and a half, a significant block of time on the new president's schedule. "We reviewed the case in detail," White recalled. "The President read significant portions of the file and peppered us with questions and asked for additional information, including the psychiatric evaluations." But Kennedy made no final decision.

The morning of March 6, Army Secretary Stahr's office phoned the JAG. The White House wanted "to be kept informed in the Bennett death case, should there be any attempt to ask [for] clemency."

General Todd called General Clifton back at the White House. He assured him everyone would be updated in these final weeks. General Clifton, though, worried the White House might miss the formal clemency plea if it was lost in the White House mail or a phone call was jammed in the switchboard. It presented "a significant problem," he warned; some forty thousand letters and mail packages already were piling up unopened in the White House mailroom. Kennedy, General Clifton stressed, "didn't want any situation developing whereby a plea of clemency by Bennett, or in his behalf, would be lost or, worse yet, would be received at the White House and not opened until after the execution if it should take place."

General Todd responded that outgoing prisoner mail from Fort Leavenworth was routinely inspected. They could easily monitor Bennett. They would do so, with the generals agreeing that this "should be held rather closely."

General Todd phoned Colonel Cox at Fort Leavenworth. He advised the prison commandant that "all information and instructions he was about to receive were to be held very closely and not to be disseminated beyond absolute necessity." He specifically directed the commandant to "telephone me immediately" if Bennett wrote "the President, the Vice President, any members of the Cabinet, the Secretary of Defense, the Secretary of the Army," or any other top Washington officials.

Colonel Cox replied that since being told he would die on April 13, Bennett had only written his lawyer. But the commandant added that he had "a feeling Bennett would get his lawyers to submit a plea for clemency to someone."

Who though, Colonel Cox could only shrug. "I don't know," he told General Todd.

Others defended the prisoner, as more mail reached the White House. His case never came near to sparking the kind of public outcry for some of the white death row prisoners. But the local papers around Leavenworth had run a brief item reporting that Bennett's execution was approaching, and that spurred a little interest. "In Leavenworth prison is a young soldier by the name of Bennett, awaiting execution next month," Mina S. Reed of Kansas City, Missouri, wrote March 11. "I do not know him, have never seen him. I am white and he is negro. But he seems to have no friends."

Four days later, on March 15, Bennett sent an airmail letter to his lawyer saying the prison's legal office had urged him to seek additional help "right away" from the JAG's defense division. The letter is difficult to read, but Bennett added a postscript: "Please over look this bad writing. I write this way when I first get up and in a hurry."

Colonel Cox forwarded a copy of the inmate's legal correspondence to General Todd. The next day, Jerry Williams wrote to Washington and asked for help from army defense lawyers assigned to the JAG office. He was desperate for someone "who has more experience in this field than I have had." His letter officially put Washington on notice: a plea for clemency was coming.

"I have exhausted legal remedies in this man's behalf," Williams wrote in a short March 22 note to Kennedy, three weeks before Bennett's execution date. "There is no remedy under the law, that I can find, that can change the sentence, except through Your Honor's power of commutation."

Nine days later, on March 31, Williams sent his formal petition for presidential clemency to the White House. "If anything I may say could possibly aid you in your consideration of this case my time is yours to command." He included his office and home telephone numbers. "Time is of the essence," he pleaded.

The petition was not long, just fourteen pages. Williams signed it, along with two JAG lawyers. They chronicled Bennett's troubled childhood and his welcome into the army despite his "very limited intelligence." He may have been suffering from epilepsy that night in Austria, they alleged, a trance that made him "stop and stare," exacerbated by heavy drinking. His lineage was marked by relatives who had committed suicide, succumbed in state mental wards, or struggled with chronic mental illness.

The lawyers contrasted Bennett with the white soldier Isaac Hurt who raped and brutally stabbed to death a five-year-old girl in Okinawa. Eisenhower commuted Hurt yet insisted Bennett must die. "The two were imprisoned together on death row for almost five years," the legal team wrote. "Hurt's life has now been spared; Bennett's life still is in jeopardy." How could this happen? "A fundamental principal of an honest judicial system must be equal justice for all," they believed.

The lawyers argued against the finality of the death penalty, against its anguish, too. "Twice Bennett was prepared for execution, twice he faced the grim specter of impending death, twice he was rescued at the last minute." Until his arrest, he had been a "quiet, pleasant and cooperative" soldier. His performance reports rated him "excellent." Even on death row under the prison Castle, he "has been no problem to the authorities," the lawyers maintained. "For the past six years John Bennett has proven that he deserves to live." To die now "would do nothing other than waste a life." Should not his life matter, rather than end with the thrust of a knotted rope one minute past midnight?

"The actual hanging will occur in the dark of the night and will be observed only by the reluctant official witnesses . . . ," the lawyers wrote. "It will be a private affair. It will pass unnoticed except by the grieving parents and family."

The attorneys ended with a prayer. They cited "psychiatrists, the clergymen, and many others" at Fort Leavenworth who awaited "with hope and fear, your word from the White House." Alone on death row "sits John himself, wondering if his life is to be snuffed out on the thirteenth of April. All of these people wait, and wonder and pray that John Bennett's life shall be spared. Mr. President, they can do no more. The decision is up to you."

In a separate letter, Bennett begged President Kennedy for his life. His letter left the prison a little after two in the afternoon of March 31, bound by airmail for the White House. He recalled four hundred "prominent doctors, lawyers, prosecutors and other families of Salzburg, Austria," who protested his death sentence. The girl today "was quite healthy," he said, as death hovered over him, the sentence harsh, and the punishment uneven, when only white soldiers were saved. "I want to live my life, Mr. President, even if it is in prison. I regret and repent the crime and I think the penalty is too severe in the light of justice and the others who have been commuted."

In Virginia, Katherine sank beyond despair. "All this time I have prayed and worked hard to do everything I possible [sic] knew to help him and have his life spared," she wrote Kennedy. "I do not ask that he is freed from this crime, [sic] but I do feel that the punishment is too severe." She pleaded, "If this sentence is carried into action, I do not see that I can continue in life." Lee White replied on April 10, just three days before the scheduled hanging. The presidential counselor however offered little hope, offering only that "I know this is difficult for you."

Exella Bennett of Chatham implored the president to spare her brother-in-law: "I do believe you have a heart, and are one of God's men . . . You are the only one can help him now." White did not have much assurance for her either, except to say that her views and those of others "will be taken into account."

Cold, dreary March gave way to a warm, sunny April in the prison yard. At the old army post at Fort Leavenworth, a wisp of hope lifted above the river bluffs. Bennett was back outside, arching his back and firing his arm at those unrelenting prison walls.

Lee White did not give up either. By April 3, he grew increasingly intrigued with an assertion in the clemency plea stating the victim "desires that Bennett's life be spared" and "requested mercy." As a death penalty opponent, White wondered how Williams could know that. JAG officials phoned Bennett's lawyer, but Williams admitted he had had "no direct communication from the victim." He had been trying to reach the advocate Elise Demus Moran in Austria for the past week, he told them, only to learn she had since died. Some in the JAG office began to think it important to find the girl; what were her feelings? "Contact could be made with victim," they advised, "if more time available." The army continued to prepare for the execution. It secured a phone line between Washington and the prison for the overnight hours of April 12–13.

Over the next three days, Lee White and General Todd debated whether Bennett's life was worth saving. In a series of remarkable phone conversations, as recorded in White House logs, they wondered how much further Kennedy should be pressed to spare Bennett's life.

"We've got a disagreeable little problem over here," White began on the late morning of April 5. "There is no legal burden on President Kennedy to review this case." And he added that "the president said he would not have any strong feelings that there should not be capital punishment in certain cases."

The president had told him, "I just don't want to get into this one." White explained to Todd, "He was saying that he was not going to upset the scheduled execution."

There remained "the girl," though. Bennett and Austrian protesters maintained she suffered "no permanent" damage. Did she really now want John Bennett to live? "If the girl feels that way," White believed, "it's a lot different than hearing it from somebody else." Find her, he instructed General Todd. "Soon."

"I am thinking it makes some difference to the President," White explained. He also wanted clarity on which soldiers were hanged. "Could [we] find out whether these boys were negroes?" he asked General Todd. "Last thing I would want to do is let this boy out because he is colored." He seemed to be worrying about any political backlash again, specifically how the public would react if Bennett was spared just to treat him like the white soldiers.

General Todd ordered army units in Austria to start searching for the girl and her family. He and White spoke again that day at 4:35. General Todd reported that the army's search was underway but likely to take at least another day. He also acknowledged to White that only black soldiers had been hanged at Fort Leavenworth. "With respect to race, all of those executed were negro," the general confirmed.

"Gosh, terrible," White replied. He added, "I assume negro soldiers are more difficult because of education and have leanings toward getting into trouble."

"That's true," agreed General Todd. "But it's something that without hard and fast statistics you just can't talk about."

They discussed again the urgency to find the girl and her parents. "I think," the general offered, "if the girl comes in favorable to them, it might favor clemency."

They were back on the phone at 9:30 the following morning, April 6. There was still no word from Europe, still nothing from the girl or her family. "I will let you know when we hear," the general promised.

The next day, they conferred at 11:25 a.m., April 7. "Four o'clock over there and the man sent to Salzburg had not returned," General Todd groused to Lee White. "So he is either having difficulty locating the girl or in getting a statement. We have nothing yet. And I'm having people alerted over the weekend so if anything comes in I can call you."

General Todd said one thing more, imploring the White House not to drag this out and make a final decision over life or death on Bennett's last day. "If you decide to do anything, it's a good idea not to wait until the last minute. It's pretty brutal to do it that way."

White understood.

Army Secretary Stahr notified the White House and Jerry Williams in Virginia that he had read the clemency petition but found "nothing in the new material warranting commutation." JAG headquarters began composing a formal letter of rejection for Private Bennett. Early the next day, the army's Southern Area Command in Munich, Germany, rushed a lengthy telegram to Washington. Army Captain Thomas F. Shea at last had located the girl and had not only talked to her but her parents as well. Some of their words were garbled by army wire operators hurrying to type the telegrams, much of it due to translation problems and the haste to transmit the statements. Munich promised to airmail the family's cleaned-up written statements later that day. But for now there was no mistaking their feelings.

"I have no objection to a commutation . . . ," announced the girl's father, the Austrian gendarme in broken English. "I know how hwrd it is for the pwrents when their own child is so close to the verge of death; it may be just as hard for the parents and relatives of the convicted Bennett . . . May daughter still suffers mental and physical pains so that rzpeated medical assistance is required. She will still have to qndergo another operation." He asked the Americans for financial help "in order to obtain further medical treatmenth for my daughter to enablz her to recover and have her health restored."

His wife agreed. "If a mother is asked to consent to a death sentence, she will say no. However, as a result of this crimz my daughter has been ruined physically and mentally for her entire life. I suffer terribly with my only child. Bennett's dath cannot give us back her health and therefore I do not object to a milder sentence. I would only have the desire thwt nothing mor should be said about the past and that no further big articles be written in the newspapers. It hurts immensely to be reminded of this terrible occurrence again and again."

She asked that the family's sentiments be "treated strictly confidential." Otherwise, "it would undoubtedly further impair Gertrude's hewlth because since the crime had been committed upon her, she has had to suffer contpnuously severely, both physically and mentally."

Even Gertie, now seventeen, felt that the execution of John Bennett would change nothing. "I consent to a commutation of the sentence since even his execution could not eradicate what has happened." But, she insisted, "In the event the convicted should ever be released from prison, I request that as long as he lives he never be permitted to return to Europe again."

White rushed the telegram consenting to Bennett's life and the army secretary's recommendation for death to President Kennedy's desk. "I recall how amazed I was that he had retained virtually every fact and point we had gone over in the first meeting," White later recalled. "He examined the new materials, discussed them extensively, stood up, paced for a bit."

White made another personal pitch for clemency. Again he recommended that Bennett be spared the gallows and resentenced to life in prison.

Kennedy stopped him. "But you don't approve of the death sentence in any situation," he said.

"That's right," White responded. Looking up at his boss, he conceded that this "crime was so heinous it could warrant the death sentence" even though the victim survived. But only, he stipulated, if "one had no basic problem with the death penalty."

Kennedy walked the room some more, still thinking. Finally he pivoted and announced he was not going to reverse Eisenhower. The death sentence would stand.

White stood to leave. He could think of nothing more to say.

"Clearly it was not an easy decision," the president's aide would long remember. "How could it be when a human life rested on that decision?"

Chapter Ten

* * * * * * *

MIDNIGHT

"After thoroughly considering all aspects of the case, it was the President's view that he should not intervene," White wrote Jerry Williams.

"Your own efforts and the concern evidenced by the petition which you submitted are deeply appreciated," he said of all of the work and time the Virginia lawyer had dedicated trying to save Bennett. For the attorney, though, the news was bitter; again he was losing a black defendant to the white man's gallows.

The Kennedy adviser also composed a short note for the prisoner, John Bennett: "It was the President's decision that he should not change the sentence imposed by the court-martial, approved by President Eisenhower and sustained by all of the military and civilian courts which have considered your case."

Late at night, the commandant Colonel Weldon Cox delivered the sealed envelope to Bennett's cell. "He read it and showed no great concern," Colonel Birch remembered of Bennett's reaction. But "because of the contents of the letter," the commandant immediately ordered the death row soldier transferred to Eight Base, the final holding cell before an execution. The soldier gathered a few personal belongings, and guards led him away. He would never again see death row or the cell that had been home these last six years.

Bennett did ask permission to make two phone calls, one to his lawyer and the other to Dr. Karl Menninger. The psychiatrist agreed to ask this second White House to reconsider, and this time he felt he had more pull—he had met Kennedy and had supported him for president.

Death was three days away when Menninger sent his telegram on April 10 to the White House, just as Kennedy was throwing out the ceremonial first pitch at the Washington Senators home opener to launch the 1961 baseball season.

"It distresses me to add to the president's concerns," Menninger wired Lee White. "But I importune him now on behalf of an undistinguished epileptic Negro soldier . . . Although no murder was committed he was sentenced to death . . . which is now scheduled for this Wednesday at Leavenworth's Disciplinary Barracks. He telephoned me yesterday from the death row begging me to wire you." The psychiatrist called it "unworthy of even military justice to hang an epileptic man for a non-seditious, non-murderous offense." In an effort to appeal to Kennedy as a former World War II sailor, Menninger noted that the navy had executed no one in more than a hundred years.

"I urge you to strike a conspicuous blow for more civilized penal methods, more scientific treatment of offenders and more nearly equitable treatment of Negroes." He told White, "I beg you to bring these thoughts to the attention of the president for his reconsideration not for the sake of John Bennett but for the sake of all the rest of us whom official executions never benefit and always degrade."

White responded crisply, "As I am sure you know, the sentence was approved by President Eisenhower and consequently the question that faced the President was whether he wished to intervene and change the sentence." Kennedy, he said, "will not intervene."

That Monday marked Bennett's twenty-fifth birthday. Prison guards presented him with a white cake from the upstairs kitchen, and prison guards started the final forty-eight-hour deathwatch. "He has stood up very well and shows no change after having been informed of the presidential decision," reported psychiatrist Captain George Berry. Colonel Birch, now back at JAG headquarters, praised the prisoner's resilience. "Bennett has firm hopes that clemency will be exercised," the captain reported, "despite the letter from the White House."

In Virginia, Williams began to falter as the hours ticked down. "I don't know where else to turn," he conceded to a local Danville newspaper after reading and rereading Lee White's letter of rejection. Bennett phoned him later in the day on Tuesday, April 11, and Williams warned him his odds were slim. The prisoner sounded hopeful nonetheless. He reminded his attorney that twice before he had been heartbeats from the gallows and never gave up.

"The last time," Bennett exclaimed, "I'd already eaten the last meal."

Wednesday, April 12, dawned on what the army, the White House, and the prison commandant expected would be Bennett's last. For his final meal, Bennett ordered shrimp with cocktail sauce, along with "hot rolls or biscuits, cake of any kind, fresh [or] frozen peaches, and milk and coffee"—to be served at four in the afternoon at his cell on Eight Base. In the power plant, technicians tested and retested the secure phone line to Washington. The commandant's office reserved an ambulance from the local Larkin funeral home, "with attendants permitted to enter the West Gate after the trap has sprung." The fort also wired Bennett's parents for instructions regarding their son's remains. The army would provide a metal casket; the family wanted him shipped home.

Bennett awoke that morning to rain pattering against the Castle walls. Thunder was rumbling in from the western plains. It was the kind of storm Bennett had feared all his life. He again wired President Kennedy. "I am taking this opportunity in the name of 'God' and the president, to make appeal in my behalf while I still have a few hours left," he pleaded. "Mr. President I beg you in the name of God to you to reconsider my case and have mercy upon me and spare my life. Because I haven't kill anyone therefore I should not be killed. The Old Testament only asks for an Eye for an Eye.' Will you please in the name of God and mercy spare my life." He signed it, "John A. Bennett."

Mail was still arriving at the White House gates. Three civil rights lawyers in Kansas, including Elisha Scott, wired the White House. "Pontius Pilate could have saved Jesus Christ from execution," they admonished. "We ask you to use your power to grant a stay to save the life of John Bennett." They cited "newly discovered evidence" and implored "that this child should not die without further consideration and investigation." At JAG headquarters in Washington, two army defense lawyers desperately compiled a second clemency petition; couldn't the White House wait until a legislative proposal abolishing the death penalty was heard on Capitol Hill?

Captain Berry again examined Bennett. "Sane, no evidence of a psychotic disorder," the psychiatrist confirmed.

Captain Thomas Carter prayed with him several times throughout the day, finding Bennett still hopeful. "He felt a special rightness with God, that God was giving him dying grace," the chaplain recalled.

Joseph Thompson, the black social worker, spoke to him several times down on Eight Base. "He said he hoped he could go like a man," Thompson remembered. "We shook hands." Driving home that evening over the small river hills toward Topeka, Thompson struggled with his sadness. "How young he is," he thought. "How they all were so young on death row."

Master Sergeant Orvill Lawson, who had built the army gallows and would head up this night's execution detail, reported to work early and headed straight for the prison records office. For the second day in a row, he pulled up a chair and poured down the coffee. For four hours, he rummaged through Bennett's case file. Smoking one cigarette after another, he read the court-martial transcript, the confession, and the psychiatric assessments. The sergeant hated child molesters; if he had caught Bennett in the act, he likely would have killed him "on the spot" in that icy stream. And yet he felt that if he had been on that army jury in Austria six years ago, he would have voted for life. After helping to hang war criminals in Japan and marching black soldiers to their deaths in Kansas, time had softened Sergeant Lawson. There was no murder here, no eye for an eye; Bennett was right about that. "But who do I tell now?" Lawson wondered.

Master Sergeant William Maddox had been there all morning too. He would stay all day and night, "until the job is done." The hangman came early because, this time, he wanted an assistant. He approached a sergeant known around Fort Leavenworth as an atheist. They met in the Castle rotunda, and when he explained why he needed help, the man "about went crazy," Sergeant Maddox recalled. "He flat-out refused."

When Maddox visited Bennett on Eight Base, Bennett was accommodating enough to stand and let him measure his height, weight, and neck size. To test his gear, Maddox hung a 210-pound railroad cross-tie from the gallows platform in the power plant and let it dangle for thirty minutes, stretching the rope out good and tight. He would test it again an hour before midnight.

Once more Bennett reached out to Menninger, desperate to try the Kennedy White House again, but he could do no more. "I thought it was damn nice of them to let him call me up on the phone, but it was such a helpless feeling," Menninger remembered. "What do you do when a man calls you because they're going to kill him at midnight?"

Even if Menninger had called Kennedy, it was doubtful he would have gotten the president on the phone. Kennedy's secretary, Evelyn Lincoln, remembered a staggering series of crises confronting Kennedy that day. "April 12," she later would write, "was an exceedingly busy day for the President."

In a stunning triumph, Russia launched the first man into space and returned him safely home that morning. A chagrined Kennedy tipped his hat to his Soviet adversary. "It is a most impressive scientific accomplishment," conceded the leader of the Free World.

During an hour-long press conference Kennedy denied rumors that the United States was immersed in a secret mission to retake Cuba from Fidel Castro. "Under no conditions," he insisted, would the United States assist in bringing about the dictator's fall. But in a Cabinet Room meeting at 5:45 p.m., Kennedy confidentially signaled his approval of the Bay of Pigs invasion, a scheme first mapped out under the Eisenhower administration. Kennedy emphasized that the clandestine assault must be seen as "an entirely Cuban affair." Five days later, as a result of his refusal to provide American air cover, more than a hundred people would die on the shores of the Caribbean island.

Kennedy also met at length on April 12 with visiting Chancellor Konrad Adenauer and pledged continued support for West Germany. Pressed over mounting fears that the Communist bloc had outflanked the United States in Western Europe, the president affirmed his resolve in the face-off over Berlin. "These dictatorships enjoy many short-range advantages," Kennedy announced in a press conference that day. "My feeling is that we are more durable in the long run."

The president also confronted divisions at home. April 12 marked the one-hundredth anniversary of the start of the Civil War in an America where deep, ragged fissures still split politics and culture. In Charleston, South Carolina, ceremonies erupted in anger when New Jersey's first black assemblywoman, Madaline A. Williams, was barred from festivities at the Francis Marion Hotel. Kennedy threatened to move the gala to a US naval base. He was speaking heatedly from the press podium in a room filled mostly with white reporters, where even the White House News Photographers Association did not admit black cameramen. Asked about that affront, Kennedy chastised the press photographers' organization. "I hope they will let everyone in," he said.

Kennedy's decision about John Bennett's execution lay several days behind him. In the midst of what would later be seen as a pivotal moment in his presidency, he showed no interest in or found any time to revisit it. Two years later, at a White House dinner party in April 1963, he discussed the death penalty with his friend, *Newsweek's* Washington bureau chief, Ben Bradlee. Kennedy mentioned the Bennett case.

"It turned out we were all against capital punishment except the president," Bradlee later wrote. "I asked him about the Catholic precept against taking a life . . . and he said that he saw no conflict." Kennedy, Bradlee added, "didn't seem to equate execution with the taking of a life in the doctrinal sense." Bradlee, however, misreported several key facts: he wrote that Bennett had been based in Germany, that the girl had been raped twice, and that Bennett had "killed her." It seems either Bradlee misremembered or that Kennedy embellished the circumstances of the case.

In the Fort Leavenworth subbasement, Bennett knew nothing of the tumult far away on the East Coast. Down on Eight Base, all he could hear were the thunderclaps closing in against the Castle walls. He was frightened as he watched streaks of lightning light up a high window. Sergeant R. W. Pinson came in around 3 p.m. and sat with him until his shift ended at 11:30. "He was up walking around, he was sure that a third time would be a charm," the sergeant recalled. "He was upbeat, jolly."

For ten minutes, they let him phone his sister Katherine. "I heard him holler for her to speak up," Sergeant Pinson remembered. "He was laughing and felt good. He was happy. He was smiling." Katherine put one of their brothers on the line, too.

"I told him that I loved him and how much I hoped he was saved," she recalled. He told her, "Sister, don't worry about that now. I've got a Bible here." He quoted from the book; he had been studying religious courses. He told her, "I've been born again."

His last meal arrived cold and late, the shrimp and cocktail sauce, the biscuits, the cake, the peaches, the milk and coffee. But Bennett could not eat. "You can have it," he offered, pushing the plates to Sergeant Pinson. Bennett did taste the coffee and then lay back on his bunk. Remnants of his birthday cake sat untouched nearby.

At nightfall, an officer appeared with the final reply to Bennett's last telegram. The officer opened the envelope and read the message from Lee White. The answer again was no, the president's decision remained "unchanged."

Sergeant Pinson recalled, "It knocked the wind out of him. He went to pieces. That's when I saw him cry." Chaplain Carter returned in a hurry, and Sergeant Pinson continued to fume. He would have preferred one of the white death row soldiers tonight, especially Maurice Schick or Isaac Hurt. They had done far worse; they had killed children.

"That wouldn't have bothered me," the sergeant said, "but not Bennett." Thirty minutes before midnight, his shift ended, and he bolted up the stairs and out into the now heavy rain. "It was a dreary night all around. I'd seen enough death in Korea. I didn't need to see this one."

Captain Carter brought Communion bread and a sip of wine. They prayed on Bennett's bunk, but when the bed springs felt loose, they moved to the floor. Bennett leaned against a small ledge. "It would be quiet and then John wanted to pray some more, once more, again, again," the chaplain remembered. "He prayed for his mother and his sister and said, 'God help those who are to take me. They are not my enemy.'"

Eleven-fifteen passed, eleven-twenty. Bennett asked about the collapse board. Would they strap him down if his knees buckled and he could not make it to the gallows? You will be fine, the chaplain promised. God will walk with you. Just control your fears, he cautioned, or the guards "will overpower you." He offered Bennett some final advice: "You decide how you're going to die, with the dignity of your own making." And Bennett, Chaplain Carter remembered proudly, "showed real human strength."

They came for him at 11:30 p.m. The six-man army execution team ordered Bennett to stand, shower, and change into an army green, two-piece, Class A uniform without insignia, medals, or belt. Guards sipped the last of the cold coffee as Bennett flung a final Camel into the toilet. Sergeant Lawson strapped a leather belt around the prisoner's waist, forcing his arms down and handcuffing his wrists in front. He pulled black slippers over Bennett's trembling feet. At a quarter before midnight, the team synchronized their watches. Sergeant Lawson leaned into the prisoner. "This is the hour," he told Bennett. "It's time to go." He radioed the power plant. "We're leaving."

They marched outside in army formation, three to a side, Chaplain Carter in front, the prisoner in the middle. In thin blue army slickers and pointed caps, the execution detail sloshed through the drenching April rain, the prison yard a mire of mud and puddles. The chaplain read from Corinthians and Psalm 23, "Even though I walk through the valley of the shadow of death." His Bible in one hand, a pen light in the other, he shouted above the wind and rain. Bennett shivered and at first answered back, his eyes fixed ahead. Gray chalky smoke wafted from the power plant chimney, drawing them nearer.

Staff Sergeant Richard Curtsinger was thinking how Bennett "would sometimes talk about his home and about Virginia and the cotton fields. From where he came, black or white, you were either rich or you picked cotton, and this kid certainly had come from the poor part of the world."

First Sergeant Ken Kramer noticed that Bennett had stopped praying. "He's been prepared for this for so long he's kind of already gone, maybe," Kramer thought. "But we can't get there too early. We have timed this and it's a very slow walk and he isn't saying a word."

Sergeant Lawson wondered, too: "We're walking with him, whatever pace he wants to go. Really, he's leading us."

High in a control tower, Private Robert Dresden could make out next to nothing in the rain and swirling fog, just the slap of boots and mud.

In another turret, Master Sergeant Holsey K. Mills shook his head as a soldier sprinted across the yard and pressed his eyes against a power plant window, trying to peer inside. "Disgusting," the tower guard muttered.

The heavy plant door swung open. Inside, the commandant, the hangman, official witnesses, and three newspaper reporters huddled against the chilled air. James J. Fisher with the *Kansas City Times*, a year younger than Bennett, was instantly struck by the prisoner's gray pallor. "He looked fearful, like a little boy with watery eyes," Fisher thought. He guessed he was sixteen years old, maybe seventeen. A former prison guard in the Marines, Fisher earlier had spotted the Pontiac hearse parked out front, glistening wet.

"I wish to make a last statement," Bennett announced. His voice was thin but clear, and heartfelt. "I want to take this last opportunity to thank you and all of your staff, whoever they may be, for all your help and all you have done for me and all the things you have tried to do for me." He turned directly to the commandant, Colonel Cox. "May God have mercy on your soul," he said.

In a blur, they rushed Bennett into the arms of the army hangman.

"He got disoriented at first," Sergeant Maddox recalled.

"He looked around and back and forth. But he didn't flinch; his eyes didn't break like he recognized me. The last words he was saying were, 'Where is the chaplain? Where is the chaplain?' and the last person he saw was me. And he wasn't shaking. He wasn't stumbling. He wasn't lurching over. He was calm, as calm as you can be when you know you're going to die, and he had known that for a god awful time."

Sergeant Maddox took Bennett's arm and centered his feet on two black spots over the trap door. He covered his head and tightened the rope. A brief silence, and then everyone remembered what sounded like another rip of thunder or a tree falling, a gunshot, a bolt lock, or a cracking noise, a harsh splintering of wood. Fisher gripped a side railing. He closed his eyes and dropped his head. The newspaperman felt embarrassed; he could not watch.

"It was so loud," he remembered, "because it was so quiet at midnight."

POSTSCRIPT

"Someone said, 'Can we smoke?'" Fisher recalled, "and we all lit up." Sergeant Kramer made it home first, but could not sleep, even after several stiff drinks. "You remember the jerking and the gyrations."

Sergeant Lawson went away angry. "It was not for murder; it was rape," he kept berating himself.

Chaplain Carter sat on his Fort Leavenworth porch, watching the last of the rain and river ice. A man in Russia flew to the heavens in the morning; tonight in Kansas, a man fell to his death. "John's execution was measured and ordered down to the last detail," the minister reflected. Army precision won out. "How cold it is," he thought.

Jerry Williams sat by the phone well after midnight, his house in Danville sadly quiet, his children careful not to disturb their father as the hour grew late. When the call at last came, the news he expected jarred him nonetheless. "It left him very disappointed in President Kennedy," remembered his son Robert.

"I went home and I went to bed," declared the hangman. He took with him the official Order of Execution, a souvenir from when the army last hanged one of its own at Fort Leavenworth. "Those things are hard to come by, you know."

Under the new day's morning sun, Mack Coles, a Bennett cousin, was tending tobacco when word swept the Virginia fields that John had died. "A black man and a white girl," Coles said shrugging. "Nothing you could do about it. They'd lynch you just for whipping a mule too hard."

The local newspaper complained that afternoon not that native son John Bennett was dead but because the army, the courts, and official Washington were slow in ending his life. "Six Years Is Too Long," griped the Danville *Bee*.

The train from Kansas chugged into the Chatham depot carrying his metal coffin and belongings, what Katherine remembered as a "trunk addressed to our mother." It included $5.82 from his prison account, plus handkerchiefs, washcloths, a tobacco pouch, a Bible, a rosary and prayer books, eyeglasses, and a three-cent postage stamp—all that remained from a life on death row. They drove him out to the Triumph Baptist Church cemetery on Fairview Road. The family could not afford a headstone, so they left a rock to mark the spot, a familiar custom among poor blacks in this rural swath of old Virginia. Over the years, the rock broke apart, either crumbled and worn down by rain and the harsh Southern sun or kicked away by children playing in the area.

Mack Coles, who became the cemetery trustee, could no longer tell where Private First Class John Bennett is buried.

EPILOGUE

Nearly six decades have passed since Private John Bennett's life came to an end at the bottom of an army rope. And in all these nearly sixty years, Fort Leavenworth has not carried out another execution. More soldiers on the army's death row have come and gone, and the old Castle was torn down and a new modern prison built, but the executions, at least so far, have stopped.

More significant is how the army's deeply flawed experiment with race and justice through the late 1950s and into early 1961 foreshadowed what was to come for inmates and punishment around this country—in state prisons, federal penitentiaries, and army brigs. Bennett remains the last of the soldiers put to death. But he is far from being the last black man—guilty or not—to face a criminal justice system stacked heavily against him.

In Bennett's time, black soldiers condemned to die were largely overlooked. Few people came to their defense, and the men themselves were forgotten, slotted away in small death row cells. The white men, however, repeatedly benefited from government officials seemingly blind to equal treatment. Army officers, military judges, Washington lawmakers, and the White House granted them not just hope but eventually commutations and, once again, their freedom. In stretching the limits to spare these white lives, government officials seemed to suggest the white prisoners were more human.

That dual system continues to thrive today.

The intervening years since Bennett's hanging have brought harsh new legislation that has sent a disproportionate number of young black and

Hispanic men to prison for the same crimes committed by white men. Tough federal sentencing guidelines, the 1990s war on crack cocaine, and popular "Three Strikes" laws are the main culprits. Ongoing efforts to seal the Mexican border have cast another wide net. The result is that people with little education or money and no political or legal contacts, much like the black soldiers on death row years ago, today fill prison tiers from Maine to California.

In many states, the penitentiaries are severely overcrowded. The situation is critical. Federal and state corrections officials have pleaded for more funds and more beds for more prisoners, yet inmates keep pouring in, a disconcerting percentage of them minorities. Instead of trying to defuse the crisis, many states have turned to private prison operators to handle the overflow.

President Obama tried to ease some of the overcrowding with a series of prison commutations for low-end offenders. President Trump has taken a different approach, pardoning a political ally here, releasing the friend of a celebrity there. And at the border, children are separated from their parents as migrant families press to reach the United States. There is little serious public discussion about the fairness of who gets released from prison and who does not.

It certainly was not recognized as an unfair system in the 1950s. What happened at Fort Leavenworth went largely unacknowledged, nor was it protested by the early leaders of the civil rights movement. They were consumed with larger issues: integrating the schools, securing fair housing and equal job opportunities. Today's generation of civil rights leaders are waging active campaigns and targeting lobbying efforts to see that all prisoners are treated alike. They hope to reform the harsh inequities in how criminal charges are filed, what kind of juries are impaneled, and when maximum sentences are appropriate. Their efforts are, in many ways, the next barricade to overcome in the fight for equal justice.

Odell Waller, the black sharecropper executed in 1942 who happened to be from Bennett's hometown, spoke this truth in his written "Dying Statement": "The penitentiary all over the United states are full of people ho [who] was pore. ... They are in prison for life that's what happens to the poor people." His words were semiliterate, but they resound with clarity and foreboding today, a warning that the nation's prisons were filling up with the poor.

Reform will not be easy. Especially not for death row men.

As of this writing, October 2018, four death row soldiers are locked up in the new Fort Leavenworth prison, awaiting their own fates. And if the army executes again, it likely will be by lethal injection, not at Fort Leavenworth but rather inside the US Bureau of Prisons death row chamber at Terre Haute, Indiana.

One of the current death row soldiers raped and murdered women in the mid-1980s around Fort Bragg, North Carolina. For thirty years he has lingered on death row, pursuing his legal appeals through the military courts and up to the US Supreme Court. He first was brought to the old Castle; now he cells on the new death row in the updated facility. Among the other three soldiers, one has done thirteen years; he killed two officers in a 2003 rifle and hand grenade attack in Kuwait in the run-up to the US invasion of Iraq. Another soldier killed thirteen people in the Fort Hood, Texas, shooting in 2009. The fourth man was sentenced to die in 2010 for stabbing to death a mother and two of her daughters in Fayetteville, North Carolina.

Of these four US Army soldiers awaiting military justice today, three of them are men of color.

ACKNOWLEDGMENTS

My heart goes out to Gertie and her parents, and the Bennett family, too. It was especially difficult and sometimes wrenching for Katherine and Ira to reopen those old wounds with me, something at first they understandably did not want to do. I will be forever grateful for their help.

Thank you also to the dozens of prison guards, army officers, psychologists, chaplains, lawyers, and others in and out of uniform who so vividly recalled Fort Leavenworth and the lives of the men on Seven Base. All were generous with their time and patience, and that includes the hangman, Bill Maddox.

The Jerry Williams family in southern Virginia helped memorialize their father and his drive and commitment during those tough David-versus-Goliath times. The world is better for men like him.

Research assistants at the Library of Congress, the National Archives, and the Eisenhower and Kennedy presidential libraries were always professional. So too were military archivists in providing Bennett's court-martial transcript, his investigative case files, and reams of internal prison records from death row, all of it invaluable. Many other materials were retrieved from the army's personnel records center in St. Louis, others from the military and federal appeals courts.

This journey has taken me down a long road, one where I was blessed to have Beacon Press see me to the end. My agent Ronald Goldfarb and Beacon's senior editor Rakia Clark have made the best of traveling companions.

NOTE ON SOURCES

Much of the written material for this book came from these key research institutes:

+ The United States Army Criminal Investigation Command's Crime Records Center in Falls Church, Virginia, housed the military police file on Private John Bennett's arrest, witness statements, and a court-martial transcript of his trial at Camp Roeder in Austria.
+ The Fort Leavenworth Disciplinary Barracks in Kansas collected and saved voluminous documents from Bennett's life on death row, including monthly progress reports, social reviews, personal histories, mental examinations, and medical records, down to his dental charts and fingerprints. Also, on file were Judge Advocate General records, communiqués, correspondence, letters, and telegrams from, to, and about Bennett and three Orders of Execution.
+ At the Dwight D. Eisenhower Library in Abilene, Kansas, individual prison records for the death row soldiers are kept, along with letters and other correspondence and, most importantly, internal White House reports and recommendations detailing the president's decision-making process.
+ The John F. Kennedy Library in Boston, Massachusetts, stores material concerning how the president and his top White House staff debated Bennett's prison fate.

+ The Law Library at the Library of Congress in Washington, DC, maintains the *Court-Martial Reports, Holdings and Decisions of the Judge Advocates General Boards of Review and United States Court of Military Appeals*—multiple volumes covering the crimes, arrests, trials, and military appeals for all those on the army's death row in the late 1950s. The Main Reading Room of the Library of Congress provides a trove of material on Fort Leavenworth, and the nation's struggle over race and capital punishment in the 1950s.

+ The National Archives in Washington, DC, keeps the records of those prisoners who were spared from execution, covering their post-death row lives inside other prisons around the country, as well as their efforts for clemency and parole.

+ The Ike Skelton Combined Arms Research Library at Fort Leavenworth retains invaluable records and histories of the fort, the prison, and iconic photographs of the old "Castle" before it was torn down.

+ The National Personnel Records Center near St. Louis, Missouri, is the home for records of US Armed Forces personnel. Although the facility was heavily damaged by fire in 1973, material for many of those sent to death row sixty years ago survived.

REFERENCES

Chapter One: Army Justice

Private First Class John A. Bennett's military history, including with his arrest, trial, and imprisonment, were found in his army personnel file, military police records, court-martial transcripts, and prison documents.

Private Louis Suttles's interrogation is recorded in army appellate records in *Court-Martial Reports: Holdings and Decisions of the Judge Advocates General, Boards of Review, and United States Court of Military Appeals*, Volume 8, *1952–1953*, 496–513, available at the Law Library of the Library of Congress. Suttles also testified about the alleged army police mistreatment in October 1953, in a federal court hearing in Topeka, Kansas, as reported by the *Leavenworth Times*, October 27, 1953.

Suttles's mother, Mrs. Gentry Collier, wrote to President Eisenhower on January 10, 1955; the letter is collected as part of his case file with the Eisenhower Presidential Papers.

Maurice Schick, interview with author, 1987.

James Rookard's comments about army segregation were found in David P. Colley, *The Road to Victory: The Untold Story of World War II's Red Ball Express* (New York: Open Road Integrated Media, 2014).

Secretary of War Henry Stimson's comments that enraged Representative William Dawson are from Douglas Walter Bristol Jr. and Heather Marie Stur, eds., *Integrating the US Military: Race, Gender, and Sexual Orientation Since World War II* (Baltimore: Johns Hopkins University Press, 2017), 25.

Rupert Trimmingham's letter titled "Democracy?" was published by *Yank, the Army Weekly* on April 28, 1944. Letters in response were printed on June 9 and July 28, 1944.

The Pearl Harbor heroics of navy messman Doris "Dorie" Miller are enshrined by the Naval History and Heritage Command collections at https://www.history.navy.mil/research/histories/biographies-list/bios-m/miller-doris.html.

General George Patton's speech to his black troops is recorded in Ulysses Lee, *The Employment of Negro Troops* (Washington, DC: Center of Military History, US Army, 2001), 661.

First Lady Eleanor Roosevelt's letter to the secretary of war, dated September 22, 1942, is included in Morris J. MacGregor and Bernard C. Nalty, eds., *Blacks in the United States Armed Forces, Basic Documents*, Volume V (Wilmington, DE: Scholarly Resources, 1977), 170.

FBI director J. Edgar Hoover's reaction to Mrs. Roosevelt and other civil rights advocates was found in Curt Gentry, *J. Edgar Hoover, the Man and the Secrets* (New York: W. W. Norton, 1991), 63, 301, and 441–42.

Protests by First Lieutenant Virginia Lawson and other black members of the Women's Army Corps were reported by the *Boston Globe*, March 20, 1945; *Boston Herald*, March 20, 1945; *Boston Globe*, March 21, 1945; *Boston Herald*, March 21, 1945; *New York Times*, March 21, 1945; *Boston Daily Globe*, April 4, 1945; *Boston Herald*, April 4, 1945; and *New York Times*, April 4, 1945.

Grant Reynolds's wartime reportage for the NAACP, titled "What the Negro Soldier Thinks About This War," was published in three installments in the organization's *Crisis* magazine in September, October, and November 1944.

Private James Pritchett's letter was found in Phillip McGuire, ed., *Taps for a Jim Crow Army: Letters from Black Soldiers in World War II* (Lexington: University of Kentucky Press, 1983), 23–24.

President Truman's executive order desegregating the army was printed in Morris J. MacGregor Jr., *Integration of the Armed Forces, 1940–1965* (Washington, DC: Center of Military History, United States Army, 1981), 312.

Thurgood Marshall recounted his investigation called, "Summary Justice—The Negro GI in Korea," for the NAACP's *Crisis* magazine, May 1951, 297–304 and 350–55.

Representative Adam Clayton Powell Jr.'s June 29, 1953, letter to the navy secretary was printed in Morris J. MacGregor and Bernard C. Nalty, eds., *Blacks in the United States Armed Forces, Basic Documents*, Volume XII, *Integration* (Wilmington, DE: Scholarly Resources, 1977), 301.

The Project Clear study was printed as Leo Bogart, ed., *Project Clear: Social Research and the Desegregation of the United States Army* (New Brunswick, NJ: Transaction Publishers, 1992).

Ira Bennett, author interview, 2016.

Protect Our Defenders' annual reports are at https://www.protectourdefenders.com/.

The three black death row inmates whose cases were commuted are Privates John T. Lee, Frank Harris, and Sherman Gravitt. Their cases files are discussed in depth in the *Court-Martial Reports: Holdings and Decisions of the Judge Advocates General, Boards of Review, and United States Court of Military Appeals*, available at the Library of Congress—Volume 14, *1953–1954*, 368–75, and Volume 16, *1954*, 145–50, for Lee; Volume 21, *1956*, 58–67, for Harris; and Volume 15, *1953–1954*, 674–92, and Volume 17, *1954*, 249–59, for Gravitt. Their cases can be further reviewed among the Eisenhower Presidential Papers at his research library in Abilene, Kansas.

Colonel Leonard Becicka, author interview, 2016.

Chapter Two: Austria

The recollections of Austrian citizens and American soldiers were collected by army military police in the wake of the sexual assault outside the US Army's Camp Roeder. Their testimony is also included in the official transcript from Bennett's army court-martial. Author interviews with other witnesses and soldiers who were there filled in additional details.

A legal review of Bennett's crime, arrest, interrogation, trial, and military appeals is at *Court-Martial Reports: Holdings and Decisions of the Judge Advocates General, Boards of*

Review, and United States Court of Military Appeals, Volume 21, *1956*, 223–28, available at the Law Library of the Library of Congress.

Sergeant Ray Lindamood, author interview, 1987.

Corporal Louis Johnson, author interview, 1986.

Lieutenant General William H. (Old Bill) Arnold's announcement to send Private Bennett to an army court-martial was carried by the *Stars and Stripes* newspaper on December 24, 1954.

The soldier who wrote home about the "long war" of occupation in Austria signed it merely as "Y.B." It was included in Ingrid Bauer and Albert Topitz, *The Encounter of the People of Austria with US Soldiers After World War II: An Austrian-American Dialogue*, a World Wide Web Project conducted in Salzburg, http://www.image-at.com/salzburg/0005.shtml.

Bill Billet's contributions in collecting funds and gifts for Austrian children were memorialized in a December 2, 1952, letter to his parents in York, Pennsylvania, signed by Major H. A. Reist at the headquarters of the Thirty-Second Statistical Services Squadron.

Major Robert Harlan Moser's recollections are drawn from Robert Harland Moser, *Past Imperfect: A Personal History of an Adventuresome Lifetime in and around Medicine* (New York: Writers Club Press, 2002), 152–95.

The army's prosecution of Private Carlos P. Johnson was covered by the *USFA Sentinel*, which served as the in-house newspaper for Camp Roeder. The guilty verdict was reported on the paper's front page of May 28, 1954.

Stefan Baier's struggles on the witness stand during Bennett's court-martial was recorded by the army's court reporter and is included in Bennett's official trial transcript.

The letter from A. Lenz was sent February 15, 1955, to the "American High Court of Justice" in Salzburg. It remains part of Bennett's official criminal case file.

President Eisenhower expressed his frustrations that it was "necessary" for Bennett to be executed during a March 9, 1960, telephone conference with Army Secretary Wilber M. Brucker. The conversation is recorded in files among the Eisenhower Presidential Papers.

Elise Demus Moran, widow of an Austrian general, wrote to the "American Military Court" on Bennett's behalf, date unknown, but most likely in February 1955.

Army Chaplain Renwick C. Kennedy's diary was quoted in William Manchester, *The Glory and the Dream: A Narrative History of America, 1932–1972*, Volume 1 (Boston: Little, Brown, 1973), 533.

The soldier's life at Camp Roeder is described in numerous articles from the post's *USFA Sentinel*, from 1950 through 1954, available at the National Archives in Washington.

Unidentified white army veteran, author interview, 2016.

For more about the Allied occupation, see Hella Pick, *Guilty Victim: Austria from the Holocaust to Haider* (London: I. B. Tauris Publishers, 2000), chapter 3; Donald R. Whitnah and Edgar L. Erickson, *The American Occupation of Austria: Planning and Early Years* (Westport, CT: Greenwood Press, 1985), and their further work, *Salzburg Under Siege: U.S. Occupation, 1945–1955* (Westport, CT: Greenwood Press, 1991); Kurt Richard Luther and Peter Pulzer, eds., *Austria 1945–95: Fifty Years of the Second Republic* (Aldershot, England: Ashgate, 1998); Hans A. Schmitt, *U.S. Occupation in Europe After World War II: Papers and Reminiscences from the April 23–24, 1976, Conference Held at the George C. Marshall Research Foundation, Lexington, Virginia* (Lawrence: Regents Press of Kansas, 1978); William Harlan Hale, "Austria Learns How to Be a Buffer

State," *Reporter*, December 22, 1953, 22–27; and Joseph Wechsberg, "The Austrians Get Austria Back," *Saturday Evening Post*, August 6, 1955, 30 and 100–102.

Major James F. Donovan's "Certificate" discussing Bennett's psychiatric evaluation is dated December 30, 1954, and written at headquarters, US Army Hospital, Salzburg. The second medical consult was written on January 13, 1955, by Major Donovan and Lieutenant Captain John R. Rollins. Second Lieutenant William J. Reid's evaluation of Bennett was recorded on January 19, 1955, for the Neuropsychiatric Service at the US Army Hospital in Frankfurt, Germany. Major Donovan C. Senter examined Bennett on January 18, 1955, for the Neuropsychiatric Service as well. Lieutenant Colonel T. A. Kiersch, chief of neuropsychiatry at Frankfurt, examined Bennett there on January 20, 1955. The three-member medical board at the US Army Hospital in Salzburg followed up with their findings on January 28, 1955. Major Robert Harlan Moser later discussed the case in his memoirs, *Past Imperfect*, 167–68.

Bennett's "confession" is recorded in an official report by Army Sergeant First Class John F. Kane, the lead investigator in the case, and taken in the hours after Bennett's arrest. Statements by Army Captain Floyd M. Wilson and his wife, Helga Wilson, were taken by military police.

Anastasia Lindamood, author interview, 1987.

Sergeant Eugene W. Cadwell, author interview, 1987.

Staff Sergeant Marvin Jacobsen, author interview, 1987.

Bennett's court-martial beginning January 31, 1955, is covered word-for-word in the official army transcript. That includes comments by the judge, lawyers, and jurors, as well as all witness testimony. In addition, the *Stars and Stripes* wrote two stories about the trial, on February 5, 1955, and February 9, 1955.

Staff Sergeant Marvin Jacobsen, author interview, 1987.

The Judge Advocate General's review is dated February 21, 1955, and attached to the start of Bennett's legal appeals record. That same day, General Arnold approved the death sentence and ordered Bennett moved temporarily to the US Army Europe Military Prison in Mannheim, Germany.

The Mannheim jail guard-turned-Fort Leavenworth hangman, Master Sergeant William H. Maddox Jr., author interview, 1987.

Chapter Three: The Castle

Henry Leavenworth's army career and early demise were highlighted in "Man for Whom Ft. Leavenworth Was Named Died 100 Years Ago Today," *Kansas City Times*, July 21, 1934. His search for a new frontier post on the Missouri River is told in the Fort Leavenworth *Lamp*, April 30, 1975.

For Fort Leavenworth history, see George Walton, *Sentinel of the Plains: Fort Leavenworth and the American West* (Englewood Cliffs, NJ: Prentice-Hall, 1973); Dr. John W. Partin, *A Brief History of Fort Leavenworth, 1827–1983* (Fort Leavenworth: US Combat Studies Institute, 1983); Elvid Hunt, *History of Fort Leavenworth, 1827–1927* (New York: Arno Press, 1979); J. Patrick Hughes, *Fort Leavenworth, Gateway to the West* (Topeka: Kansas State Historical Society, 2000); Edward R. DeZurro, "A Report on Cantonment Leavenworth," *Kansas Historical Quarterly* (November 1947): 353–59; and Arthur J. Stanley Jr., "Fort Leavenworth: Dowager Queen of Frontier Posts," *Kansas Historical Quarterly* (Spring 1976): 1–23.

Otis Wheeler's letter is reproduced in Elvid Hunt, *History of Fort Leavenworth, 1827–1927* (New York: Arno Press, 1979), 28–29.

The author John Treat Irving and artist George Catlin are quoted in Walton, *Sentinel of the Plains*, 42–43. In addition, Catlin recalls Henry Leavenworth's death on page 17 in the Walton book.

Invaluable histories of the old prison "Castle" include Henry Shindler, *History of the United States Military Prison* (Fort Leavenworth: Army Service Schools Press, 1911); Richard Whittingham, *Martial Justice: The Last Mass Executions in the U.S.* (Chicago: Henry Regnery Co., 1971), 1–11; Peter J. Grande, *Images of America: United States Disciplinary Barracks* (Mount Pleasant, SC: Arcadia Publishing, 2009); Lieutenant Colonel Ralph Herrod, "The United States Disciplinary Barracks System," *Military Law Review* (April 1960): 35–72; George V. Strong, "Administration of Military Justice at the United States Disciplinary Barracks Fort Leavenworth, Kansas," *Journal of Criminal Law and Criminology* 8, no. 3 (1917): 420–22; Peg McMahon, "Inside 'The Castle' at Fort Leavenworth," *Kansas City Star Magazine*, October 18, 1970, 17–20; Raymond R. Youngs, "A History of U.S. Army Corrections," a thesis presented to the faculty of the College of Criminal Justice, Sam Houston University, Huntsville, Texas, May 1983; Richard Farmer, "Life as a USDB Guard and Inmate During 1870–1900," a May 1, 1989, study on file at the fort's Ike Skelton Combined Arms Research Library; and Howard N. Jones, "U.S.D.B. History, June 1957," published in a prisoner publication, *Stray Shots*.

The 1919 riot at the Fort Leavenworth Castle is told in "Historical Tidbits from the U.S. Disciplinary Barracks," *Corrections Today*, December 2003, 72–76; and *Leavenworth Times*, May 22, 1919.

Colonel Weldon Cox's pronouncements can be found in his "Fort Leavenworth, Kansas, U.S.D.B." history published by the fort in 1962.

Reflections by Donald Powell Wilson are from his memoirs, *My Six Convicts: A Psychologist's Three Years in Fort Leavenworth* (New York: Rinehart & Company, 1948), 216.

Lieutenant Louis H. Diamond, author interview, 2016.

First Sergeant Kenneth Kramer, author interview, 1987.

Joan Bateman, author interview, 2016.

The 1956 escape was reported by the *Kansas City Times* on September 21, 1956, and September 22, 1956.

The escape in 1959 was reported by the *Kansas City Star* on February 13, 1959.

The March 1959 break-out was reported by the *Kansas City Times* on March 23, 1959.

The murder of Fred Alexander in 1901 was drawn from Christopher C. Lovett, "A Public Burning: Race, Sex and the Lynching of Fred Alexander," *Kansas History, a Journal of the Great Plains* (Summer 2010): 94–115.

The 1906 city bus incident involving Fort Leavenworth black soldiers was reported by the *New York Times* on December 27, 1906.

Private Charles O'Neil's arrest, trial, and commutation from death row are recounted in James J. Fisher, "Obscurity Punished the Victim," *Kansas City Times*, October 29, 1986.

The triple hanging of black soldiers at Camp Dodge, Iowa, in the summer of 1918 is told in Bill Douglas, "Wartime Illusions and Disillusionment: Camp Dodge and Racial Stereotyping, 1917–1918," State Historical Society of Iowa, *Annals of Iowa* (Spring 1998): 111–34. See also *New York Times*, July 6, 1918.

The USDB 1947 melee was reported by the *New York Times* on May 4, 1947, and the news-paper's editorial decrying segregation at the prison, "The Sweep of Prejudice," ran on May 5, 1947. The riot also is found in Youngs, "A History of U.S. Army Corrections," 48.

Levi Brandon's crime, arrest, trial, and appeals are examined in *Judge Advocate General's Department, Board of Review*, May 8, 1943, available at the Law Library of the Library of Congress. Newspaper coverage from July 26, 1943, describing his hanging, is in the Kansas City *Kansan*, and the *Leavenworth Times*, both on page 1, and the *Kansas City Star*, July 26, 1943.

Copies of the Procedure for Military Executions for 1944, 1947, 1953, and 1959 are housed at the Fort Leavenworth Prison and the Ike Skelton Combined Arms Research Library on the post grounds. Copies also are available at the Army Library at the Pentagon. See also Michelle Daniels, "Executions at the United States Disciplinary Barracks," a study on file at the Ike Skelton Combined Arms Research Library.

Neal Harrison, author interview, 2016.

The army's board of review turned down the appeals by Warrant Officer Bernard O'Brien in its opinion printed in *Court-Martial Reports: Holdings and Decisions of the Judge Ad-vocates General, Boards of Review, and United States Court of Military Appeals*, Volume 9, 1952–1953, 201–10, available at the Law Library of the Library of Congress. More material can also be found in the Eisenhower Presidential Papers, including an October 16, 1953, report from the secretary of the army to the president summarizing the case.

Master Sergeant William H. Maddox Jr., author interview, 1987.

More about the hangman Maddox can be found in John L. Ginn, *Sugamo Prison, Tokyo: An Account of the Trial and Sentencing of Japanese War Criminals in 1948 by a U.S. Partici-pant* (Jefferson, NC: McFarland & Company Publishers, 1992), 279; Jon Roe, "Execu-tioner Ready If Kansas Passes Death Penalty," *Wichita Eagle-Beacon*, January 8, 1977; and Maddox's obituary in the *Topeka Capital-Journal*, September 24, 1999.

Harrison, author interview, 2016.

Chapter Four: Seven Base

Schick, author interview, 1987.

Richard Hagelberger, author interview, 1987.

"The Green Door," performed by Jim Lowe with the High Fives, composed by Bob "Hutch" Davie and Marvin Moore, Dot Records release, 1956.

Command Sergeant Major Shirley Strange, author interview, 1987.

Master Sergeant Orvill K. Lawson, author interview, 1987.

Master Sergeant Holsey K. Mills, author interview, 1987.

Master Sergeant Thompson Biggar, author interview, 1987.

Staff Sergeant Richard C. Curstinger, author interview, 1987.

Sergeant Elgie Maiden, author interview, 1987.

Sergeant R. W. Pinson, author interview, 1987.

Staff Sergeant Ted Ray, author interview, 1987.

Captain Thomas E. Carter, author interview, 1987.

Father Anthony A. Dudek, author interview, 1987.

Frank Harris, author interview, 1987.

Joseph A. Thompson, author interview, 1987.

Sherman Gravitt, author interview, 1987.

Harris, author interview, 1987.
USDB records show Bennett arrived at the Fort Leavenworth prison on April 20, 1955, under sentence of death, and was placed in "administrative segregation custody per order of the commandant"—US Army jargon for death row.

Chapter Five: White Death Row
KUNAK
Lawson, author interview, 1987.
Kunak's murder, his trial, and his appeals are reviewed at length in *Court-Martial Reports: Holdings and Decisions of the Judge Advocates General, Boards of Review, and United States Court of Military Appeals*, Volume 10, *1953*, 198–208; Volume 17, *1954*, 346–74, and Volume 18, *1954–1955*, 361–62, all available at the Law Library of the Library of Congress. His case is further discussed in Arthur L. Hillman Jr., "Federal Criminal Law: Insanity; Reaffirmance of M'Naghten's Rule," *California Law Review* (October 1957): 538–42; and Aaron Malo, Matthew P. Barach, and Joseph A. Levin, *The Temporary Insanity Defense in California*, a Public Law Research Institute report, 1994. For more on the homicide, see "G.I., Seeking 'to Get Out,' Kills an Officer in Texas," *New York Times*, April 1, 1952; "GI Kills Officer to Get Out of Army," *Times* of San Mateo, California, April 1, 1952; and an eyewitness account, written by reporter Robert Mooney, titled "Newspaperman Tells How He Almost Was Shot When Man Shoots Officer to Get Out of Army," *Brownsville (TX) Herald*, April 1, 1952.
Maiden, author interview, 1987.
Lawson, author interview, 1987.

HAGELBERGER and VIGNEAULT
Their double homicide, separate trials, and legal appeals are reviewed in *Court-Martial Reports: Holdings and Decision of the Judge Advocates General, Boards of Review, and United States Court of Military Appeals*, Volume 9, *1952–1953*, and Volume 12, *1953*, both available in the Law Library at the Library of Congress.
Claudia Vigneault, "U.S. Soldier Guilty; Slew 2 Germans," *Daily American* (Somerset, PA), May 23, 1952.
"Has Justice Triumphed?" editorial, *Daily News* (Newport, RI), May 28, 1952.
Hagelberger's letters from death row can be found among the Eisenhower Presidential Papers at the research library in Abilene, Kansas, and in the National Archives in Washington, DC.
Curtsinger, author interview, 1987.
Maiden, author interview, 1987.
Dr. Anna L. Philbrook's letter to the Eisenhower White House is dated January 25, 1955.
Claudia Vigneault's letter to Mrs. Mamie Eisenhower is dated January 19, 1955.
Raymond E. Sullivan wrote the Eisenhower White House on February 9, 1955.
Mrs. Anna Stacy of Chula Vista, California, wrote the White House on February 7, 1955.
Vigneault's handwritten letter thanking the president for his commutation was written December 26, 1955.
The lawyer Anne Mack wrote on Hagelberger's behalf on December 26, 1955.
Sergeant Elmer Peterson, author interview, 1987.
Maiden, author interview, 1987.
Hagelberger, author interview, 1987.

Hagelberger wrote directly to Eisenhower on January 16, 1956.

Newspaper editorials: Chula Vista, California, *Star*, February 9, 1956, and *Chicago Daily Tribune*, June 5, 1956, and June 10, 1956.

Hagelberger's letters to his former high school teacher were printed January 5, 1956, in the Buffalo, New York, *Evening News*, and used by Representative John R. Pillion of New York to lobby on his behalf for a commutation.

Hagelberger, author interview, 1987.

The official President Ford pardons are stored at the National Archives in Washington, DC.

Hagelberger, author interview, 1987.

SCHICK

Schick's slaying of the young girl, his trial, and appeals are reviewed in depth in *Court-Martial Reports: Holdings and Decisions of the Judge Advocates General, Boards of Review, and United States Court of Military Appeals*, Volume 20, *1955–1956*, 209–11, Volume 21, *1956*, 343–47, and Volume 22, *1956–1957*, 209–19, all available in the Law Library at the Library of Congress. Also of note are two high court cases dealing with whether Eisenhower should have been permitted to commute Schick from death to life but also insist he never be released from prison. Titled *Schick v. Reed*, the case was argued before the US Court of Appeals, District of Columbia Circuit, on June 18, 1973, and decided July 23, 1973, and reached the Supreme Court as 419 U.S. 256 (1974). See also Washington University open scholarship, "Presidential Power of Commutation: From Death to Life Without Parole, Schick v. Reed, 483 F.2d 1266 (D.C. Cir 1973)," in *Washington University Law Quarterly* 4 (January 1973): 919–30.

Colonel Karl D. MacMillan's comments to the press were made November 27, 1953.

Curtsinger, author interview, 1987.

Ron Rothschild, author interview, 2017.

Schick, author interview, 1987.

Maiden, author interview, 1987.

Pinson, author interview, 1987.

Harris, author interview, 1987.

Phyllis Rothschild's mercy for the Schick family was announced on November 28, 1953, through a statement released by an army spokesman.

Ron Rothschild, author interview, 2017.

Jeanne Schick's comments to reporters were made on February 18, 1954.

Dr. Winfred Overholser's letter is dated December 27, 1956, and included in the Eisenhower Presidential Papers.

Schick, author interview, 1987.

Sergeant George W. Dull wrote the president on February 20, 1957. His letter is part of the Eisenhower Presidential Papers collection.

The internal debates among senior Eisenhower administration officials, as well as mental health examinations and other reviews, are part of the Eisenhower Presidential Papers collection.

Schick, author interview, 1987.

Homer Davis, author interview, 1987.

Effie Schick wrote to President Johnson on October 9, 1968. Her son's clemency petition was filed on October 11, 1968.

J. J. Parker's letter urging clemency was written April 1, 1975, and is part of Schick's case file stored by the National Archives.

the federal prison report in Pennsylvania describing Schick's "nightmares" after World War II was compiled on August 14, 1975, and is part of Schick's case file now at the National Archives.

Schick, author interview, 1987.

DUNNAHOE

The murder of the German boy in the woods, Dunnahoe's court-martial, his military appeals, and his sentence reduction from death to life are laid out in *Court-Martial Reports: Holdings and Decisions of the Judge Advocates General, Boards of Review, and and United States Court of Military Appeals*, Volume 21, *1956*, 67–83, and Volume 22, *1956–1957*, 477–82, available in the Law Library at the Library of Congress. *Stars and Stripes* reported his criminal charges on September 15, 1954, and his death sentence on September 25, 1954. Dunnahoe's home state newspapers also reported on his case: the Arkansas *Democrat* on September 24, 1954, and the Arkansas *Gazette* on September 25, 1954. The *Gazette* on April 24, 1957, and the *Kansas City Times* on April 25, 1954, noted that his life had been saved.

Schick, author interview, 1987.

Thompson, author interview, 1987.

HURT

Isaac Hurt's murder of a child in Okinawa, his trial and appeals, the public outcry, and the US Army's public response are drawn from *Court-Martial Reports: Holdings and Decisions of the Judge Advocates General, Boards of Review, and United States Court of Military Appeals*, Volume 22, *1956–1957*, 630–37, Volume 23, *1957*, 573–80, and Volume 27, *1958–1959*, 3–60, in the Law Library at the Library of Congress.

The uproar and protests in Okinawa are also covered in Miyume Tanji, *Myth, Protest and Struggle in Okinawa* (London: Routledge, 2006), 70–71; Yuki Takauchi, "Rape and the Sexual Politics of Homosociality: The U.S. Military Occupation of Okinawa, 1955–56," part of the *History of Asian Sexualities Series*, www.notchesblog.com.

Davis, author interview, 1987.

Thompson, author interview, 1987.

Peterson, author interview, 1987.

Ray, author interview, 1987.

The extraordinary pressure from Kentucky and Texas politicians on behalf of Hurt is evident in letters stored among the Eisenhower Presidential Papers. Representative Carl D. Perkins wrote the White House on January 15, 1959; Senator Thruston B. Morton forwarded the VFW letter to the White House on January 29, 1959. The VFW statement was dated January 17, 1959. Senator John Sherman Cooper pressed the White House on June 30, 1959. Texas lawyer Robert J. Hearon Jr. wrote the White House on July 24, 1959, and August 4, 1959; on August 7, 1959, he advised that Texas politicians were engaged in Hurt's behalf as well. Representative Eugene Siler lobbied the White House on October 28, 1959.

Homer Davis's argument at the federal court hearing in Kansas City, Kansas, was brought on December 28, 1959, and reported by the *Kansas City Star* on December 28, 1959, and the *Kansas City Times* on December 29, 1959.

Internal White House memos, including assistant counselor Phillip Areeda's doubts about the death sentence and Army Secretary Wilber Brucker's approval of death, are available among the Eisenhower Presidential Papers.

Hurt's petition for a "Commutation of Sentence," in which he claimed he was "sacrificed" to
quell the Okinawa protests, was signed August 11, 1975. It is available at the National
Archives.
Lura Hurt's "Character Affidavit" to win her husband a full presidential pardon was dated
July 8, 1982, and is at the National Archives.

McFARLANE
*Court-Martial Reports: Holdings and Decisions of the Judge Advocates General, Boards of
Review, and United States Court of Military Appeals*, Volume 23, 1957, summarizes Mc-
Farlane's arrest, trial and military appeals.
Media coverage of the case includes *Time* magazine, July 16, 1956, 24; *Stars and Stripes*,
June 14, 1956, June 16, 1956, and June 30, 1956; and an editorial in the Corpus Christi,
Texas, *Times*, July 23, 1957. The *Kansas City Times* reported on November 16, 1957,
that McFarlane's life had been spared.
McFarlane's criminal history in Wyoming was provided by the Wyoming Department of
Corrections.

HEILMAN
*Court-Martial Reports: Holdings and Decisions of the Judge Advocates General, Boards of Re-
view, and United States Court of Military Appeals*, Volume 31, 1962, 234–44. Note: The
army board of review reduced Heilman's sentence of death in 1960 to a fixed term of
fifty years, removing him from death row. The army's Court of Military Appeals in 1962
analyzed the Heilman case and affirmed the board's decision to spare Heilman's life. The
Oklahoma City *Daily Oklahoman* reported Heilman's conviction and death sentence on
October 23, 1959, and October 25, 1959.
Roy Hahn, author interview, 2017.
Sue Hahn, author interview, 2017.

Chapter Six: Eisenhower
Private Leroy Henry's arrest and trial, and the protests over his death sentence lay with the
records maintained by the National Personnel Records Center near St. Louis. For more
on this case and the experiences of black troops in England during World War II, see
David Reynolds, *Rich Relations: The American Occupation of Britain, 1942–1945* (New
York: Random House, 1995), 234–37; J. Robert Lilly and J. Michael Thomson, "Exe-
cuting US Soldiers in England, World War II, Command Influence and Sexual Racism,"
British Journal of Criminology 37, no. 2 (Spring 1997): 262–83; "The Trial of a Negro,"
London *Tribune*, June 9, 1944; "Eisenhower Frees Soldier," Pittsburgh *Courier*, June 17,
1944, and July 1, 1944; and "Is This England?," *Time*, June 12, 1944, 27–28.
President Truman described his November 18, 1952, conversation with President Elect Eisenhower in his diary; it is included in Robert H. Ferrell, ed., *Off the Record: The Private
Papers of Harry S. Truman* (New York: Harper & Row Publishers, 1980), 274–75. The
diary entry is dated November 20, 1952.
For more insight into Eisenhower the army officer and his attitude toward race relations, see
a May 29, 1967, letter he wrote to Bruce C. Clarke, regarding the role of black volunteers
in the army, included in Morris J. MacGregor and Bernard C. Nalty, eds., *Blacks in the
United States Armed Forces, Basic Documents*, Volume V, *Black Soldiers in World War II*
(Wilmington, DE: Scholarly Resources, 1977), 511–12; and David P. Colley, *Blood for*

Dignity: The Story of the First Integrated Combat Unit in the U.S. Army (New York: St. Martin's Press, 2003), 43–56.

Much has been written about Eisenhower as president and his "go slow" policy for racial integration. Of note are Robert Frederick Burk, *The Eisenhower Administration and Black Civil Rights* (Knoxville: University of Tennessee Press, 1984); David A. Nichols, *A Matter of Justice: Eisenhower and the Beginning of the Civil Rights Revolution* (New York: Simon & Schuster, 2007); Robert Griffith, ed., *Ike's Letters to a Friend, 1941–1959* (Lawrence: University Press of Kansas, 1984); Terrence J. Roberts and Rocco C. Siciliano, *President Dwight D. Eisenhower and Civil Rights* (Gettysburg, PA: Eisenhower World Affairs Institute, Gettysburg College, 2000); William Manchester, *The Glory and the Dream: A Narrative History of America, 1932–1972*, Volume 1 (Boston: Little, Brown, 1973), 338, 745, 751; and William Manchester, *The Glory and the Dream, A Narrative History of America, 1932–1972*, Volume 2 (Boston: Little, Brown, 1973–1974), 900–903, 984–85, 989–90.

The telegram from Emmett Till's mother was wired on September 1, 1955. J. William Barba, assistant to the special counsel of the president, sent a brief reply the following day. Both are on file among the Eisenhower Presidential Papers. See also Stephen J. Whitfield, *A Death in the Delta: The Story of Emmett Till* (New York: Free Press, 1988), 71–84.

Private Henry Nevin, imprisoned at Fort Leavenworth, sent an undated letter to Morrow. The White House aide drafted a response on October 29, 1959. The Nevin letter and Morrow's reply are included in the Eisenhower Presidential Papers collection.

For more, see E. Frederic Morrow, *Black Man in the White House* (New York: McFadden-Bartell, 1969). See further: Burk, *The Eisenhower Administration and Black Civil Rights*, 77–88; David Halberstam, *The Fifties* (New York: Villard Books, 1993), 424–28; Taylor Branch, *Parting the Waters: America in the King Years, 1954–63* (New York: Simon & Schuster, 1988), 203; Milton S. Katz, "E. Frederick [sic] Morrow and Civil Rights in the Eisenhower Administration," *Atlanta University Review of Race and Culture* XLII, no. 2 (June 1981): 133–44; and "People of the Week," *US News and World Report*, July 22, 1955, 14.

Derrick Bell, *Confronting Authority: Reflections of an Ardent Protester* (Boston: Beacon Press, 1994), 9–25.

Richard Delgado and Jen Stefancic, eds., *The Derrick Bell Reader* (New York: New York University Press, 2005).

John S. D. Eisenhower, *Strictly Personal* (Garden City, NY: Doubleday & Company, 1974), 289–91.

David Eisenhower with Julie Nixon Eisenhower, *Going Home to Glory: A Memoir of Life with Dwight D. Eisenhower, 1961–1969* (New York: Simon & Schuster, 2010), 189–90. For more regarding John Markoe, see Bob Reilly, "It Has Been the Few Who Have Acted, Who Have Saved Us from Unspeakable Scandal," *Window* magazine, Creighton University, Winter 1995–96, 3–9.

Earl Warren, *The Memoirs of Earl Warren* (Garden City, NY: Doubleday & Company, 1977), 290–97. See also Bernard Schwartz and Stephan Lesher, *Inside the Warren Court* (Garden City, NY: Doubleday & Company, 1983), 86–99, 156–59; and James F. Simon, *Eisenhower vs. Warren: The Battle for Civil Rights and Liberties* (New York: W. W. Norton & Company, 2018).

For additional discussion about Eisenhower and the impasse at Little Rock, consult Morris J. MacGregor and Bernard C. Nalty, eds., *Blacks in the United States Armed Forces, Basic*

Documents, Volume V, *Black Soldiers in World War II*, Volume XIII (Wilmington, DE: Scholarly Resources, 1977), 390–409; Cary Fraser, "Crossing the Color Line in Little Rock, the Eisenhower Administration and the Dilemma of Race for Foreign Policy," *Diplomatic History* 24, no. 2 (Spring 2000): 233–64; and Richard H. Rovere, "Letter from Washington," *New Yorker*, October 5, 1957, 167–72.

Sherman Adams, *First-Hand Report: The Story of the Eisenhower Administration* (New York: Harper & Brothers, 1961), 331–59.

Arthur Larson, *Eisenhower, the President Nobody Knew* (New York: Charles Scribner's Sons, 1968), 124–33.

William O. Douglas, *The Court Years, 1939–1975: The Autobiography of William O. Douglas* (New York: Random House, 1980), 120–21.

Jackie Robinson's letter to the president was dated May 13, 1958, and Eisenhower's reply, June 4, 1958. They are housed with the Eisenhower Presidential Papers at his library in Abilene, Kansas.

Chapter Seven: Black Death Row

BEVERLY, RIGGINS, and SUTTLES

The triple hanging in March 1955 of privates Chastine Beverly, James L. Riggins, and Louis M. Suttles was covered extensively by local newspapers, especially the *Kansas City Times* and the *Leavenworth Times* on March 1, 1955, both page 1.

The Fort Leavenworth prison also published several initial press releases describing preparations for the executions and details about their deaths. This is reflected in army documents on internal "guidance" on how to hang three men in one night, dated September 19, 1953, and September 21, 1953, all part of the prisoners' records. The press releases are dated February 23, 24, and 28, 1955.

Thompson, author interview, 1987.

Martin Kiger's comments were published in the Junction City, Kansas, *Union*, January 24, 1957.

Maiden, author interview, 1987.

Their crime, arrest, trial, and legal appeals are detailed in army appellate records in *Court-Martial Reports: Holdings and Decisions of the Judge Advocates General, Boards of Review, and United States Court of Military Appeals*, Volume 8, *1952–1953*, 496–513, and Volume 9, *1952–1953*, 81–90, both in the Law Library at the Library of Congress.

McMillin's editorial ran without a headline but instead began simply, "Dear Friends: A very tragic thing happened in Waynesville . . ." It was published in the Pulaski County *Democrat*, September 27, 1951.

Biggar, author interview, 1987.

Curtsinger, author interview, 1987.

Thompson, author interview, 1987.

Hagelberger, author interview, 1987.

Davis, author interview, 1987.

Other recollections about Homer Davis came from author interviews in 2016 with Ed Chapman and Lee McGuire, fellow Leavenworth attorneys who had worked on legal cases with Davis. For more on Davis, see Sandra L. Thomas's lengthy profile, "Homer Davis Chose Law Career Over Two Others," Leavenworth *Times*, February 22, 1987, and his obituary, "Thomas Homer Davis Dies at 89," October 27, 1992.

lisha Scott was profiled in Thom Rosenblum, "Unlocking the Schoolhouse Doors: Elisha Scott, 'Colored Lawyer, Topeka,'" *Kansas History: A Journal of the Central Plains* (Spring 2013): 40–55. Scott's obituary in the Kansas City *Kansan* was published April 24, 1963. Other brief obituaries ran in the Topeka *State Journal*, April 24, 1963, and the *Kansas City Star*, April 24, 1963.

The federal court hearing for Beverly, Riggins, and Suttles was held on October 26, 27, and 28, 1953, in Topeka, and covered extensively those three days by the Topeka *State Journal* and the Leavenworth *Times*. Records of the federal appellate case were found in the annals of the federal Tenth Circuit Court of Appeals in Denver.

Scott's plea to the White House is dated December 6, 1954. Shanley's reply was written December 9, 1954. Scott wrote again on December 21, 1954. The correspondence is stored with the Eisenhower Presidential Papers.

Cassie Beverly's letter to Eisenhower is dated September 17, 1953. Her second letter is February 5, 1955. May Lee Jones wrote to Eisenhower on December 14, 1954. The Sarabelle H. Eldridge letter is dated January 11, 1955. All are part of the Eisenhower Presidential Papers collection.

EDWARDS and MOORE

Harrison, author interview, 2016.

Private Robert Dresden, author interview, 1987.

Biggar, author interview, 1987.

Lawson, author interview, 1987.

Studies of the death penalty from that era include Robert G. Elliott with Albert R. Beatty, *Agent of Death: The Memoirs of an Executioner* (New York: E. P. Dutton & Co., 1940); Franklin H. Williams, "The Death Penalty and the Negro," *The Crisis* magazine, October 1960, 3–14; Colonel Dwight H. Sullivan, "A Matter of Life and Death, Examining the Military Death Penalty's Fairness," *Federal Lawyer* 45, no. 5 (June 1988): 38–44; Jacques Barzun, "In Favor of Capital Punishment," *American Scholar* 31, no. 2 (Summer 1962): 181–91, Paul C. Kochan, "Source Book on Capital Punishment and Penal Reform," *Penal Study Committee, Kansas Council of Churches*, 1962; and F. A. Grass, "Who Hangs the Hangman?," *Nongqai* (South Africa) 52, no. 2 (February 8, 1961). Also of interest are the congressional debates beginning in the spring of 1960 to abolish the death penalty in the United States, transcripts available in the Congressional Record.

For more on hangman John C. Woods, see the Wichita *Eagle*, January 8, 2018, and *Los Angeles Times*, November 24, 1996.

Army plans and after-action reports for the double execution of Edwards and Moore are unveiled in internal correspondence at the Fort Leavenworth prison, from December 18, 1956, through February 14, 1957, noting that the hangings were carried out "in the first minutes of Thursday morning, February 14, 1957." These documents are from Fort Leavenworth's Ike Skelton Combined Arms Research Library and other sources.

Maddox, author interview, 1987, and also from his detailed notes in his personal spiral notebook.

Master Sergeant Tom Dunham, author interview, 1987.

Curtsinger, author interview, 1987.

Peterson, author interview, 1987.

Harris, author interview, 1987.

Edwards's arrest, trial, and military appeals are covered in *Court-Martial Reports: Holdings and Decisions of the Judge Advocates General, Boards of Review, and United States Court of*

Military Appeals, Volume 11, *1953*, 350–55; Volume 14, *1953–1954*, 292, and Volume 15, *1953–1954*, 299–307, all in the Law Library at the Library of Congress.

Charlie Mae Edwards wrote to the president on June 30, 1955. Attorney General Herbert Brownell's conclusions are undated but numbered as 77–727. Barba's recommendations were made September 17, 1956. All are available in the Eisenhower Presidential Papers collection.

Edwards's two letters to Eisenhower are dated February 7, 1957, and February 8, 1957.

Moore's arrest, trial, and military appeals are covered in *Court-Martial Reports: Holdings and Decisions of the Judge Advocates General, Boards of Review, and United States Court of Military Appeals,*" Volume 13, *1953*, 311–19, and Volume 16, *1954*, 56–62.

Peterson, author interview, 1987.

Maiden, author interview, 1987.

W. Francis Taylor Jr. wrote to the president on July 22, 1954. Brownell's recommendation to Eisenhower was made in an undated memo, titled 77–726-Moore. Barba's concurrence is dated September 14, 1956.

The double hanging was reported in various newspapers, including the Garden City, Kansas, *Telegram*, February 14, 1957, 12.

Maddox, author interview, 1987.

Bateman, author interview, 2016.

RANSOM

Peterson, author interview, 1987.

Kramer, author interview, 1987.

Dunham, author interview, 1987.

Tech Sergeant Harold L. Baldwin, author interview, 1987.

Ransom's crime, arrest, trial, and military appeals are covered in *Court-Martial Reports: Holdings and Decisions of the Judge Advocates General, Boards of Review, and United States Court of Military Appeals*, Volume 12, *1953*, 480–90, and Volume 15, *1953–1954*, 195–203, both in the Law Library at the Library of Congress.

Ransom's escape was reported in the *Pacific Stars & Stripes*, June 7, 1953, 2.

Ransom's mother's remembrance of her son is cited in a June 13, 1955, Lindsay memo to the attorney general. Barba's synopsis is dated January 25, 1957. Father Harold Livingston Thomas wrote the White House on April 1, 1957. All these materials are available in the Eisenhower President Papers collection.

The final army execution planning reports leading up to the hanging, retrieved from Fort Leavenworth's Ike Skelton Combined Arms Research Library and other sources, are dated February 23, 1957, February 26, 1957, March 21, 1957, March 27, 1957, and hours after his death "in the first minutes of Wednesday morning, 3 April 1957." Of further note is an oral interview of retired Master Sergeant John L. Harris by Sergeant Rex Berry on December 11, 1989. Titled *Life of a Prison Guard at the Disciplinary Barracks in the 1950's*, the history is part of a U.S.D.B. term paper collection housed at the Fort Leavenworth Ike Skelton Combined Arms Research Library. Harris is asked to describe his best and worst experiences working at the army prison. "The worst?" he replied. "I would have to say the execution and burial of Ransom. . . . He deserved it, but it was [an] unfortunate thing. I actually felt sorry for him."

Maddox, author interview, 1987, and from diary notes in his spiral notebook.

Schick, author interview, 1987.

Peterson, author interview, 1987.

THOMAS

Thomas's pleas to Eisenhower were made in June and July 1958, and the telegrams and
 letters are stored with the Eisenhower Presidential Papers.

Thomas's crime, arrest, trial, and military appeals are covered in *Court-Martial Reports:
 Holdings and Decisions of the Judge Advocates General, Boards of Review, and United States
 Court of Military Appeals*, Volume 19, *1955*, 218–26, available in the Law Library at the
 Library of Congress.

Felton's initial letters to the White House admitting he was ill-equipped to handle a capital
 case are dated September 13, 1956, and October 9, 1956. On February 20, 1957, he
 wrote to Walter F. George, special assistant to the president, hoping to see Eisenhower
 during the president's golf outing at Thomasville, Georgia.

Brownell's recommendation to the president is not dated; however, it is identified as Number
 78–714-Thomas. Barba concurred on January 28, 1957.

Davis, author interview, 1987.

On November 27, 1957, Davis asked the Supreme Court to hear the Thomas appeal. Solicitor General J. Lee Rankin and his staff in January 1958 opposed the petition for a writ
 of certiorari with the Supreme Court. The Supreme Court denied Davis's request on
 January 20, 1958.

Schick, author interview, 1987.

Harris, author interview, 1987.

Curtsinger, author interview, 1987.

Peterson, author interview, 1987.

Thomas suffered the stroke on November 26, 1957. Part of the report by Captain Lawrence
 S. Sonkin regarding the stroke is incorporated in a February 12, 1958, letter from Felton
 to Morgan in the White House Counsel's Office. The medical evaluation of Thomas
 at Fort Leavenworth was conducted by Captain R. B. Callahan, an army psychiatrist,
 on March 10, 1955. It is in that report that Thomas is quoted as saying, "It doesn't feel
 good to have to go for an offense you didn't commit. But I'm willing." All this material is
 available in the Eisenhower Presidential Papers collection.

Davis, author interview, 1987.

Felton telegrammed Morgan saying the Thomas family was "reluctant to give up" on July
 14, 1958.

Army Secretary Brucker's Order of Execution is dated July 15, 1958.

Missouri Thomas wrote to Eisenhower on February 14, 1958. Morgan replied on February
 24, 1958. She wrote again on July 1, 1958. There is no White House reply to the second
 letter in the Eisenhower Presidential Papers.

Thomas's letters and telegrams in July 1958 to Eisenhower are part of the Eisenhower Presidential Papers collection.

Henry Roemer McPhee, assistant special counsel to the president, replied to Thomas's letters
 on July 17, 1958.

Thompson, author interview, 1987.

Ray, author interview, 1987.

The hanging was reported by the Leavenworth *Times* on July 23, 1958.

DAY

Day's crime, arrest, trial, and military appeals are covered in *Court-Martial Reports: Holdings
 and Decisions of the Judge Advocates General, Boards of Review, and United States Court of*

Military Appeals, Volume 8, *1952–1953*, 424–34, and Volume 9, *1952–1953*, 46–60, both in the Law Library at the Library of Congress. The case is further discussed in detail in a "Confidential" army police summary titled "Case No. 51–0-161-A," which included witness statements and was used by army prosecutors at Day's court-martial.

Army Secretary Robert T. Stevens on October 16, 1953, recommended death. Barba's analysis is dated May 5, 1954. He cited a letter from South Korean president Syngman Rhee urging "sympathy and compassion." Barba also noted that Day is a "negro" and that "two members of the court-martial were negroes."

The victim wrote to Eisenhower, pleading for Day's life, on August 12, 1954.

Davis, author interview, 1987.

Judge Arthur J. Mellott ruled against Day on November 19, 1955; see the *Kansas City Times*, November 19, 1955. The Supreme Court, on October 22, 1956, declined to hear the appeal.

The prisoner's mother, Martha Day, wrote the president on June 9, 1958.

Day's lawyer, Harry C. Wood, wrote to Eisenhower on January 16, 1959, attaching a letter from Day.

Day wrote to Army Secretary Brucker on March 15, 1959.

Eisenhower re-approved the death sentence on July 10, 1959.

Wood again wrote the president on July 14, 1959. "While Day's life is cheap," the lawyer pleaded, "mercy to him would be priceless."

Davis wrote Eisenhower on July 17, 1959.

Day wrote to Eisenhower on July 20, 1959.

You Chan Yang, Korean ambassador to the United States, on August 4, 1959, reiterated his country's plea for mercy.

Thompson, author interview, 1987.

Pinson, author interview, 1987.

Day's final telegram to Eisenhower was sent on September 22, 1959.

Dr. Karl Menninger's *Reader's Digest* article, "Verdict Guilty—Now What?" was published in the magazine's October 1959 edition, 180–84. Menninger later described his conversation with Day in a "Personal" note in *Harper's* magazine, December 1959, 20–21.

Davis, author interview, 1987.

Ray, author interview, 1987.

The hanging was reported by the Leavenworth *Times* and the *Kansas City Star* on September 23, 1959.

Chapter Eight: A Great Trouble

On April 4, 1955, Delma M. Easley, executive secretary of the Red Cross chapter in Chatham, Virginia, filed her report of the visit with the Bennett family on April 1, 1955. She titled it, "Social History of Bennett, John A. (GP) Negro, unmarried" and further identified her report as file number #28, 799. The army declassified the report on April 24, 1963.

Katherine Bennett Younger (from here on, identified simply as Katherine), author interview, 2016.

Ira Bennett, author interview, 2016.

Robert Gilbert, author interview, 2016.

To learn more about Odell Waller, see Richard B. Sherman, *The Case of Odell Waller and Virginia Justice, 1940–1942* (Knoxville: University of Tennessee Press, 1992).

Dresden, author interview, 1987.

Jacobsen, author interview, 1987.

Sergeant Walter Beckerjeck, author interview, 1987.

Curtsinger, author interview, 1987.

Peterson, author interview, 1987.

Harris, author interview, 1987.

Jacobsen, author interview, 1987.

Thompson, author interview, 1987.

Schick, author interview, 1987.

Angenette Pompey, author interview, 1987.

Captain Thomas Carter, author interview, 1987.

The new "Personal History" for John Bennett was written at the army prison in New Cumberland, Pennsylvania, and forwarded to the Fort Leavenworth Disciplinary Barracks. It is dated April 12, 1955.

The Elise Demus Moran letter, April 15, 1955, was addressed to the army's "Military Justice Division."

The new round of interviews and mental health examinations for Bennett at the Fort Leavenworth prison were detailed in an "Admission Classification Summary" dated February 3, 1956. It was compiled by First Lieutenant John J. Bateman, army psychiatrist at Fort Leavenworth.

The board of review and Court of Military Appeals opinions, which researched Bennett's crime, his arrest, his trial, and his army appeals, can be found in *Court-Martial Reports: Holdings and Decisions of the Judge Advocates General, Boards of Review, and United States Court of Military Appeals*, Volume 21, 1956, 223–28, available in the Law Library at the Library of Congress. For a separate and excellent legal analysis, see Lieutenant Commander Stephen C. Reyes, "Dusty Gallows," *Military Justice Naval Law Review* I, Volume 62, 2013, 103–38.

Ollie Bennett wrote to Eisenhower on June 11, 1956. Morgan, the White House Counsel, replied on June 13, 1956, saying "his case has not yet been forwarded to the president." Ollie Bennett and her daughter Katherine wrote to the Judge Advocate General's office in Washington on July 2, 1956, asking if Eisenhower had reached any decision about John. The letter was placed in Bennett's army file; there is no evidence though that Washington responded to that second letter, according to what is available in the Eisenhower Presidential Papers.

Bertha Banks, who was Bennett's former teacher, wrote to Eisenhower on August 13, 1956. The letter from the Chatham neighbor complaining that "drinking is too popular among our service men" was written by Carrie Shelton and arrived in Washington on July 2, 1956.

Captain William M. Fuller's letter urging a commutation for Bennett is dated September 1, 1956, and was addressed to Eisenhower.

Army Secretary Brucker on August 2, 1956, recommended death for Bennett; in October 1956, Attorney General Brownell concurred. There was no specific date on Brownell's memo to the president, but he identified his memorandum as Misc.-56-Bennett. Barba, on February 7, 1957, decided that death was appropriate as well. On July 2, President Eisenhower approved death for Bennett.

The Thompson interview with Bennett was one of a series of brief, monthly examinations to monitor Bennett's adjustment on death row.

The Muse-Parker telephone conversation is memorialized in a transcript produced by Parker on that day, July 30, 1957.

Bennett wrote Eisenhower on August 14, 1957. His parents wrote the president on August 18, 1957. They ended their short, one-page letter with: "Yours in Christ, Percy and Ollie Bennett."

Much of Jerry Williams's life and times and his labors in the field of civil rights was provided by his sons, fellow attorneys Jerry and Robert Williams. He is mentioned prominently in Danville's *News & Advance*, June 9, 2013, and his obituary ran in the *Sunday Bee* in Danville, Virginia, January 3, 1988.

Williams is mostly remembered for his legal struggles, often bravely fought against long odds. The Buford Russell Morton case, for example, was followed closely, often with racial overtones, by the Danville *Bee*, in articles on May 23, 1947, June 7, 1947, July 8, 1947, July 22, 1947, July 23, 1947, July 24, 1947, July 25, 1947, October 7, 1947, October 10, 1947. The *Bee*'s editorial that "justice had been done" with Morton's death sentence ran in the paper's October 17, 1947, edition.

For more on the Martinsville Seven case, another that Williams helped defend, see Eric W. Rise, *The Martinsville Seven, Race, Rape and Capital Punishment* (Charlottesville: University Press of Virginia, 1995), and Eric W. Rise, "Race, Rape and Radicalism: The Case of the Martinsville Seven, 1949–1951," *Journal of Southern History* 58, No 3 (August 1992): 461–90. The Danville *Register* ridiculed the black lawyers defending the seven men in its January 26, 1951, editorial.

Robert Williams, author interview, 2016.

Jerry Williams, author interview, 2016.

Williams filed the emergency petition on August 19, 1957. Judge Hill on August 20, 1957, granted the stay of execution.

Katherine, author interview, 2016.

The federal court hearing on Bennett's appeal was held in Topeka on October 29, 1957. Court testimony and legal debate come from the court reporter's transcript.

For more on Lieutenant Colonel Peter S. Wondolowski and the My Lai cases, see "Patient Army Judge in Mylai [sic]Case Peter Stanislaus Wondolowski, *New York Times*, December 17, 1971.

Judge Hill denied Bennett's petition on January 28, 1958. Williams appealed to the Tenth Circuit on December 17, 1958. The appellate court ruled against him on May 12, 1959. On December 11, 1959, Judge Hill dissolved the stay of execution. On January 28, 1960, the army scheduled a new execution date: March 10, 1960.

The results of Dr. Bernard Foster's February 8, 1960, examination of Bennett at the Menninger Clinic was forwarded to the army hospital at Fort Leavenworth on February 16, 1960. The next day, February 17, 1960, the army's board of medical examiners determined the "significant possibility" that Bennett was suffering an epileptic attack during the assault in Austria.

Katherine on March 2, 1960, notified Fort Leavenworth Legal Officer Lieutenant Robert J. Smith that Williams was preparing a "last-minute appeal for clemency," according to a memo prepared that day by Colonel William M. Smoak Jr., chief of the JAG's Military Justice Division. Secretary Brucker again advised Eisenhower, this time on March 7, 1960, that Bennett's execution should be carried out.

Bennett's telegram to Eisenhower was wired on March 8, 1960.

Williams on March 14, 1960, filed a new legal petition for Bennett, on the strength of the new findings of epilepsy.

Carter, author interview, 1987.

Maddox, author interview, 1987.

Katherine, author interview, 2016.

Dr. Menninger, author interview, 1987.

Dr. Menninger's telegram to the White House was sent March 9, 1960.

The Eisenhower-Brucker phone conversation the night of March 9, 1960, is memorialized in the "DDE Diary Series" under "Briefings-March 1960" among the Eisenhower Presidential Papers.

Pinson, author interview, 1987.

Carter, author interview, 1987.

For more on the judge, see his own work, Arthur J. Stanley Jr., "Fort Leavenworth: Dowager Queen of Frontier Posts," *Kansas Historical Quarterly* (Spring 1976): 1–23.

Testimony, legal arguments, and the judge's comments in the March 23, 1960, hearing come from the court reporter's transcript.

Dr. Menninger, author interview, 1987.

Most valuable in understanding Dr. Menninger are his letters, a countless trove of personal and professional missives stored with the Kansas Historical Society in Topeka. Many also were compiled in Howard J. Faulkner and Virginia D. Pruitt, eds., *The Selected Correspondence of Karl A. Menninger, 1919–1945* (New Haven, CT: Yale University Press, 1988); and Howard J. Faulkner and Virginia D. Pruitt, eds., *The Selected Correspondence of Karl A. Menninger, 1946–1965* (Columbia: University of Missouri Press, 1995).

A longtime opponent of capital punishment, Dr. Menninger suggested the best way to do away with executions might be to televise them, as he offered in the Topeka *Daily Capital*, February 30, 1979. In a typical letter to a state or Washington senator, he would admonish that "killing doesn't stop killing," as he did in a mass mailing on February 23, 1987. In an April 3, 1963, letter to California state officials, he decried capital punishment as too costly, with the odds of a man being executed 200 to 1. He also spoke widely against legal executions, as he did in 1960, telling the American Psychiatric Association that the ultimate punishment was generally meted out on minorities—see the *New York Times*, May 13, 1960.

Crime reduction and prison reform were also Dr. Menninger's long-held causes, and they drove some of his most vigorous writings. His works include *Man Against Himself* (San Diego: Harvest/HBJ Book, Harcourt Brace Jovanovich Publishers, 1936) and *The Crime of Punishment* (New York: Viking Press, 1966). For insight into how he interacted with inmates, see Charles Hammer, "Prison Decency His Goal," *Kansas City Star*, January 9, 1977.

Judge Stanley ruled against Bennett on June 28, 1960. Colonel Robert J. O'Connor's reaction to Bennett's testimony was prepared earlier, on April 6, 1960, when he memorialized his thoughts as chief of the JAG's Military Justice Division.

Captain George J. Berry's evaluation of Bennett was conducted on September 20, 1960.

Mills, author interview, 1987.

Chapter Nine: Kennedy

Biggar, author interview, 1987.

Pinson, author interview, 1987.

The January 12, 1961, "Psychiatric Summary" was prepared for Lieutenant Colonel Thomas W. Birch.

The Court of Appeals rejected Bennett's petition on January 17, 1971.

Williams telegrammed Scott at 4 p.m. on February 4, 1961. That same day, Scott asked the appellate court for more time to raise more money. On February 6, 1961, Scott and Williams filed a petition with the court asking that their appeal be reinstated. The appellate court said no, and Judge Hill on February 9, 1961, lifted the stay of execution.

Major General Charles L. Decker's February 16, 1961, memo to the secretary of the army is titled "Information Concerning Pending Court-Martial Cases in Which a Death Sentence Has Been Adjudged."

Army Secretary Elvis J. Stahr Jr.'s February 16, 1961, memo to the president includes a written history of Bennett's crime, arrest, trial, and appeals.

The Fifth Army's Order of Execution was written on February 20, 1961.

Major William D. Myers wrote the first-person account describing how Bennett was told on February 17, 1961, that his stay of execution had been lifted and the army would soon set a new date for his hanging.

Chaplain Carter and Father Joseph E. X. Frain each wrote on Bennett's behalf on February 21, 1961.

Captain David J. Anderson wrote the first-person account of how Colonel Cox approached Bennett's prison cell door on February 27, 1961, and informed him he would be put to death "starting at 0001 hours, CST, 13 April, 1961."

Birch wrote to Percy Bennett on February 17 and February 28, 1961, apprising him of the fast-moving developments in his son's pending execution.

Katherine, author interview, 2016.

Ira Bennett, author interview, 2016.

Lee C. White, author interview, 2000.

For more on the presidential adviser, see Lee C. White, *Government for the People: Reflections of a White House Counsel to Presidents Kennedy and Johnson* (Lanham, MD: Hamilton Books, 2008); and Gerald S. and Deborah H. Strober, *"Let Us Begin Anew": An Oral History of the Kennedy Presidency* (New York: HarperCollins Publishers, 1993), 153, 293, 308–309, 320, and 524.

The attorney general's lament about dogs being treated better than black people in parts of the South comes from Robert F. Kennedy, *The Pursuit of Justice* (New York: Harper & Row, 1964), 76.

Robert F. Kennedy's February 27, 1961, report to White discusses the "field and scope of Executive clemency" and includes a list of which prisoners were executed or spared and provides their racial breakdown.

Katherine, author interview, 2016.

Robert Williams, author interview, 2016.

Brigadier General Alan B. Todd's March 2, 1961, notes come from his memorandum titled, "White House Briefing in the Case of Prisoner John A. Bennett (formerly Private First Class, US 52 342 347)."

Gertrude H. Wilkinson's letter is dated March 3, 1961.

White's March 4 memo for President Kennedy is brief, just one page long, but covers eight key points. His handwritten notes are three pages on legal-size paper.

White, author interview, 2000.

In a March 6, 1961, "Memorandum to File," Todd recounts his discussions with Major General Chester "Ted" Clifton and, separately, with Colonel Cox at the Fort Leavenworth prison

Bennett wrote to Williams on March 15, 1961, and a copy was sent from Cox to Todd that
    same day. Williams wrote to the JAG office in Washington asking for help from army
    defense lawyers on March 16, 1961.
Williams's letter to Kennedy was dated March 21, 1961.
Williams's March 31 formal plea to the president is titled, "A Petition for Clemency in the
    Court-Martial of John Bennett."
Bennett's March 31 handwritten letter to Kennedy was first typed "for clarity" by the Office
    of the Judge Advocate General's before it was forwarded to the White House.
Katherine, author interview, 2016.
Katherine and Exella Bennett sent separate letters to the president on March 29, 1961.
The White and Todd conversations were transcribed and initially stamped "FOR OFFICIAL
    USE ONLY."
Stahr's review of the clemency petition is noted in a "Memorandum for the Record" prepared
    by White and dated April 7, 1961. White notes that Stahr spoke with Williams and that
    the army secretary was not persuaded by the clemency petition.
The April 8, 1961, telegram from the girl and her parents was sent from the army's Southern
    Area Command in Munich, Germany, to the JAG office in Washington, DC, and then
    rushed to the White House.
White, author interview, 2000.

Chapter Ten: Midnight
White's letters to Williams and Bennett are dated April 8, 1961.
Birch's April 10, 1961, recollections of Bennett receiving the news from the Kennedy White
    House come from his memo to the Assistant Judge Advocate General for Military Jus-
    tice. In addition, Captain Anderson, who, like Birch, was present at Bennett's cell door,
    recalled the incident in an April 11, 1961, "Disposition Form," and said Colonel Cox let
    Bennett keep the telegram ordering his execution.
Dr. Menninger, author interview, 1987.
Dr. Menninger's telegram was sent on April 10, 1961. White replied the same day.
Berry's mental exam of Bennett is described in a Birch memo on April 10, 1961, to the Assis-
    tant Judge Advocate General for Military Justice. Birch also praised Bennett's resilience,
    saying the prisoner "has firm hopes that clemency will be exercised despite the letter
    from the White House."
Williams's frustrations were expressed in the Danville *Bee*, April 11, 1961; the lawyer also de-
    tailed his phone conversation with Bennett. The article is headlined "President Refuses
    to Commute County Soldier's Death Sentence."
Bennett's last meal request is detailed in another Anderson "Disposition Form," this one also
    dated April 11, 1961.
Final execution preparations are outlined by Anderson in an April 11, 1961, order titled
    simply, "Execution."
Bennett's April 12, 1961, telegram to Kennedy was sent as a "PRIORITY" alert.
The plea from civil rights lawyers in Kansas, including Elisha Scott, arrived at the White
    House at 7:46 p.m. on April 12.
Attempts by JAG defense lawyers to postpone the execution were described by Williams in
    the Danville *Bee*, April 11, 1961.
Berry's mental exam is memorialized in an April 12, 1961, "Certificate" from the Directorate
    of Mental Hygiene, United States Disciplinary Barracks, Fort Leavenworth, Kansas.

Carter, author interview, 1987.

Thompson, author interview, 1987.

Lawson, author interview, 1987.

Maddox, author interview, 1987. Additional details were gleaned from the hangman's personal spiral notebook.

Dr. Menninger, author interview, 1987.

"April 12 was an exceedingly busy day for the President." See Evelyn Lincoln, Personal Secretary to the President, *My Twelve Years with John F. Kennedy* (New York: David McKay Company, 1965), 253–56.

Benjamin C. Bradlee, *Conversations with Kennedy* (New York: W. W. Norton and Company, 1975), 165–66.

Pinson, author interview, 1987.

Katherine, author interview, 2016.

White's telegram responding to Bennett reemphasized that Kennedy's "decision to accept the sentence imposed by the court-martial, approved by all military courts, approved by President Eisenhower, and sustained by civilian courts remains unchanged."

Pinson, author interview, 1987.

Katherine, author interview, 2016.

Pinson, author interview, 1987.

Carter, author interview, 1987.

Lawson, author interview, 1987.

Curtsinger, author interview, 1987.

Kramer, author interview, 1987.

Lawson, author interview, 1987.

Dresden, author interview, 1987

Mills, author interview, 1987.

James J. Fisher, author interview, 1987.

Maddox, author interview, 1987.

Fisher, author interview, 1987.

For newspaper coverage of the execution, see "A Soldier Is Hanged," *Kansas City Times*, April 13, 1961; "Bennett Hanged After Appeal To the President Is Denied," Leavenworth *Times*, April 13, 1961; "Soldier Dies on the Gallows," Lawrence, Kansas, *Journal-World*, April 13, 1961; "Death Ends Long Fight For Freedom; County Negro Dies on Gallows," Danville *Bee*, April 13, 1961; and "Bennett Hanged at Leavenworth," Danville *Register*, April 13, 1961.

The death certificate, filed with the state of Kansas, gave the cause as "fracture cervical vertebrae with cord injury" due to "Judicial hanging." The certificate added: "Interval between onset and death 16 Min 5 Sec." Death began at 12:05 a.m.

Separately, the overnight Duty Officer's Journal in the Adjutant General's Office stated the following: "Bennet (sic) dropped at 0005 + 17 seconds. Pronounced dead by Senior Medical Officer at 0021 + 22 seconds. No special requests by the prisoner." The journal notes, compiled by Major Robert H. Ingle Jr., added in conclusion, "There were no unusual incidents."

Postscript

Fisher, author interview, 1987.

Kramer, author interview, 1987.

Lawson, author interview, 1987.
Carter, author interview, 1987.
Robert Williams, author interview, 2016.
Maddox, author interview, 1987.
Mack Coles, author interview, 2016.
"Six Years Is Too Long," Danville *Bee*, editorial, April 13, 1961.
The items shipped home with his coffin are listed in an army "Inventory of Personal
    Effects of John A. Bennett, Deceased."

INDEX

ABOUT THE AUTHOR

RICHARD A. SERRANO was a longtime reporter for the *Kansas City Times* and the *Los Angeles Times*. In twenty-five years as a Washington correspondent, he covered the Pentagon and the Justice Department, the FBI, and the War on Terror. In March 2003 he witnessed and wrote about the legal execution of Louis Jones, a decorated black Army veteran put to death in Indiana for the rape and murder of a young white female recruit.

Serrano shared in three Pulitzer Prizes for his reporting after the Hyatt Hotel skywalks disaster in Kansas City, the Los Angeles race riots, and, most recently, the 2015 terror attack in San Bernardino, California. The author of four other books, he has written about the 1995 Oklahoma City bombing, profiled the last veterans of the Civil War, and chronicled the fading days of America's Wild West.